ARAB VOICES

ARAB VOICES

WHAT THEY
ARE SAYING TO US,
AND WHY
IT MATTERS

JAMES ZOGBY

 ST. MARTIN'S GRIFFIN ✖ NEW YORK

First published in hardcover in 2010 by St. Martin's Griffin in the
US—a division of St. Martin's Press LLC, 175 Fifth Avenue, New York, NY
10010.

St. Martin's Griffin are registered trademarks in the United States, the
United Kingdom, Europe and other countries.

ISBN: 978-0-230-12068-6

The Library of Congress has cataloged the hardcover edition as follows:
Zogby, James J.
    Arab voices : what they are saying to us, and why it matters / James Zogby.
        p.   cm.
    Summary: "The co-founder of the renowned polling firm Zogby
International draws from 40 years of the most extensive polls from the Arab
World to lift the fog that has obscured this culture for centuries"—Provided by
publisher.
    ISBN 978-0-230-10299-6 (hardback)
    1. Arabs—Attitudes.   2. Public opinion—Arab countries.   3. National
characteristics, Arab.   4. United States—Foreign public opinion, Arab.
I. Title.
DS36.7.Z64   2010
303.3'809174927—dc22

                                                        2010012507

A catalogue record of the book is available from the British Library.

Design by Letra Libre Inc.

First St. Martin's Griffin paperback edition: January 2012

To Eileen, for her unfailing judgment and commitment to justice.

CONTENTS

4

GETTING IT RIGHT

INTRODUCTION

ON OCTOBER 2, 2001, less than a month after the worst terrorist attacks in American history, a former ad executive named Charlotte Beers assumed leadership of the U.S. State Department's efforts to improve communication with the Arab World. Beers had started out as a product manager for Uncle Ben's rice—a modest beginning to an impressive career. In 1997, she retired as vice president of marketing powerhouse Ogilvy and Mather. That same year, *Fortune* magazine put Beers on the cover of an issue dedicated to the most powerful women in America. By naming her the State Department's undersecretary for public diplomacy and public affairs, the White House was betting that Beers, with her experience from campaigns for Head and Shoulders and American Express, could help to rebrand America in a part of the world where we desperately needed goodwill and cooperation.

Though many of my colleagues who specialized in Middle East affairs were skeptical, I gave qualified support to the appointment. I knew that Beers had not worked in Washington and knew little about the Middle East. But I figured that if she were faithful to the rules of the world she did know—marketing and advertising—she could have a positive impact on Arab–American relations.

Several weeks later, just before Beers left on her first tour of the Middle East, we met at the State Department. New to both the Arab World and the world of public policy, she asked my advice. I kept it simple: "Listen," I urged her. "Hear what Arabs are saying. Understand what they are thinking and what they are telling us they need to hear from us. Know the questions they are asking before attempting to give them answers." Really, my advice was just another way of saying what my mother used to tell me: "If you want someone to hear you, listen to them first."

Beers then embarked on a multination trip to engage directly her new target demographic: the Arab people. She was planning to get to know the region by having conversations with the people whose opinions she was trying to understand. "Smart," I thought.

However, as I later learned from a State Department official who accompanied Beers, the listening tour produced mixed results. During her stops in Morocco and Egypt, Beers received a warm official welcome. But when the discussion turned to U.S. policy, Arabs repeatedly asked Beers tough questions about Palestine and the double standards America demonstrated in siding with Israel against the Arab states. Though I had warned Beers that these topics would be foremost on the minds of Arabs, I was told this line of questioning frustrated her because it distracted from the message she sought to project: America as a good and tolerant country.

When she returned to the United States, Beers authorized the opening of a media outreach center in London that could respond to the issues she herself was not equipped to handle. This was a good decision. However, undeterred from her original plan, she also proceeded with her mission to use advertising campaigns to rebrand al-Qaeda and America, with the goal of winning the hearts and minds of Arabs and Muslims worldwide.

From then on, things went downhill. It wasn't that Beers had failed to heed my advice; rather, she had ignored the basic rules of her world: marketing. Ogilvy and Mather, Beers's former employer, maintains a branch in the Arab World that promises clients, via its Web site, "a unique insight into Arabic culture in its many forms and a unique ability to produce communication solutions that are perfectly in sync with it"[1]—a typical marketing approach. Yet after her unsuccessful trip, Beers instead chose a well-worn path in U.S. engagement with the Arab World: acting without listening.

Not surprisingly, Beers's resultant advertising drives were less than "perfectly in sync" with Arabic culture. There was, for example, the Osama Bin Laden "Wanted: Dead or Alive" poster that she attempted to place as a paid advertisement in Arab newspapers. Not only did it fail, but the ad gave Bin Laden free publicity. The poster produced a backlash, with Arab commentators charging that its bellicose language smacked of a cowboy mentality.

Another central part of Beers's campaign was a series of advertisements and videos portraying happily integrated Muslims from various walks of life going about their lives in America. One such ad featured a Muslim American paramedic saying, "I have never gotten disrespect because I am a Muslim."[2] However, because Beers offered to pay substantial amounts to have these pieces appear on television stations in the Muslim World, she created the negative perception that the United States was trying to buy influence. Equally problematic was that the positive theme of the ads was in direct competition with hard news reports about large numbers of Muslim immigrants being rounded up by the Department of Justice for deportation.

I previewed another one of Beers's television spots and found it visually striking. Promoting the ideas of tolerance and respect for diversity, it featured a female Moroccan Olympic medalist running alone while her internal voice spoke beautifully of the need for mutual respect. The production was simple, powerful, and quite eloquent.

Although I was moved, I could also tell that this impressive bit of advertising was destined for failure in the Arab World. For one, the language in the ad was written by Americans for Americans—it didn't really reflect an understanding of the target audience and would not resonate in an Arab context. What's more, the female athlete was running in shorts! The very people the United States hoped to positively affect would not watch it and, if they did, would probably be offended. Like many other ads produced during Beers's tenure, this one also flopped.

Beers was smart and experienced, and had excelled in her field, but her public diplomacy efforts were widely regarded as a failure. At the time, I noted that if she had attempted to sell rice the same way she had sought to market America, Uncle Ben's never would have left the shelf. The White House began to look for other ways to promote its message. In March 2003 at the onset of the Iraq War—an undertaking that was to brand America more profoundly than any of her efforts—Charlotte Beers stepped down.

With the exception of the media outreach center, Beers's brief time at the State Department was striking mainly for the way it reduced the recent history of U.S.–Arab relations to its essence. The campaigns she produced did not lack for technical skill or funding, but they undercut their many positive qualities by substituting politically driven agendas for real understanding. The same would hold true for other U.S. endeavors in the Arab World. From corporate initiatives to public diplomacy, from direct negotiations to military invasions, efforts that replace on-the-ground reality with stale perceptions and rigid ideology are ultimately self-defeating. In today's Middle East, the stakes are extremely high; the United States can no longer afford to gamble money, talent, resources, and lives in a loser's game.

The truth is that the Middle East is critical to both America's own self-interest and global security and stability. Since the end of the Vietnam War in the early 1970s, the United States has been more deeply enmeshed and invested in this region than anywhere else. During this nearly forty-year period, Americans have spent more money, sold more weapons, devoted more political capital, sent more troops, fought more wars, and lost more lives in the Middle East than in any other part of the world. As I write, more than 150,000 young American men and women, joined by nearly 50,000 British and other NATO forces, are fighting wars in and near the region. Hundreds of thousands more Americans and other Westerners are directly involved in the Middle East through businesses and partnerships that are vital to their countries' economic well-being. Conflicts there can threaten the flow of essential resources to Europe and Asia, and hostility toward American policies can aggravate relations between the Arab World and other Western nations. With the United States taking a lead role in both war and peace in the Middle East, how American policy makers handle critical issues in this part of the world is of vital importance to global peace and prosperity. It is the United States that mobilized NATO and other allies to depose the Taliban and hunt down and bring to justice al-Qaeda terrorists being sheltered in Afghanistan. And it is the United States that left the job in Afghanistan unfinished and, bypassing the United Nations, forged a coalition of its own to invade and occupy Iraq. Finally, it is also the United States that reserves for itself the principal leadership role in negotiating an end to the Arab–Israeli conflict.

For all these reasons, gaining a better understanding of the Arab World is not a parochial U.S. interest or merely a collegiate intellectual exercise; nor is it an optional form of culture-stretching. The United States exercises massive economic, diplomatic, and military heft in the region, making it vitally important that Americans know what the people of the Arab World think, want, and hope for. We need to recognize what our mistaken assumptions about Arabs are and, more importantly, what the realities are. Americans need this knowledge to help the United States—and the larger world—avoid the disastrous policy failures of the recent past.

My relationship with the Arab World began early—at birth to be exact. My mother's family had immigrated to America from Lebanon at the turn of the last century. My father came from Lebanon as an adult in the 1920s. My parents married and settled in Utica, New York, where I was raised in a community rich with ethnic heritage. Growing up, I was a Boy Scout, attended Catholic school, served as an altar boy, played American Legion baseball, learned Arabic folktales from my grandmother, danced the *dabka* (a traditional folk dance) at family gatherings, and followed news from the "old country" with my father and uncles.

As I grew older, my involvement with the Arab American community deepened. I have founded and led a number of national Arab American organizations; I write a weekly column that appears in twelve Arab countries and host a current-events talk show that is televised across the Arab World. Both because of the access I gained with Arab leaders and opinion shapers and the recognition my brother John's polling organization, Zogby International, earned through its work in the United States, John and I have been given the opportunity to conduct groundbreaking opinion polls in the Arab World since 1996.

Initially our surveys were limited in scope, measuring consumer satisfaction for the water authority in Saudi Arabia or the performance of the Saudi Chamber of Commerce. Later we were asked to conduct regionwide polls looking at television viewer preferences; consumer confidence levels; and attitudes toward the United States, the United Kingdom, France, and other countries around the world.

In the past decade, we have been asked to survey more complex internal concerns, as we did with the poll we conducted for this book that measures attitudes toward reform, tracks issues of Arab identity, and ranks top political concerns. Efforts such as these have made it possible for us to see more clearly the inner workings and deeper feelings of an entire population and culture.

The full picture of a people emerges not only from high-profile discussions and methodical polling, but also from the countless number of chance encounters with Arabs going about their daily lives. Several years ago, on a flight to Jeddah from Washington, I sat next to a young Saudi woman who had just graduated from Georgetown University. Her English was without accent, and her attire (fashionable jeans and a T-shirt) made her indistinguishable from many American twenty-year-olds. But as we were approaching the kingdom, she—like the other Saudi women onboard—opened her carry-on and removed an *abaya* (traditional robe) before landing. I wasn't surprised, but because we had been talking about her life in Washington, I asked if she minded covering—especially the *niqab*, or face veil. "No," she said without hesitation, "in fact I miss it. In the States, I get tired of being leered at. Covered, I'm in control. I can walk where I please and engage only when it suits me, and I can be seen only by those whom I want to see me." Most debates in the United States don't even begin to make room for a woman who is educated, intelligent, and Westernized and yet happily dons a *niqab*. But that's not because she doesn't exist.

My adult life has been composed of thousands of seemingly small, but revealing moments like these. There's no right or wrong to many of them and frequently no great moral lesson to be drawn. These random episodes simply reflect the Arab World that is, not the one that isn't; the real lives of real people, not the conjured lives of stereotypes that continue to crowd Western media channels.

The fact is that no one, no matter how bright and no matter how committed, can "explain" Arabs and the Arab World secondhand. You can't understand Arab radicalism unless you've sat, as I have, for long afternoons in Tunisia, talking with young recruits to the Muslim Brotherhood. You can't appreciate the Arab fascination with American pop culture until you've spent time in the Kingdom Center in Riyadh, rubbing elbows with young Saudis decked out like teenagers in New York or Los Angeles. You can't comprehend the complicated feelings of Arab Americans without trying to find out what it's like to live inside their skins. And you can't even begin to fathom what drives the "Arab mind" until you engage it on its own ground, on its own terms.

A more positive and successful Western relationship with the Arab World is vital—both to America's and the world's interests. But I also realize that such an engagement is not possible without broadening our understanding beyond the all-too-often outdated and limited debate that misrepresents the region and its people. Only by grasping the real Arab World can America avoid stumbling down the same paths that have repeatedly tarnished our prestige, compromised our allies, and harmed our collective interests in the Middle East.

Though many Western nations have seemed particularly distant from the Arab World in recent years, the simple act of listening can bridge enormous gaps. One person I've met who best understands this is Sheikh Abdullah bin Zayed. Abdullah, who now serves as the minister of foreign affairs for the United Arab Emirates (UAE), is by inclination and lineage both quiet and reflective. His father was Sheikh Zayed, the founder and first president of the UAE, who was revered throughout the Arab World for his strong leadership, humanitarianism, and peaceful dignity.

Though young enough to be my son, Abdullah possesses a quality for which my own father was known: he listens. In meetings, as arguments crisscross the room and, as my mother would say, "lesser men display what they don't know at the tops of their voices," Abdullah sits, hands folded, eyes focused, absorbing. When he speaks, like my father, he speaks softly so that others will listen. And because he is wise (though only in his thirties), many often do.

A number of U.S. ambassadors to the UAE know Sheikh Abdullah's reputation. These diplomats also realize that, although deeply respectful of his country's relations with the United States, he can also be a strong critic of American policy.

In early 2002, Sheikh Abdullah, then minister of information, invited me to participate in a meeting with other ministers from the Gulf Arab countries. They were concerned with the deteriorating image of Arabs and Islam in the West and were seeking ways to change that perception. I was asked to brief the group on what Americans did and did not know about the region and what could be done to improve the public's opinion, and also to describe what I knew of U.S. efforts to engage in public diplomacy in the Arab World.

A discussion ensued with the ministers criticizing U.S. endeavors and arguing among themselves as to what they, as Arabs, could and should do to improve their image in the United States. Through it all, Abdullah listened. He understood what many of his colleagues did not: Americans didn't understand Arabs, and Arabs didn't understand Americans. Therefore, despite best intentions, the efforts of both groups would miss the mark. Finally he spoke, slowly and precisely. Reflecting on failed attempts at public diplomacy on both sides, Sheikh Abdullah noted, "You know, in the end, we Arabs will never be able to help you Americans understand us unless we understand you first. Similarly, you Americans will never succeed in your efforts to communicate to us who you are unless you take time to know us first."[3] My hope for this book is that it will help bridge this gap.

PART 1
HEARING PROBLEMS

1
THE DAY THAT DIDN'T
CHANGE EVERYTHING

WHEN AMERICANS went to bed on the night of September 10, 2001, the Arab World felt very far away. Despite the growing importance of the region, most of us in the West only fleetingly directed our attention its way—during crises like political flare-ups or oil price hikes. Once the various crises passed, the Arab World all but disappeared. Floating on the periphery of our consciousness, its realities were largely shrouded in myths and ignorance.

Then, on September 11, nineteen Arabs hijacked four planes in the worst terrorist attacks in U.S. history. Thousands were killed, and a shocked nation all but shut down for days, while most of the world stood in solidarity with mourning Americans. Long neglected, the Arab World now had our full attention. But as we went about figuring out how to prevent future tragedies, separating the real Arab World from the hype that inundated us via newspaper headlines, overheated talk shows, workplace rumors, and ideologically driven policy was a real chore. Listening is simple—but not easy.

On September 11, 2002, the first anniversary of one of the darkest days in American history, I sat alone in the well of a theater at Rockefeller Center in New York. Facing me in the audience were more than a hundred family members of victims in the 9/11 attacks. Because of my academic work in Islamic Studies and my role within the Arab American community, NBC's Tom Brokaw had invited me to be his guest on a special, commemorative live broadcast.

Of course, I knew this exchange might be painful and difficult. During the past year I had been in touch with several survivors—they had the right to ask tough questions, and I felt a personal responsibility to provide answers and, if possible, to help their healing. I had spent the last several decades of my life trying to share the Arab reality that I knew with other Americans. This meeting was an important part of that job.

Early on in our discussion that day, audience members asked me to explain how such an act of violence could be justified. I immediately replied that there was "no justification, period."

From there, most of the conversation went well, focusing on understanding Arabs and Muslims. I wanted to make clear that Arab Americans had also died in the attacks—that we, too, had mourned. I pointed out that many Arab Americans were first responders at Ground Zero and the Pentagon, and even more serve in the military and law enforcement agencies committed to keeping our country secure.

However, two audience members kept asking: Why can't you Arabs just condemn what happened and not try to justify it? Each time I made clear, with Brokaw's concurrence, that I had unequivocally condemned all terrorist acts and would never tolerate anyone else attempting to justify these heinous acts of murder.[1] But no amount of repetition could get my message across. Most people understood, but in their pain and fear, some had simply stopped listening.

Though I wish I had been able to get through to every member of the audience that day at Rockefeller Center, I respected the effects of such intense trauma. For these people, a national calamity had also resulted in an intensely personal loss. I also understood that it is one thing for private citizens dealing with emotional pain to shut down, but it is quite another when our public commentators stop listening.

Later that same day, I was at Ground Zero. Abu Dhabi Television, the Arab satellite network that carries my weekly political talk show, had purchased the rights to a program called "The Roots of 9/11," produced by the well-known *New York Times* columnist Thomas Friedman.

After the special aired, Friedman joined me in discussion from the former site of the World Trade Center. We were connected by satellite to a student audience in the United Arab Emirates (UAE). For more than an hour, the students reacted to the program they had just seen, and Friedman responded.

The exchange, thoughtful for the most part, became testy at times, with Friedman pontificating that although Americans understand Arabs, Arabs have only surface knowledge of the United States—derived mainly from watching television programs and movies. To bolster his point, Friedman noted that he himself had taken multiple courses on Middle East history in college, and later at Oxford, where he had earned a master's degree in Middle East Studies. Dumbstruck at this sign of unintended arrogance, one very bright young woman pointedly responded, "But we're having this discussion in English"—a fact that Friedman, a widely read columnist on Middle East matters, had apparently missed.[2]

Following the trauma of 9/11, we were repeatedly told that it was a day that changed everything. This made sense: terrorists had been able to kill thousands of innocent Americans, a situation we could hardly accept as status quo. But although the United States was now focusing enormous talent and resources on the Middle East, one critical element hadn't changed: the real Arab World was still largely shrouded in myths. A mixture of fear, arrogance, ignorance, and bias made listening to and understanding Arabs and their world an elusive goal. Sadly, this was a road I'd been down before.

In the very early morning hours of April 20, 1995, I found myself being shuttled in the back of a car through Washington's nearly empty streets. Exhausted from a nonstop stream of interviews, I was headed to one final session.

About sixteen hours earlier, a U.S. Army veteran named Timothy McVeigh had parked a Ryder truck full of explosives outside the shiny Alfred P. Murrah building in downtown Oklahoma City. Minutes later, as McVeigh made his escape on foot, an explosion tore the front off the building, killing 168 people in what was then the worst case of terrorism in U.S. history.

The media quickly seized on the fact that the explosion came on the second anniversary of the final raid by federal agents on the Branch Davidian compound in Waco, Texas. They were right: McVeigh had, in fact, timed his bombing to coincide with both the events in Waco and the 220th anniversary of the Revolutionary War battles at Lexington and Concord. But just as quickly, the media gave space to rumors linking Arabs and Muslims to the attack.

Less than two hours after the explosion, for example, former Oklahoma Congressman David McCurdy—echoing comments made on CBS-TV by a professional Muslim basher, "terrorism expert" Steven Emerson[3]—speculated that Muslims or another Middle Eastern group might well have perpetrated the attack. There was, he noted, a large and active Middle Eastern community in Oklahoma known to support radical causes.[4] He was flat-out wrong: there has never been any evidence connecting Oklahoma's Arab American population to anything untoward. Further, aside from superficial similarities to the bungled but still lethal 1993 World Trade Center bombing, there was simply no evidence linking al-Qaeda or any other Islamic or Arab group to the crime.

Eventually, Congressman McCurdy—who was a finalist for the job of CIA director in the Clinton administration—seemed to realize how far off base he had been. After first suggesting there was Arab or Muslim involvement, McCurdy caught himself, cautioning that we should not jump to conclusions. But it was too late; with McCurdy now seen as validating the speculations of the "experts," the story played out all day that perhaps Arabs had been responsible for the attack.

For my part, I tried to keep the frenzied postattack media coverage grounded in reality. Throughout the day, I defended Arab Americans via radio and television. At 8 P.M., my live call-in television talk show, A Capital View (the precursor to my current show Viewpoint), went on air. We received calls from Arab Americans across the country, outraged over the assault and the loss of life it caused. Many were also deeply concerned with the inevitable consequences that would flow from the suggestions linking Arab Americans to this heinous act.

We even received calls from a number of Arab Americans who were experiencing the beginnings of the backlash. By far, the most poignant calls came from the Arab American community in Oklahoma City. They responded first and foremost as Oklahomans—hurt and grieving for their neighbors and friends who were killed or wounded in the attack. "Oklahoma has always been home to us," one caller noted with pride.[5] But another Oklahoma City family called in, terrified, reporting that an angry mob had gathered outside their house.

Finally, on that early April morning, I had one more stop to make—one more chance to appeal to reason and calm. Washington, DC's CNN studio is tucked away in a concrete maze of high-rise office buildings beside Union Station, the capital's train hub. By day, this area is hardly attractive. At night, it can be a lonely and foreboding place. But I was going there again, as I have many times since, to say two things: like virtually all our countrymen, Arab Americans and American Muslims condemned the Oklahoma City bombing; and the media, congressmen, and would-be CIA directors must take responsibility for their casual speculation. These things would have been obvious to anyone who took the time to listen.

For millions of Americans, 9/11 began as just another Tuesday morning. I was stuck in downtown Washington traffic. While stopped at a light, I noticed the woman in the car next to me signaling. As I rolled down my window, she shouted, "Did you hear?"

"No." I had been meaning to get my car radio fixed.

"A plane just crashed into the World Trade Center!" she yelled. "My father works in that building." Then the light changed, and she moved on. I never saw her again, but I can't forget her look of sheer horror.

By the time I got to the office, everyone was watching television. That was when the second plane hit. Like my colleagues, I was stunned and transfixed by the images of planes slicing through the walls of the World Trade Center, of people jumping from the buildings, and, finally, of the two towers collapsing into a pile and disappearing forever. By then, though, the nightmare had become more personal. My daughter worked near the Pentagon, the third target. She called, frightened and also concerned for me because the White House seemed another likely target, and my office building is only three blocks away.

Building security came to evacuate us around noon. We refused to leave because there was too much work to do. Although no one yet knew for certain the identity of the hijackers, speculation was rife that Arabs were involved, and Arab American community leaders were already phoning us for advice and support. They wanted to know how to respond and what to say to the inevitable media requests.

From early calls and e-mails, we could see signs of a brewing backlash. During this period, my office was under police protection because of what quickly became a flood of hate mail and death threats. Some were personal: "Jim, you towel head. Death to every Arab. We'll slit your throat and kill your children."[6] Others were more general. On October 12, 2001, I was asked by the chair of the U.S. Commission on Civil Rights, Mary Berry, to present testimony on the extent of hate-crime violence that had occurred in the wake of 9/11. In my testimony to the commission, I catalogued hundreds of documented hate crimes against Arab Americans, Muslims, and those thought to be Arabs and Muslims. I noted that there had been seven murders as well as other acts of violence and threats of violence.[7]

This backlash was profoundly disturbing and quite frightening to Arab Americans. We, too, were pained by the horror that had been inflicted on our country. We, too, needed to mourn. But we were pulled away from our grieving and forced to look over our shoulders to respond to those who struck out against us with hate, telling Arab Americans, in effect, "You are not a part of us." This produced a double hurt.

Another thought plagued me. I was angry, of course, at the threats and prejudice. But more than that, I was angry at the terrorists who had violated the openness and freedom of my country. They had killed thousands of my fellow citizens. And in so doing, they had also caused incalculable damage to the millions in the Arab American and Muslim American communities.

Each day after the attack, as I read new reports detailing the activities of the hijackers leading up to 9/11, I was struck by how sinister it was that these men, armed with such hideous intent, were able to take advantage of the opportunities and the almost naïve goodwill of so many Americans. The hijackers had found homes in which to live and schools to train them, and they had moved about without question—all the while planning their deadly mission.

How was it, I wondered, that as these hijackers prepared to kill thousands, they weren't moved to question their intended evil by the good they saw around them every day? The answer lies in the perverse logic of closed ears. Fundamental to terrorism is a willful abstraction, a dehumanizing of victims, and a blunt refusal to understand. The terrorist's mind-set relies on an active denial of reality.

Concerned with the growing backlash, leading Arab American organizations called on the Bush administration to speak out against this bigotry. We took our appeal to the national media and, using our national network, to grassroots Americans. The Ad Council of America sponsored an ad from my organization promoting greater understanding of Arab Americans and American Muslims. The ad appeared in the newspapers of more than 10,000 communities, and it was ultimately converted into a TV ad carried by the Starz-Encore networks and seen in 64 million households nationwide.

The response was immediate and profoundly gratifying. In the weeks following the attacks, I made multiple daily television appearances on every major network. I did radio shows and interviews with dozens of newspapers. Soon, the Civil Rights Division at the Department of Justice (DOJ) called us to an emergency meeting. We had requested that the DOJ issue a statement condemning hate crimes against Arab Americans and American Muslims. We had also asked that it set up a mechanism to prosecute those who committed hate crimes against our community. They agreed to both of our requests. The FBI began to investigate possible civil rights violations with the intent to prosecute quickly in order to set an example of enforcement.

Two days after the attacks, I had received personal calls and messages from leaders across the political spectrum—from Senator Ted Kennedy to Senator John McCain, and from Senator Joe Lieberman to former Congressman Jack Kemp. All offered support and acted to defend Arab American and American Muslim rights. Within two weeks, the tone of the e-mails we were receiving had changed: they were now either expressing support and opposing prejudice or asking for information about Arab Americans, Arab history, and Islam. A month after the attacks, the acts of hate had declined precipitously. This was the good news about America in the aftermath of 9/11—the overwhelming generosity and understanding of the American people, even in a time of great stress.

From a distance, Americans have followed many traumatic events in the media age. But there was something quite different about 9/11. This time Americans, along with their many supporters around the world, did not simply suffer for the victims; they suffered with them. Because the weapons were ordinary civilian aircraft, the death scene a place of work, the buildings iconic—the World Trade Center and the Pentagon—and the casualties so many, those of us who watched were affected to our core. Each of us said, "It could have been any one of us." And in a way it was. People from virtually every nationality, race, and faith had died. As we listened to the stories of those who survived, each of us was able to relate to the horror, the loss, and the fear. As a nation, Americans were filled with an almost inconsolable sadness.

As time went on, out of this enormous anguish, fear, and confusion there arose an honest curiosity about the region from whence the nineteen hijackers had come. There was a real chance that, as Americans reached deep inside to rebuild, this tragedy could actually lead to understanding. Clearly, this was not what the terrorists or the purveyors of hate had wanted. They wanted to show they could make the West bleed. They welcomed talk of a religious war or a clash of civilizations. But the opportunity for mutual understanding was there just the same.

2
LISTENING IN
THE LEVANT

IN 1971, I TOOK MY first trip to the Middle East and got my first lesson in Arab realities on the ground. After visiting Beirut and my family's home up in the mountains, I continued on to a Palestinian refugee camp, Ein al Hilweh in south Lebanon, where I planned to conduct research for my doctoral dissertation. Based on the perceptions I had grown up with, I expected to find a huge tent city full of broken and displaced people. But when I got there, instead of a morose and gray place, the camp was incredibly vibrant. There was movement everywhere—people, cars, and donkeys pulling carts. The refugees did not live in tents, but in densely populated two- or three-story concrete buildings. Though the camp was clearly poor, people weren't sitting around weeping into blankets. Instead, they had built lives and were going about living them as best they could.

The camps weren't located near fertile land, so there was dust everywhere. Yet the refugees had planted grapevines in oil barrels and grew smaller plants in coffee tins placed on windowsills or anywhere else they could, creating a green landscape. I was amazed that I could walk into somebody's house in a refugee camp, and it would look almost like my father's home in the mountain village. We would sit and have coffee on the patio under a grape arbor. The chairs were a bit frayed perhaps and the air dustier, but these Palestinians, making do with what was available, had transplanted their village lifestyle into this camp.

In Arabic, the word *samoud* means "steadfastness," and it perfectly describes the Palestinian refugees—they held on to and protected the memories of what they had previously. One day during my visit, I talked to an old woman who, as was common, carried on a string around her neck the key to her old house in Palestine—now appropriated by Israeli settlers.

"Do you want to see my home?" she asked. When I replied, "Yes," she pulled out an old, faded picture album of her house. This gesture certainly revealed a sense of loss, but remarkably, her simple nostalgia and longing for her past life far exceeded any raw bitterness.

In addition to witnessing this astonishing ability of the human spirit to overcome grim circumstances, I learned the importance of listening and logged the personal stories of dozens of Palestinians I met in Ein al Hilweh camp. When I was leaving, the grandmother of my friend, who had acted as my guide, asked me: "Now that you have heard our stories, what will you do with them?" Her challenge taught me a life-altering lesson: when you really listen and learn, you have the responsibility to act.

It was during my dissertation research that I first became acquainted with the King-Crane Report, the first modern survey of Arab opinion. In many ways the survey has been my polestar ever since.

In 1919, following the mind-bending violence of the first modern World War, the victorious Allied Powers met in Paris to remake the world. The prime ministers of Italy, France, and Great Britain as well as U.S. President Woodrow Wilson, collectively known as the "Big Four," were the decisive diplomatic players at the meeting. Under their leadership, the defeated Central Powers were picked apart. The Austro-Hungarian Empire was dissolved into smaller central European countries. Germany lost territory and was served with an extremely punitive and expensive peace treaty. In several cases, the triumphant Big Four parceled out bits of land to themselves. France grew at Germany's expense, and Italy expanded to the north into former Austro-Hungarian territory.

Beyond these great powers exercising the prerogatives of victory, the meeting was generally marked by self-interested scrapping for territories among the leaders of dozens of additional nations and international groups. Australia, for example, tried (and failed) to extend its territorial borders all the way north to the equator. Even the most isolated Allied nation, New Zealand, managed to extend its boundaries with the acquisition of a Pacific island formerly known as German Samoa. It was in this context of self-serving agendas that the fate of the traditionally Arab lands of the defeated Ottoman Empire was decided.

During WWI, the Allies had overcome the Ottomans with the important assistance of local Arabs who had rebelled against Turkish rule.

Among these former Ottoman subjects was Emir Faisal, the son of Sharif Hussein of Mecca. Faisal arrived at the Paris conference—with a delegation that included T. E. Lawrence—seeking assurance that the British would honor the commitments they had made to his father: postwar independence for all the Arab lands that had been liberated from Turkish control.

The conference also heard from Chaim Weizmann, a leader of the British Zionist movement. Weizmann soon would be named head of the World Zionist Organization and eventually would become the first president of Israel. In Paris, Weizmann argued for the establishment of a Jewish homeland in the Arab territory known as Palestine. During his presentation, Weizmann cited in its entirety the Balfour Declaration, British Foreign Secretary Lord Arthur James Balfour's 1917 promise to the Zionist movement that the British government favored the establishment of a Jewish homeland in Palestine.[1]

It was exactly this type of conflicting maze of treaties and agreements that had led to the outbreak of the Great War. And it was with the aim of preventing another such calamity that in 1919 Woodrow Wilson proposed the foundation of a League of Nations—a body designed to bring international diplomacy into the light of day and under the rule of law. Wilson believed that by preventing the caustic buildup of labyrinthine, contradictory allegiances and by promoting democracy, sovereignty, liberty, and self-determination, an environment for a lasting peace would be created.

The idealism of the League of Nations made Wilson the highest-minded of the Big Four. American ambitions in 1919 were largely limited to Latin America; Americans generally had little interest in Old World entanglements. As a result, Wilson did not arrive in Paris with an agenda of expanding U.S. territory but with the idea that a lasting peace was achievable and laying its foundation was the best possible outcome.

So when the question of how to divide the formerly Ottoman lands arose, Wilson made a proposal in keeping with his ideals of self-determination: ask the people who live there. This was, of course, an idea completely alien to the imperial objectives of France and Britain, and certainly out of place at the Paris conference, where the unofficial motto was "to the victor belong the spoils." Yet Wilson was undaunted by the perceived radical nature of his suggestion. Instead, he declared that the newly liberated Arabs should shape their own destiny and that any settlement "of territory [or] of sovereignty [should be determined on] the basis of the free acceptance of that settlement by the people immediately concerned."[2] With that, Wilson commissioned a survey of Arab views.

In June of 1919, an American commission, led by the president of Oberlin College, Dr. Henry King, and businessman and diplomat Charles Crane, arrived in the Mediterranean coastal city of Jaffa to begin the first-ever Arab public opinion survey. The commission traveled throughout what was then known as Greater Syria, including modern-day Lebanon, Syria, Jordan, and Palestine/Israel. Commission members visited three dozen towns, met with representatives of 442 organizations (153 political associations, 41 economic and social institutions, and 248 religious groups), and received nearly 2,000 petitions. At each stop they tried to ascertain what the local population wanted for their political future—to be independent or placed under the mandate of a foreign power. The commission asked how the people viewed British and French plans to divide their region. They also questioned local populations about Britain's intention to support the Zionist goal of a "Jewish homeland" in Palestine. At the time, the population of the region in question was 3,247,500, of whom 2,365,000 were Muslim, 587,560 were Christian, 140,000 were Druze, and 110,000 were Jewish.

The results showed particularly adamant views on certain issues. According to the report, "The non-Jewish population of Palestine—nearly nine-tenths of the whole—are emphatically against the entire Zionist program. . . . There was no one thing upon which the population of Palestine were more agreed than upon this." This feeling was also shared by the broader population of the entire Arab East: "Only two requests—those for a united Syria and for independence—had a larger support" (see Table 2.1).[3]

Based on the responses of the local populations, the King-Crane report made a series of suggestions. To answer the broad question of how to manage the formerly Ottoman lands, the authors proposed that a united Syria be led by Emir Faisal. The report recommended that this greater Syria first be placed under the control of a temporary American mandate that would follow certain international rules. This recommendation was based on the fact that 60% of those whom King and Crane surveyed favored an American role in the transition, as opposed to only 14% who supported French intervention and 3% who advocated British involvement. The report also suggested that the Zionist project, to which the authors claimed to have been initially sympathetic, be dramatically scaled back by

TABLE 2.1   PERCENTAGE OF PETITIONS TO THE KING-CRANE COMMISSION ADVOCATING
VARYING POSITIONS ON THE "ZIONIST PROGRAM"*

Issue Under Consideration	Greater Syria**	Only Palestine
For the complete Zionist program of a Jewish state and open Jewish immigration to Palestine	0.6	2.7
For a modified Zionist program	0.4	3.0
Against the Zionist program	72.3	85.3
For a united Syria	80.4	—

*The King-Crane findings are based on 1,863 petitions received from mayors, municipal councils, societies, religious communities (Muslim, Christian, Jewish), professional and trade associations, chambers of commerce, and youth organizations.

**This region included present-day Syria, Lebanon, Jordan, and Israel/Palestine.

limiting Jewish migration and by questioning the advisability of a Jewish state in Palestine.

The report's suggestions on specific issues continued for pages, but what is most striking is its overall theme—that local, in this case largely Arab, opinions mattered. Like Wilson, King and Crane fully accepted that imposing policy against the will of the population would generate massive resistance. However, the British and French—old hands at the colonial game—were undeterred.

Lord Balfour, for one, sharply rejected the Wilsonian approach. "In Palestine," he declared, "we do not propose even to go through the form of consulting the wishes of the present inhabitants of the country, though the American commission has. . . . Zionism, be it right or wrong, good or bad, is rooted in age-long tradition, in present needs, in future hopes, of far profounder import than the desire and prejudices of the 700,000 Arabs who now inhabit that ancient land."[4]

In the end, Lord Balfour had his way. Instead of granting independence, France and Great Britain drew boundaries, dismembering the Arab East: France imposed its influence on the newly created states of Lebanon and Syria, and Great Britain enforced its role in Transjordan, Iraq, and Palestine (with the understanding that it would become the "Jewish homeland").

In March 1920, Emir Faisal was proclaimed King of Greater Syria by a pan-Arab conference, but later that year he was deposed by the French, who had been awarded the mandate for Syria by an international conference in April in San Remo, Italy. Faisal then fled to the United Kingdom. A year later, the British decided to install Faisal as the head of Iraq, where most people had never heard of him.

The King-Crane report itself was sealed and disappeared from public view until 1922. When it reemerged, initially in the pages of New York's *Editor & Publisher* magazine, the report was heralded by the *New York Times* as the document "desired by every editorial writer in the world; every teacher and student of history . . . every person doing business in the Near East; every member of Congress; every Foreign Office everywhere."[5] Unfortunately, the die had been cast: Britain and France had already carved up the territory in question, and the U.S. Congress had just passed a resolution endorsing the Zionist program in Palestine.

Thus the stage was set for the multiple conflicts that have plagued the region ever since. For years, the British and French ruled swaths of the Arab World without much feel or concern for Arab opinions or realities. But reality always resurfaces. As British Foreign Secretary Jack Straw told the *New Statesman* in 2002: "A lot of the problems we are having to deal with now, I have to deal with now, are a consequence of our colonial past. . . . The Balfour declaration and the contradictory assurances which were being given to Palestinians in private at the same time as they were being given to the Israelis—again, an interesting history for us but not an entirely honourable one."[6]

Thus, too, was established the precedent of ignoring Arab concerns whenever it was convenient to do so.

Nearly a century after Western powers divvied up the Middle East in the aftermath of World War I, the landscape has changed in many ways. The Jewish state, only a theory then, has been firmly established for more than sixty years. The commerce of oil has turned once dusty outposts into vibrant modern cities. Colonialism has waned, taking the old colonial power structure along with it. Today, the United States is the dominant international player in the Middle East, but the fundamental lesson from all those years ago remains the same: Arab opinions matter.

Back then, Henry King and Charles Crane compiled their survey of Arab opinion by immersing themselves in the region. As revealing as their findings were, today's polling methodologies create opportunities for a more scientific assessment and detailed examination of public attitudes. For nearly four decades, I have been doing essentially what King and Crane did: talking with Arabs and listening to what they say. Most recently, I've been involved in polling and interviewing Arabs and then using that information to help make certain that the Arab World we, in the West, see is—to paraphrase President Barack Obama's historic Cairo speech—the world that is, not the one that isn't. Blindly imposing foreign notions—no matter how well intended—often has disastrous consequences. Worst of all, not listening closes us off to truths that, rightly understood, would further our ability to constructively engage the region.

Following 9/11, I received an invitation to travel to the Arab World to meet with the leadership of a newly formed think tank, the Arab Thought Foundation (ATF). Launched in June 2001, the ATF brought together prominent Arab intellectuals and business leaders. Their goal was to promote self-understanding and to encourage public debate on critical issues in order to help foster better understanding between Arabs and the world community. My hosts had invited me because they wanted to learn more about American and Arab public opinion. They wanted to explore ways to communicate more effectively with Americans, and they sought to inform U.S. public opinion about Arabs and Islam.

My first conversation was with the chair of the foundation, Prince Khalid al Faisal, son of the late Saudi King Faisal. Like his brothers (Saud, the current Saudi foreign minister, and Turki, who served for a time as Saudi Arabia's ambassador in Washington), Prince Khalid is a thoughtful and deeply reflective man. At the time of our meeting, he was clearly troubled by the growing rift he could sense was developing between the United States and the Arab World, and he was seeking ways for the ATF to play even a modest role in addressing the situation. My suggestion to him was a simple one: "You need to tell your story to America. They need to hear from Arabs and get to know what Arabs want and who you are."

Though he agreed that such a campaign was necessary, he paused at one point to observe, "But do we really know who we are? Can we even give a clear answer to that question? And if we attempted such a campaign, whose answers would we use to describe our reality?"[7]

Prince Khalid's questions were, in fact, difficult and sensitive ones to ask and answer, because no society gives one uniform answer to fundamental questions of beliefs, values, and identity. Addressing these questions would be a complex task, but we at Zogby International resolved to work with the ATF to conduct an in-depth poll of Arab public opinion for the first time since King and Crane had undertaken the same job eight decades earlier. We did so because we believed that there were two distinct audiences—Arab and Western—who would benefit from an effort to learn "what Arabs think."

Zogby International had developed the necessary expertise for this project through our previous work on a number of multi-nation Arab polls. Working with the Arab Thought Foundation, we selected eight countries comprising a diverse range of Arab experience. We chose two countries from Africa (Morocco and Egypt), two from the Levant (Lebanon and Jordan), three Arab Gulf states (Saudi Arabia, the UAE, and Kuwait), and the Arab citizens in Israel. We then worked with the ATF to construct a survey composed of ninety-two questions designed to measure Arabs' sense of identity, political concerns, values, and attitudes toward their own and other countries.

In each of the eight countries, we hired fieldworkers and outlined a methodology for them to ensure that our survey included a representative sample of opinions reflecting the full range of demographics (gender, age, education level, etc.) in each area. We also defined for our fieldworkers the selection process to be utilized in conducting the required face-to-face interviews. At the end of the project, our team had conducted 3,800 interviews, tallied the responses, and presented reports with detailed examinations and comparisons of each country's views as a whole and of views categorized by demographic.

What did we find in this in-depth examination of Arab attitudes?[8] For one, we learned that Arabs are largely focused on issues close to home. When we asked our respondents what mattered most to them in their lives, they identified "the quality of [their] work," "family," "religion," and "job security." Similarly, when we asked those surveyed to rank their top political concerns in order of priority, the overall focus once again appeared to be on their personal and family life, with an interesting twist: ranking number three, just after "protecting civil and personal rights" and "health care," and just ahead of "personal economic security," was "the rights of the Palestinian people."

When we asked our respondents to describe their attitudes toward a number of countries around the world, the United States ranked poorly everywhere, with the United Kingdom faring only slightly better. However, France and Germany had overall favorable ratings in half of the countries we surveyed, and Canada received the highest ranking of all Western countries covered in the survey.

In October 2002, I traveled to Cairo to release our findings at the Royal Nile Hilton Hotel in a press conference convened by the ATF and attended by more than one hundred international journalists. I also fielded press inquiries for the next two days from reporters seeking more details on the survey, including seven calls from Canadian news outlets excited to cover the story of their country's high ratings across the region.

After the press conference, I watched as small groups of Arabs involved in the ATF's yearlong effort gathered to pore over the findings. Some checked out how their countrymen answered specific questions; others examined where their demographic group stood on various issues. The ensuing discussions lasted well into the night. By following in the steps of Henry King and Charles Crane, we had helped create a tool that allowed both Arabs and those of us in the West to better understand the answers to Prince Khalid's thoughtful questions. But our survey, no matter how groundbreaking, was only the beginning of our wider effort to define and listen to the voices of the Arab World.

3
KNOWLEDGE
WARS

- Americans who incorrectly identify Iran as an Arab country: 65%
- Americans who know that Iraq shares a border with Syria: 23%
- Americans who can identify 1948 as the year of Israel's War of Independence: 37%
- Americans who believe that Muslims tend to be religious fanatics: 42%
- Americans who say they would like to know more about Arab countries and people: 59%

From Zogby International
Poll of American Opinion
—December 2009[1]

ON OCTOBER 15, 2001, I happened to be visiting the Hart Senate Office Building in Washington, DC, when anthrax spores were discovered in an envelope addressed to South Dakota Senator Tom Daschle. Anthrax, though dangerous, is generally treatable. However, authorities had already confirmed one death—a photo editor at the south Florida offices of American Media Inc., publisher of the *Sun* and other tabloids—and the media and politicians were all over the story. When I was instructed a week later to show up at the Dirksen Building across the street from the Capitol to be tested for the bacteria, I expected a grim time of waiting in line with more than one thousand grumbling Senate staff members, Capitol Hill police, lobbyists, news reporters, unlucky deliverymen, and others like myself who had happened to be at the wrong office at the wrong time. My fears were misplaced.

The line moved slowly—I was in it for four hours—but quietly and calmly. Washingtonians are normally not patient people. To be sure, some worked while they waited, and others talked on their cell phones, but just about everyone was in good spirits, cooperative, and friendly. The terrifying images of 9/11 are easy to recall, but the widespread generosity and fraternity that blossomed in the autumn of 2001 are often forgotten. We had been attacked and humbled, but the terror had also suddenly bonded Americans together with a common purpose.

Just a few months earlier, whenever Washington residents heard a siren, they would speed up their cars in an effort to beat the ambulance or fire truck through the next intersection. If they had to wait, they complained. They were, of course, important people with important business, and they couldn't be held up even for an emergency. But after the horror of 9/11—and the heroism of police, firefighters, and other first responders in the face of those attacks—Washingtonians became more attentive and patient, more solicitous and thoughtful. At the sound of a siren, they actually stopped and waited—and toward the end of 2001, there were lots of sirens.

This new attitude went beyond courtesy—it created a unique opportunity for listening. Standing in line that day waiting to be tested for anthrax, we strangers, brought together by accident, fell into conversation about our children and what we did for a living. Almost invariably, when I mentioned my work with the Arab American Institute, ears would perk up. My neighbors in line knew little about the Middle East and even less about Islam, but they were curious and asked thoughtful questions.

What we needed right then, I came to realize, was not to shut the door but to swing it wide open. Americans and Arabs already worked and traded together to the tune of almost $200 billion annually, but we still did not know each other. There were minority factions on both sides—religious fanatics and ideological hard-liners—working to push us apart, but given a real opportunity, the vast majority of Arabs and Americans would be able to recognize our common bonds.

I wasn't the only one in the wake of 9/11 who sensed a need to increase American understanding about the Arab World. Concerned by the anti-Arab backlash that followed the terrorist attacks, school districts and groups of educators around the United States launched efforts to enhance their limited curricula pertaining to the Middle East. My office in Washington was deluged by calls from teachers and principals requesting new and better information about Arab Americans, the Arab World, and

Islam. Encouraged and supported by the Community Relations Service of the Department of Justice and the National Education Association, we prepared materials for educators covering topics ranging from the role of Arab Americans in American life to the contributions of Arabs to world civilization.[2]

These materials were distributed to thousands of school districts and individual educators seeking information in the immediate aftermath of 9/11—an initial attempt to confront years of neglect. At the high school level, Arabs barely appeared in history lessons—and then only as the losers of the Battle of Tours or the Spanish Reconquista. When the contemporary Arab World was mentioned, it was often depicted as stuck in the past.

The issues of bias and lack of information about Arabs in American textbooks have been highlighted in academic studies for decades. For example, an extensive study of secondary school social studies textbooks first undertaken in the mid-1970s and periodically updated by the Middle East Studies Association (MESA), the premier organization of American academics dealing with the region, found that secondary school textbooks "often convey an oversimplified, naïve, and even distorted image of the Middle Eastern cultures, history, and politics."[3] The researchers found a "prevalence of error and stereotypes"[4] and "major cultural bias."[5] Depictions of Arabs as "backward," "nomads," or "Muslim warriors" distorted the history of the region and diminished its people and culture.[6]

Twenty years later, the situation was little improved. After poring over history and geography textbooks, the author of one 1995 scholarly review described "an over-portrayal of deserts, camels and nomads" in chapters on the Middle East. (This was fifteen years ago, and these were the very textbooks that taught the young men and women who are now teaching.) As for the numerous distortions in the presentation of Islam, the study concluded that "it is perhaps time for educators at the college and university level to send a red alert to their colleagues at the pre-collegiate level."[7]

In 1998, I visited a school in Dearborn, Michigan, and the trip brought the issue of educational neglect home for me. I had been asked by a group of Yemeni American students and their parents to come to Dearborn, home to 29,000 Arab Americans—the largest concentration in any American city. Most are of Lebanese descent, mainly Shi'a from south

Lebanon. There is also a sizable group of Yemenis and, more recently, Iraqi Shi'a who escaped Saddam Hussein's regime. Most are recent immigrants or first-generation Americans, and most are Muslim.

During that year's Ramadan, the month when Muslims fast during daylight hours, the students at one of the city's high schools reported problems with the school's administration. Instead of allowing the fasting students to go to a study hall during lunch period, the school had insisted that they sit in a cafeteria where some of their non-Muslim peers teased, taunted, and on a few occasions even threw food at them. Fights had broken out, and parents and students were asking for advice on how to ease tensions.

At a town meeting convened at a Yemeni community center, one young and very eloquent Yemeni American girl rose to tell me her story. After witnessing the growing conflict in the cafeteria, she had made an effort to discuss the matter with the school's principal. She had told the principal that she did not blame the other students because she recognized that Islam and Arab culture were strange to them. She had asked the principal to arrange a discussion so that she and other Muslim students could help their classmates better understand their culture. The principal had rejected the girl's proposal, telling her that his job was not to help her explain Muslim culture to her peers but to teach the Muslim students about American culture.

Despite urgent warnings from the Middle East Studies Association, it wasn't until after 9/11 that our educational system got a real jolt. Following the attacks, the Chicago Council on Foreign Relations examined the problems faced by educators who were seeking to meet their students' need to learn more about the Arab World and Islam. The group's report concluded that 9/11 had created a "pedagogical challenge" in which teachers found that they "lacked the curricular materials with which to assist their students in understanding the world, the US, their city, and their lives after these events. . . . Suddenly, they needed to teach about Islam, the Arab World, and Afghanistan, parts of the world most teachers knew little or nothing about."[8] Although a few resourceful educators were able to locate additional classroom materials, they "sometimes found that their efforts were undone by other teachers whose biases and stereotypes, nourished by lack of knowledge, influenced their teaching."[9]

In short, making up for decades of institutionalized ignorance was a tall order, but suddenly there was not just an *opportunity* for Americans to better understand the Arab World, but an obvious, gaping *need* to do so. More articles were appearing in U.S. newspapers about Islam than ever before, and more thoughtful questions were being asked about the Middle East than I could ever remember. Moreover, as anti-Arab hate crimes across the United States quickly reverted to pre-9/11 levels, Arab American communities were increasingly being called upon to teach and share their specialized knowledge about Arab culture and Islam.

Under the headline "For Linguists, Job Is Patriotic Duty," *USA Today* described the efforts of Arab Americans to help fill FBI Director Robert Mueller's September 17, 2001, call for applicants who could translate Arabic. These language skills were no longer merely academic. As the *USA Today* piece and many similar articles pointed out, numerous American intelligence agencies were frustrated by the lack of translators for confiscated documents, videotapes, secret wiretaps, and other electronic surveillance with possible links to terrorist plots.[10]

America's thirty-year distant embrace of the Arab World—despite the mountains of money invested there, the many high-profile but uneven diplomatic pursuits, and the occasional dispersion of tens of thousands of U.S. soldiers to the region—was now history. The Middle East was obviously America's top foreign-policy priority, and there was a lot of catching up to do. Colleges and universities made a determined effort to expand course offerings in Arabic language study, Arab history, and Islam. Congress appropriated $20 million to augment the budget of a few premier U.S. Middle East studies programs, and, as I noted, school districts sought additional materials about the Arab World in response to the growing need to know more about the region. However, despite the clear need in the early 2000s for more U.S. citizens fluent in Arabic language and culture, opposition quickly emerged.

In November 2001, a Washington-based group called the American Council for Trustees and Alumni issued a report entitled "Defending Civilization: How Our Universities Are Failing America and What Can Be Done About It," which accused higher-education institutions of "moral equivocation" for their failure to support "the War on Terrorism."[11] They further charged that in rushing to add courses in "Islam and Asian Studies," universities "reinforced the mindset that it was America—and America's failure to understand Islam—that were to blame" for 9/11.[12]

Then in 2003, an ad hoc group of conservative activists came together to oppose the congressional expenditure on Middle East studies. The effort was initiated by Stanley Kurtz, a fellow at the Hoover Institution and a contributing editor to the conservative Web site *National Review Online*. Kurtz criticized the congressionally funded Middle East studies programs for having a pro-Arab bias and fostering "extreme and one-sided criticisms of American foreign policy."[13]

Kurtz's effort was supported by two other longtime critics of Arab and Muslim studies, Martin Kramer and Daniel Pipes. Kramer, a scholar at the Washington Institute for Near East Policy, made his views on this subject known in his book *Ivory Towers on Sand: The Failure of Middle Eastern Studies in America*—an indictment of academics as too pro-Arab and left wing. Pipes, also an author who has written books and columns attacking Muslims in the United States, is probably best known for launching Campus Watch, an Internet blacklist that encourages students to report on and harass teachers who are "pro-Arab sympathizers" or "apologists for . . . militant Islam."[14]

Together, the group promoted the International Studies Higher Education Act, a bill before Congress that purported to encourage college programs that "reflect diverse perspectives and the full range of views."[15] What they actually sought was the establishment of a board to monitor academic programs and report on whether or not they complied with the "diversity of views" mandate. According to the bill, those programs not in compliance would be stripped of funding. Supporters of the Middle East studies centers warned that allowing such a board would amount to the creation of a government education censor that could align university scholarship with a specific political orientation. As New York University history professor Zachary Lockman pointed out in *Salon,* "There's the threat that [educational] centers will be punished for not toeing the official line out of Washington, which is an unprecedented degree of federal intrusion into a university-based area studies program."[16]

Although the bill in the form proposed by Kramer, Pipes, and Kurtz did not pass in the Senate, some of its proposed language has been inserted into congressional legislation authorizing higher education funding,[17] justifying Kramer's boast: "Well, academic colleagues get used to it. Yes, you are being watched. Those obscure articles in campus newspapers are now available on the Internet, and they will be harvested. Your syllabi, which you've also posted, will be scrutinized. Your websites will be visited late at night."[18]

Daniel Pipes's activities were not limited to cyberstalking university professors; he also targeted some of the public school teachers and school districts that had embraced the monumental task of broadening America's knowledge of the Arab World. Among his more ambitious plans to this end was bringing down New York City's Khalil Gibran International Academy (KGIA), planned to open in 2007 as the first Arabic–English dual-language school in the United States.[19] Like many other dual-language schools across the country, the Khalil Gibran International Academy sought to teach native speakers alongside non-native speakers, with the expectation that all students would develop functional language skills in both Arabic and English by graduation. Beginning with a pioneering sixth-grade class, the school would steadily expand into a middle and high school.

Though ambitious, those involved in the academy's founding—including the New York–based nonprofit New Visions for Public Schools—were not naïve. Aware of the long-standing political tensions that might be mobilized by a public school dedicated to Arabic language and culture, the founders took several precautions. The school's name, for one, was selected in part for political reasons. Kahlil Gibran was a Christian, Lebanese-born poet who grew up largely in Boston before later moving to New York—in short, an uncontroversial Arab American figure. Likewise, the woman who would lead the new school was Debbie Almontaser, a Muslim and Arab American veteran of the New York City school system who also had a long history of fostering interfaith dialogue.

After years of planning, the academy's September 4, 2007, opening was promising enough. There was a clear demand to begin fostering both a new generation of U.S.-born Arabic speakers and an educational environment where these students might not be such rare commodities. However, within a year both Almontaser and her successor were gone, victims of a withering barrage of attacks. By the time the school reopened for year two, it was in a new location, run by a third principal, with a radically altered vision: Arabic language instruction would be limited, and high school extension was a fast-receding dream. The school staff was ever-changing—many teachers quit because of stress—and textbooks were tattered because teachers felt compelled to cut out all the pictures of mosques.[20]

This dismantling of the Khalil Gibran school actually began months before a single student passed through its doors. Its seemingly uncontroversial name alone had been enough to cause hate blogs to pillory the school.[21] Then, several months before the first day of school, the *New York Sun* published an op-ed by Daniel Pipes, "A Madrassa Grows in Brooklyn," in which he blasted the school. In the article, Pipes, beginning in the best rhetorical fashion, praised the necessity of schools like the Khalil Gibran academy and the theoretical importance and value of Arabic language skills. Those pleasantries out of the way, he went into attack mode: "In practice, however, I strongly oppose the KGIA and predict that its establishment will generate serious problems," Pipes wrote. "I say this because Arabic-language instruction is inevitably laden with pan-Arabist and Islamist baggage."[22]

Then, instead of giving examples of how an acceptable, depoliticized version of Arabic might be taught, Pipes went on to cite examples that he claimed prove even Arab grammar lessons carry the dictums of certain political stances. Pipes even claimed that merely learning Arabic carries the assumption of an eventual conversion to Islam. Instead of wrestling with what—even by his arguments—would seem to be the bigger issue of how to create our much-needed Arabic speakers, Pipes simply called for the shuttering of the nation's first Arabic dual-language school before it even opened. Pipes pledged that "the fight goes on. The next step is to get the academy itself canceled."[23]

Even though three years later the Khalil Gibran International Academy still exists, its total enrollment is limited to sixty sixth-grade students. The school has shed students and staff, all of whom learned a lesson crystallized by one twelve-year-old: "I don't read the articles, but everyone is against learning Arabic as a second language."[24] In short, Pipes and the broader campaign of enforced ignorance toward the Arab World have been—to date—largely successful.

Another approach taken to thwart efforts to expand educational offerings was to alarm parents about materials and workshops designed to better educate students on Islam and the Arab World. A 2005 report issued by the Jewish Telegraphic Agency (JTA) wire service warned that "teaching programs funded by Saudi Arabia [are making] their way into elementary and secondary classrooms." The report charged that Saudi-supported materials were influencing U.S. educators through "teacher-training seminars," "the dissemination of supplemental teaching materials," and "school textbooks paid for by taxpayers, some of them vetted by activists with Saudi ties."[25]

The JTA report also singled out as suspect respected university-run programs at Harvard, Georgetown, and Columbia, as well as groups of educators and diplomats who have committed decades of their lives to correcting omissions in U.S. educational programs. In its lengthy piece, however, the JTA only suggested one example of alleged "Saudi influence": the Arab World Studies Notebook (AWSN). In fact, the AWSN is an extraordinary and comprehensive program to provide secondary and post-secondary teachers with supplementary materials and training sessions that will enhance their teaching of Islam and Arab history. The JTA attempted to discredit the effort and to portray the materials as alien and suspicious by linking the AWSN to some Saudi contributions, mentioning a donation from Saudi Aramco (Saudi Arabia's state-run oil company) and the Middle East Policy Council (MEPC), a Washington-based think tank. Although at the time of the JTA report the MEPC was headed by former U.S. Ambassador to Saudi Arabia Charles Freeman, the group's sponsorship of the AWSN began under Freeman's predecessor, former U.S. Senator George McGovern. The JTA report did acknowledge denials by the MEPC and by the AWSN's author of any Saudi influence, but continued to assert the Saudi connection, citing only guilt by association.

Despite this negative pressure, after 9/11 secondary- and university-level courses teaching Islam as well as Arabic language, history, and culture did experience a spike in enrollment, but serious problems and shortages remain. Of the more than 2,400 four-year colleges in the United States, only 370 offer any Arabic language classes. And although the number of students taking Arabic has doubled—now more than 23,000 are enrolled in Arabic courses—only 2,400 are in advanced-level classes that can lead to proficiency in the language. By comparison, four times as many students are taking German, and three times as many are studying Italian or Japanese. In fact, the number of students enrolled in Arabic is roughly equal to those taking ancient Greek.[26] And only sixty-one universities offer degree programs in either Middle East studies or Islam. At the K–12 level, the status of Arabic language instruction in the United States is even more dire. A 2009 report released by the Center for Applied Linguistics found that in 2008 only 1% of America's elementary schools and less than 1% of high schools provided students with opportunities to learn Arabic.[27]

Likewise, despite America's deepening engagement in the Arab World, there remains a severe shortage of Arabic language speakers. A 2009 Government Accountability Office report found that more than a

third of federal government employees in Arabic-language public diplomacy posts in 2006 were unable to speak Arabic at the designated level of
proficiency required for their position.[28]

A similar metric of this lack of progress is the continued inability of
the FBI and other intelligence agencies to recruit Arabic-speaking agents.
As a 2006 *Washington Post* article put it, "Five years after Arab terrorists attacked the United States, only 33 FBI agents have even a limited proficiency in Arabic, and none of them work in the sections of the bureau that
coordinate investigations of international terrorism, according to new FBI
statistics."[29]

These shortcomings still exist despite the best efforts of Arab American organizations, which, upon request, widely posted and circulated FBI
recruitment notices after 9/11. In fact, this recruitment effort was perhaps
too successful in attracting applicants. A few weeks after these notices
went up, the Bureau asked the same Arab American organizations to take
them down because they were overwhelmed by the response. The problem
had now shifted: the FBI had plenty of Arabic-speaking applicants, but
many of them were foreign-born or American citizens with roots overseas,
groups that unfairly face enormous hurdles securing clearances. Unless
there are changes in these FBI screening practices and an expansion of opportunity for Arabic education for native-born Americans, we will remain
mired in a familiar situation—unable to directly communicate with a majority of the 350 million people in the most geostrategically important region in the world.[30]

As if the campaign to roll back Americans' efforts to better educate themselves about the Arab World wasn't enough, there is another component in
our national hearing problem: the stereotyped Arabs found in our popular
entertainment. Though television drama, entertainment programs, and
movies may not be a big part of most formal educations, their influence on
public perceptions of everything from race to gender to current events is
broadly accepted in the United States and other countries. What's more,
because Americans have so little exposure to the Arab World in school, the
influence these pop-culture creations have can be outsized. Tracing the
historical development of these stereotypes also shows them to be anything but apolitical. In fact, in Zogby International's recent survey of
American attitudes we learned that the vehicles of popular culture are
among the most important sources of information shaping Americans' attitudes about the Arab World.[31]

In the earliest days of film, Arabs were often romanticized. Rudolph Valentino, one of the biggest stars of the silent-film era, had a career largely based around roles as Latin lovers and Arab sheikhs. Arab stereotyping *a la* Valentino was a decidedly mixed bag: Arabs were seen as violent and savage but also passionate and romantic. The prejudices written into Valentino's Arab characters were generally less pointed than those that would follow. Not coincidentally, the United States was largely uninvolved in the Middle East in this era.

After WWII, as U.S. ties in the region grew and strengthened, more was at stake in defining Arabs to Americans. But in fact, few Arabs and Arab Americans were involved in the pop-culture effort to characterize Arabs. Instead, the first politically monumental movie about Arabs was the 1960 film adaptation of Leon Uris's *Exodus,* a novel that explained the creation of Israel from the viewpoint of the Israeli settlers. Seen by tens of millions of Americans, this film transferred the American cultural mythology of courageous, brave pioneers and cowboys confronted by hostile, savage Indians to the Middle East conflict. Israelis were portrayed as "people like us," bright and energetic visionaries filled with hopes and dreams of a better life, confronting soulless Arabs, who only wanted to kill Israelis and their dreams.

In critical ways, the conflict seen through these stereotypes still plays out. To be sure, the image of Israeli "cowboys" has taken some lumps over the last decades. But with rare exceptions, Arabs in U.S. pop culture are still largely demonized as assassins, terrorists, greedy sheikhs—or all three at once.

In 1984, I completed my own study of the way Arabs had been depicted in U.S. television programs. I exhaustively reviewed four years of entertainment programs on all three major networks. Remarkably, the only "Arab" television characters I found in those four years—almost two decades before 9/11 and nearly a decade before the first Gulf War—were negative stereotypes of terrorists or oil sheikhs. In my study, I acknowledged that other groups had also been stereotyped. But I noted that in each case the networks' overall programming also included other characters, who presented a more honest and complex portrait of Italians, Jews, the Irish, and African Americans. These more balanced depictions helped to offset the negative stereotypes. However, in the case of Arabs the only portrayals were negative caricatures, and the impact was profound.

Armed with this research, I wrote to each of the networks requesting meetings. ABC did not respond. Executives at CBS met with me but dismissed my concerns, telling me that everyone has a complaint. One CBS exec noted that an organization representing potato farmers had come in to see him the week before, furious that a character on one of CBS's shows had suggested that potatoes were fattening. Needless to say, it was not a productive session.

Only NBC took the issue seriously and convened a meeting of producers and writers to explore ways of remedying the situation. The late Bruce Paltrow, the creative genius behind the 1970s and '80s award-winning television series *The White Shadow* and *St. Elsewhere,* was moved by my presentation. Paltrow offered to have one of his writers work with me to introduce an Arab doctor into the cast of *St. Elsewhere.* This was appropriate enough because the Arab World's "brain drain" had led to a substantial number of Arab doctors working at U.S. hospitals.

A few days later a writer called. We talked about ideas and plotlines in what seemed a very positive mode, and he promised to send me a "workup" in a few weeks. When it arrived, here's what I found: The scene opens with a stretch limousine pulling up in front of the hospital and discharging a Saudi doctor, dressed in white robe and headdress. He enters the hospital and first goes to the gift shop, where he looks through the magazines until he finds a *Playboy.* He opens it to the centerfold, looks approvingly, and says his first words: "I like this. We do not have this in my country."

The rest of the storyline was, in fact, entertaining, and the Saudi doctor did come through as a good man. But I couldn't let the silly opening scene go. The writer and I spoke, but he was adamant. I realized the problem of our cultural biases was so great that this screenwriter had to lean on Saudi caricatures even while trying to help combat stereotypes—he simply had no other images of Arabs to draw on. Ultimately, the writer explained that he hadn't shown the script to Paltrow; it was too near the end of the season, and he was too busy to redo the script. In any case, the robed, lecherous, and limo-driven Saudi doctor never appeared. *St. Elsewhere* ended, and my initial attempt to expand the range of Arabs appearing on American television proved interesting but somewhat fruitless.

Just as the tragedy of 9/11 led many Americans to try to better understand the Arab World, some in Hollywood have made a small effort to broaden big screen portrayals of Arabs. But this improvement can be measured in baby steps. In 2008, a study of American movies released pre-9/11 found a scant 12 positive portrayals of Arabs out of 900. The same study found that, since the terrorist attacks, Hollywood has produced 200 Arab characters with less than 30 of them being positive.[32] Statistically speaking, this improvement from 99% negative to only 85% negative is significant. But it also speaks volumes about how far we have left to go: the Arabs in our favorite movies are still distant images, shrouded in myths and ignorance. Unfortunately, these stereotypes—combined with a widespread raw lack of knowledge about real Arabs—have left the door wide open for a seriously flawed discussion about how to best engage the Arab World.

4
LORD BALFOUR,
THEN AND NOW

A R T H U R   J A M E S   Balfour—the first Earl of Balfour—was an imposing figure. Educated at Eton and Trinity College, Cambridge, Balfour served as British prime minister from 1902 to 1905. He was a leading light of Britain's Conservative Party for half a century and one of the dominant aristocratic intellectuals of his age.

Since Balfour's day, some elements in the West's relationship with the Middle East have been transformed. Beginning at the end of WWII, just a few decades after Balfour's famous 1917 declaration, the struggles for independence and self-determination spread across the globe. Within the space of the next decade, the territory controlled by the British Empire—at its apogee following the First World War—diminished rapidly. As colonialism officially died, a general consensus arose reflecting the view President Wilson had advanced: that it was no longer acceptable (or at least politically possible) to merely declare oneself uninterested in the desires and rights of local populations.

Today, the United States is the dominant international player in the Middle East. Yet the era of Wilsonian idealism is long past. In too many instances, American political leadership has acted more like Balfour than Wilson, operating in the region without regard for the desires and opinions of the Arab people. How both American political parties and the U.S. Congress have dealt with the status of the city of Jerusalem is a case in point.

It has long been understood that Jerusalem is one of the most sensitive issues in the Arab–Israeli conflict. Because the city holds special significance for Jews, Christians, and Muslims, the 1948 United Nations partition plan for Palestine created both a Jewish state and an Arab state but kept Jerusalem as a separate entity. Instead of dividing the city between the two competing groups, the U.N. sought to establish the city as an "international zone" to be administered by the U.N. itself.[1]

Israel's military victory and declaration of independence in 1948 saw Jerusalem divided, with the western side under Israeli control and the east under Arab rule. Israel's decision to name Jerusalem as its capital was not accepted by either the U.N. or the overwhelming majority of its members. The United States, Britain, and other major powers kept their embassies in Tel Aviv.

After the 1967 Six-Day War, Israel occupied all of what had been Palestine, including the eastern side of Jerusalem. Almost immediately, Israel made clear that it was annexing not only the eastern side of Jerusalem but large swatches of land around the city, creating a "Greater Jerusalem." Israel formalized this unilateral action in its 1980 "Basic Law on Jerusalem," which declared Jerusalem the "unified" capital of Israel.[2] This decision was condemned in a U.N. Security Council Resolution, which deemed the Israeli act "null and void."[3] Today, no nation recognizes Israel's annexation or has its embassy in Jerusalem.

Since 1967, Jerusalem has remained a flash point for tension and violence in the ongoing Arab–Israeli conflict. Not only the Palestinians but also the Arab League (representing the twenty-two Arab nations) and the Organization of the Islamic Conference (OIC) (representing fifty-seven majority-Muslim countries) have taken strong stands opposing Israel's annexation and denouncing Israeli measures in and around the city. In 2008, for example, the Council of Foreign Ministers of the OIC endorsed a resolution that "Reaffirms the centrality of the cause of Al-Quds Al-Sharif [Jerusalem] for the whole Muslim Ummah [community]."[4] A year later, in November of 2009, an OIC meeting in Morocco went further, declaring that "the question of the Holy Haram in Al Quds is a red line that can absolutely not be addressed with laxity or be subject of any debate."[5] As Shibley Telhami, who holds the Anwar Sadat Chair at the University of Maryland, notes: "In the Arab and Muslim worlds, no issue with Israel mobilizes more people. Jerusalem is celebrated and invoked in political, religious and social rallies."[6]

Recognizing this sensitivity, the United Kingdom and the European Union have rejected Israel's annexation, supported the original U.N. concept of an "international zone," and maintained that the future status of the city should be resolved in negotiations between Arabs and Israelis.[7] This, too, has been the official position of the U.S. government. But this international consensus regarding the importance of Jerusalem and the sensitivities of Arab and Muslim opinion about the city hasn't stopped Congress or both the Democratic and Republican parties from periodically turning Jerusalem into a political football.

For much of the past four decades, both parties have included language in their official platforms either urging recognition of Jerusalem as the "undivided capital of Israel" or calling on the White House to authorize moving the U.S. Embassy in Israel to Jerusalem.[8] In 2008, for example, the Republican Party platform stated, "We support Jerusalem as the undivided capital of Israel," and then called for "moving the American Embassy to that undivided capital."[9] Democrats, for their part, were somewhat more equivocal, noting: "Jerusalem is and will remain the capital of Israel. The parties have agreed that Jerusalem is a matter for final status negotiations. It should remain an undivided city accessible to people of all faiths."[10]

Congress, too, has gotten into the act, periodically proposing legislation pressing the president to ignore Arab opinion and recognize Israel's exclusive claim to Jerusalem. During the 1980s there were two such efforts, both partisan in nature. The "game" is described by a former official of the pro-Israel lobby, the American Israel Public Affairs Committee: "The party out of the White House tries to embarrass the one inside with legislation to move the embassy. . . . Republicans tried it in 1980 to embarrass President Jimmy Carter. . . . Four years later, Ronald Reagan was President and Democrats, led by Sen. Patrick Moynihan of New York and Tom Lantos of California, raised the Jerusalem flag."[11] Both efforts ultimately failed owing to warnings from the White House and U.S. intelligence services of the dangers such a move would pose to U.S. interests and security.

Then in 1995, in the midst of a delicate phase of Israeli–Palestinian peace negotiations, Senator Robert Dole introduced the Jerusalem Embassy Act. The legislation termed Jerusalem the "undivided capital of Israel" and threatened to withhold a significant portion of State Department funding until the United States opened an embassy in Jerusalem.[12] Because the bill was passed with significant majorities, President Clinton felt compelled to sign it into law. But the act also included a provision allowing the president to waive implementation for reasons of "national security," which Clinton promptly did (as have presidents George W. Bush and Barack Obama), and so the embassy has not been moved.

Undeterred, Congress has continued to press this issue. In 2009, Senator Sam Brownback (R-KS) introduced the Jerusalem Embassy Relocation Act, once again attempting to pressure the White House to act by threatening to cut the State Department's overseas operating budget if the White House fails to begin construction of the U.S. embassy in the city.[13]

Congressional insensitivity toward Arab concerns doesn't stop with Jerusalem. Each year dozens of similarly biased bills are introduced and letters to the president are circulated seeking the endorsement of members of Congress. These documents are all designed to pressure the White House to take one-sided positions on a range of sensitive Middle East issues.

When President Obama launched his effort to restart Israeli–Palestinian peace negotiations, he attempted to strike a balance. He called on all sides to take steps that would create the mutual confidence needed for talks to begin. Obama pushed for the Israelis to freeze settlements in the territories they occupied in 1967. He urged the Palestinians to stop violence and verbal incitement against Israel. And he pressed the other Arab states to make clear their intent to fully normalize ties with Israel as part of a final peace agreement.

While the president's envoys were meeting with Israelis and Arabs in an effort to secure their commitment to take these steps, Congress jumped into the fray. Undermining the president's efforts to balance his requests to all parties, letters signed by a majority of senators and representatives focused pressure on the Arab side alone. The Senate letter to the president, for example, begins, "We write in support of your efforts to encourage Arab states to normalize relations with the State of Israel."[14] The letter goes on to praise Israel, ignoring the matter of settlements, and then concludes by calling on the president to "continue to press Arab leaders to consider dramatic gestures toward Israel."[15] Although letters of this sort do not, in and of themselves, make policy, they send a message to the White House that can constrain presidential action, and an unmistakable message to the people of the Arab World that their views do not matter.

More recently, Congress denounced the findings of a U.N. investigation into the December 2008–January 2009 Gaza War between Israel and Hamas forces. The conflict, which killed roughly 1,400 Palestinians and left large segments of Gaza destroyed, provoked outrage both inside and outside the Arab World.

Charged with determining what had happened during the war was internationally respected jurist Richard Goldstone, a South African lauded for his investigations into war crimes in the former Yugoslavia and Rwanda, and for his lead role in the South African Truth and Reconcilia-

tion Commission. On September 15, 2009, after five months of investigation, Goldstone's report concluded that both Israel and Hamas were guilty
of possible war crimes.[16] Despite Goldstone's reputation, the thoroughness
of his work, and continuing Arab concern over the devastation wrought by
the war, a bipartisan collection of U.S. representatives almost immediately
issued a flood of harsh statements attacking Goldstone and his report.[17]

Within hours of the release of the 575-page report, Representative
Gary Ackerman (D-NY) issued a statement calling it a "pompous, tendentious, one-sided political diatribe" and accusing Goldstone of inhabit-
ing a "self-righteous fantasy-land."[18] Representatives Elliot Engel (D-NY)
and Shelley Berkley (D-NV) called the report "biased against Israel from
the very beginning."[19] Representative Dan Burton (R-IN) was even less
kind, "categorically" rejecting the report because it was issued by the
Human Rights Council, which he termed "despot-controlled."[20] Acceler-
ating the rhetoric further, Representative Todd Tiahrt (R-KS) claimed
that the Human Rights Council was "[d]ominated by anti-democratic and
anti-Semitic nations."[21] Representative Ileana Ros-Lehtinen (R-FL) casti-
gated the entire United Nations, which she said is "where the inmates run
the asylum."[22]

And then on November 3, 2009, the U.S. House of Representatives
passed—by a vote of 344 in favor, 36 opposed, and 22 present—a resolution
denouncing the findings of the Goldstone report and calling on the
Obama administration to reject it.[23]

This penchant for ignoring Arab concern is not the special reserve of Congress or U.S. political parties; administrations, both Republican and Democratic, have also failed to take into account Arab attitudes.

Veterans of the Clinton administration's Middle East efforts have
noted instances in which, despite the White House's sincere efforts to
achieve peace, Arab sensitivities were ignored. In my many dealings with
the Clinton team, I found that while they were in fact deeply committed to
peace, they tended to see the region and the Arab–Israeli conflict from the
perspective of Israel looking out at the Arab World and could not balance
that view with an understanding of an Arab perspective.

Referring specifically to Jerusalem, a former Clinton official is quoted
in the U.S. Institute of Peace's study of the history of peacemaking, *Negotiating Arab-Israeli Peace*, saying: "There was no expert on our team on Islam or
on Muslim perspectives . . . [so] when it came to dealing with Jerusalem,

there's some very embarrassing episodes that betrayed our lack of knowledge or bias."[24] As noted by Aaron David Miller, who served as an adviser
to six secretaries of state and was a deputy special Middle East envoy during the Clinton administration: "Far too often the small group with whom
I had worked in the Clinton administration, myself included, had acted as
a lawyer for only one side, Israel."[25]

The problem, though, went beyond the Clinton administration's handling of the Arab–Israeli conflict. One episode in which I personally became involved was the administration's opposition to U.N. Secretary
General Boutros Boutros-Ghali's reelection bid. As a former Egyptian foreign minister, he was widely respected, and his role at the U.N. was a matter of pride not only to Arabs but to African nations as well. Boutros-Ghali
had sought my help with his reelection. When I hosted him on my weekly
program, A Capital View, he expressed frustration that the United States had
not made clear the reasons for its opposition to his reelection.[26] He had the
support of not only the Arab and Muslim states but also a number of U.S.
senators, the U.S. Catholic Bishops Conference, and the National Council
of Churches. Senator Paul Simon, a Democrat from Illinois, charged that
the administration was "letting our own domestic politics determine a
choice that should be made in our own national interest, and in the interests of the U.N. and the international community."[27] New York Times columnist A. M. Rosenthal concurred, urging the president to reconsider his
opposition in order to demonstrate that the United States "had not taken
leave of common sense, self-interest or a decent respect of the rights and
opinions of friends."[28] U.S. opposition continued, and despite Boutros-
Ghali's winning the support of a majority of nations, a U.S. veto doomed
his reelection, causing Simon to charge that the administration's behavior
was "not worthy of a great power."[29]

There are still other examples of U.S. failure to pay attention to Arab
sentiments, one notable case being the long and deadly sanctions regime
instituted against Iraq during the 1990s. Although the sanctions program
was intended to punish the Ba'ath regime in Baghdad, following Iraq's brutal invasion and occupation of neighboring Kuwait in 1990, sanctions had
resulted in widespread suffering and the impoverishment of the Iraqi people. Iraq's leadership had lost Arab support because of their behavior in
Kuwait, but the enormous toll that sanctions took on the people of Iraq
was widely denounced across the Arab World.[30]

That the Clinton administration did not understand this growing
Arab concern was made evident in the now infamous May 12, 1996, tele-

vised exchange between then Secretary of State Madeleine Albright and CBS News's Lesley Stahl:

> Lesley Stahl [on U.S. sanctions against Iraq]: We have heard that a half-million children have died. I mean, that's more children than died in Hiroshima. And, you know, is the price worth it?
> Secretary of State Madeleine Albright: I think this is a very hard choice, but the price—we think the price is worth it.[31]

Though years later Albright expressed regret over her choice of words,[32] at the time they reinforced a view that the West was indifferent to the loss of Arab lives.

And during the Clinton administration's efforts to secure an Arab–Israeli peace agreement at Camp David in the summer of 2000, when the president publicly blamed the late Palestinian President Yassir Arafat for the failure and sided with Israel's then Prime Minister Ehud Barak (breaking the promise he had made to both Arafat and Barak not to assess blame), Arab opinion once again saw the United States, as Miller would later note, playing "Israel's lawyer."[33]

Up until 2001, there was little in the way of reliable and relevant public opinion polling in the Arab World to inform our discussion. However, what we at Zogby International found during the Bush administration, when polling became more frequent and covered topics related to public policy, was that Washington either rejected Arab views they didn't like or twisted them to meet their own goals. Two personal examples come to mind.

In mid-November of 2002, shortly after the release of our first eight-country Arab poll, I received an invitation to speak to a group of about sixty regional experts and intelligence analysts from the departments of State and Defense, the CIA, and the White House. During my presentation, I highlighted two items from the poll that struck me as running counter to conventional wisdom. The first ran contrary to the widely held assumption that young Arabs and people who watched news programs on Arab satellite television were more anti-American than the older Arabs who did not have access to satellite television—the idea of a radicalized population glued to Al Jazeera all day. In fact, the opposite appeared to be true. For example, attitudes toward the American people were twenty-eight points higher (more positive) in Egypt and eight points higher in

Saudi Arabia among those who watched satellite television than among those who did not.[34] It appeared that access to U.S. culture through advertising and entertainment programs resulted in more positive attitudes toward the American people, which helped to offset the negative attitudes toward U.S. policy that came from watching the news.

Second, I observed that because the U.S. administration was advocating for women's rights in Saudi Arabia, it was important to consider the poll's finding that Saudi men were slightly more liberal in their social views than Saudi women. By a five-point margin, Saudi men were also more likely than their female counterparts to support expanding women's rights.

Attending my presentation was Liz Cheney, Vice President Dick Cheney's daughter, who had just been appointed to a State Department post overseeing the president's Middle East Partnership Initiative. One of the initiative's goals was to advocate for women's rights. Cheney was quick to dismiss the numbers, telling me that she flat out disagreed with the findings. She noted that she had met with four Saudi women in her office just one week earlier and that she felt they would disagree, too.[35]

I explained to her that although I respected the views of those four Saudi women who were visiting the United States as part of a State Department–funded tour, I also respected the collective opinions of the more than 800 randomly interviewed individuals covered in our survey of Saudi opinion.

Further, I made it clear that I was not personally arguing against expanding women's rights, nor was I claiming that absolutely no Arab women (or men) were in favor of Western-style feminism. What I was doing was giving a real picture of where Arab attitudes were and, therefore, what problems we might face in shaping a policy initiative on that issue. That Cheney was unswayed was no surprise. She and other hard-liners in the Bush administration frequently displayed a tendency to reject empirical data about the Middle East in favor of a convenient anecdote—or to twist the data when a useful example didn't present itself.

The invasion and subsequent occupation of Iraq in 2003 provides a case study of just how out of touch our leadership was with the real Arab World—and the brutal toll that a submerged reality eventually takes. Leading up to and during the invasion of Iraq, Americans were repeatedly told that Iraqis loved the United States and were thankful that we brought them democracy.[36] The U.S. military would be greeted as liberators with flowers and sweets. Although this was certainly true for some Iraqis, polling that Zogby International did in September of 2003—just six months after the invasion—showed that a disturbingly high percentage of Iraqis wanted the United States to leave their country and did not have a favorable opinion of the U.S. military.[37]

For example, 55% of Iraqis surveyed complained of harsh treatment from the U.S. military, and only 20% gave a positive rating to how our troops were dealing with Iraqi civilians. Taken as a whole, these polling numbers should have caused U.S. policy makers some concern—even at that early stage in the conflict. However, these facts were a mere bump in the road for American political leaders following in the footsteps of Lord Balfour.

A few days after our poll was released, I was at home watching Vice President Dick Cheney on NBC's *Meet the Press*.[38] Cheney was appearing as part of the Bush administration's public-relations campaign to rebuild U.S. support for the war effort in Iraq. Attempting to make the case that the United States was winning in Iraq, Cheney referenced our data. "There was a poll done," said Cheney, "just random in the last week, first one I've seen carefully done; admittedly, it's a difficult area to poll in. Zogby International did it with *American Enterprise* magazine. But that's got very positive news in it."[39]

Now warmed up for his spin, Cheney continued, "One of the questions it asked is: 'If you could have any model for the kind of government you'd like to have'—and they were given five choices—'which would it be?' The U.S. wins hands down."[40]

"If you ask how long they want Americans to stay," Cheney added, "over 60 percent of the people polled said they want the U.S. to stay for at least another year. So admittedly there are problems, especially in that area where Saddam Hussein was from, where people have benefited most from his regime. . . . But to suggest somehow that that's representative of the country at large or the Iraqi people are opposed to what we've done in Iraq or are actively and aggressively trying to undermine it, I just think that's not true."[41]

I was both furious and deeply troubled, and I wrote an op-ed for the *Guardian* titled "Bend It Like Cheney."[42] I set the record straight about what the poll really found and pointed out that the administration's abuse of poll numbers resembled the way it used intelligence data to make a false case justifying the war.

For example, Cheney claimed that when asked what kind of government they would like, Iraqis chose the American system. The results of the poll were actually quite different.[43] Twenty-three percent of Iraqis did say that they would like to model their new government on that of the United

States, but 17.5% said they would like their model to be Saudi Arabia, 12% cited Syria, 7% said Egypt, and the clear plurality—37%—stated they wanted "none of the above." That's hardly "win[ning] hands down."

More damning for the vice president was the fact that when an actual majority expressed an opinion about their future government, it was decidedly antidemocratic. When asked if "democracy can work well in Iraq," 51% said, "No; it is a Western way of doing things and will not work here."

As for Cheney's claim that Iraqis were quite happy with an American military presence in their country for at least a year, the deeper truth revealed by the poll numbers was less rosy. Respondents were given the choice as to whether they "would like to see the American and British forces leave Iraq in six months, one year, or two years." The plurality—34% of Iraqis—said they wanted to see our forces out in a year, 31.5% said we should leave in six months, and only 25% said two or more years. Although technically Cheney can claim that "over 60% [actually it was 59%] . . . want the U.S. to stay at least another year," it is also correct—and maybe more honest—to state that 65.5% of Iraqis wanted the United States and Britain to leave in a year or less.

And if Cheney had looked more closely into the poll numbers to compare the attitudes of Iraq's different subgroups, he would have found that it was the Kurds, who were effectively living in a U.S. protectorate, who wanted Western forces to stay. Conversely, Sunni Arabs—who eventually formed the core of the bloody anti-U.S. insurgency—were almost uniformly in favor of a quick departure.

Finally, although Cheney admitted that there were a few problems, "especially in that area where Saddam Hussein was from," his thrust was that we generally had the support of the Iraqi people. This was simply not true; attitudes toward the U.S. occupation were already—just six months after the invasion—clearly quite negative. When asked whether over the next five years, they felt that the "U.S. would help or hurt Iraq," 50% of Iraqis said that the United States would hurt Iraq, but only 35.5% felt the United States would help the country. Asked the same question about Saudi Arabia, 60.5% of Iraqis felt that country would help them. When asked the same question about the United Nations, 50.5% felt that the United Nations would help Iraq, but 18.5% felt the U.N. would hurt the country (see Table 4.1).

In other words, America's poor rankings were not a simple case of animus being directed at foreign, non-Arab entities. To put these numbers in a larger context, America's help-hurt ratio was only slightly better than

TABLE 4.1   IRAQI OPINIONS ABOUT IMPACT OF FOREIGN ENTITIES IN THE NEXT FIVE YEARS

	Help (%)	Hurt (%)
Iran	21.5	53.5
Saudi Arabia	60.5	7.5
United States	35.5	50.0
United Nations	50.5	18.5

that of Iran. This put the United States in the same category as Iraq's bitter rival in a war that lasted most of the 1980s and cost hundreds of thousands of lives.

The poll that Vice President Cheney had twisted for his own ends was more than just a bunch of numbers. Through their responses, the Iraqi people were telling us that they did have hope for the future, but wanted the help of others more than that of the United States. These opinions clearly weren't popular in Washington, but our policy makers ought to have listened nevertheless. This mass of data held important lessons for how to move Iraq forward—as well as how not to. An honest reading of the data would have pointed toward the anti-U.S. sentiments in Iraq that eventually made the occupation significantly longer, costlier, and bloodier than most Americans could have imagined at the outset of the war.

The hard fact is that whether you are Lord Balfour imperially preempting discussions of Arab opinion or Vice President Cheney making torturous analyses of polling data—or his daughter ignoring data she didn't want to hear—forcing policies on unwilling populations ultimately carries a cost. Remember, our polling took place in 2003, long before the war's supporters began abandoning the effort in droves. If the findings had been heeded, the lessons in these numbers could have provided us an opportunity to adjust our approach in Iraq. Instead, the Bush administration continued to tell itself and the American people that the situation was under control. That worked, as it often does, until reality intervened—in the form of hundreds of billions of dollars spent, thousands of dead American soldiers, and hundreds of thousands of dead and wounded Iraqis. Reality *always* wins in the end.

This disregard for Arab opinion took a toll on America's standing across the Middle East. By 2006, Arab favorable attitudes toward the United States were at precariously low levels—ranging from a high of 28% in Morocco to a low of 9% in Jordan.[44]

Neither Vice President Cheney, nor his daughter, nor other luminaries from the Bush administration can be dismissed as spent forces. They continue to speak out regularly and receive considerable media attention in their effort to shape the public debate. They have continued to defend their administration's use of torture and the maintaining of a prison at Guantanamo Bay, Cuba[45]—two issues that our polling across the Arab World demonstrates are of significant concern.[46] When an April 2009 survey of the Arab World asked respondents to note the most positive action the Obama administration had taken to improve relations with the Arab World, "closing Guantanamo and banning torture" placed a close second to "announcing the withdrawal from Iraq."

At home, however, critics have been hostile to the Obama administration's outreach efforts to develop new understanding with the Arab and Muslim World. I had one such antagonistic encounter, again with Liz Cheney, on CNN's *Situation Room with Wolf Blitzer* following President Obama's historic speech in Cairo in June of 2009.[47] In response to the president's claim that both Israelis and Palestinians had their own narratives that we must make an effort to understand, Cheney wrongly accused the president of "moral equivalency," saying that he had equated the suffering of Jews during the Holocaust with the suffering of Palestinians. Cheney further charged that, by pledging to end torture and close the prison at Guantanamo because these practices were not in keeping with America's best values, Obama was, in effect, selling his own country short in an effort to curry favor with the Muslim World. She concluded by saying that "the biggest problem" in the Middle East "is not the perception of the United States . . . [but] the Iranians attempting to get nuclear weapons," and that the United States should not be making "policy decisions here based on polls in the Arab World."[48] In short, according to Cheney, there is no need to listen to Arab voices or to pay attention to what they are saying.

President Barack Obama came to office inspiring hope across the Arab World that Arab views would matter. Those expectations soared when, on his third day in office, he gave his first television interview to an Arab satellite network. Obama said that he had instructed his newly appointed Middle East envoy, former Senator George Mitchell, to "start by listening, because all too often the United States starts by dictating—in the past on some of these issues—and we don't always know all the factors that are involved."[49] And when Obama called on Israel to freeze settlements, Arab expectations rose even higher.

But the Obama administration has not been immune to the "tone deafness" that has plagued Washington in the past. When the Goldstone Report was first issued, and even before reading it (as they later admitted), the administration's immediate response was to term it "unbalanced, one-sided, and basically unacceptable."[50] Before the report was to be submitted to the Human Rights Council for a vote, the administration pressured the Palestinian Authority to withdraw it from consideration. Arab expectations were let down.[51] This frustration was further compounded when Israeli Prime Minister Benjamin Netanyahu decided not to freeze settlements but only to temporarily restrain them (exempting 3,000 units already under construction or new construction planned in and around Jerusalem). At the time, Secretary of State Hillary Clinton praised the "concession" as unprecedented and set off an avalanche of Arab protest.[52]

Another display of disregard for Arab concerns on the part of the Obama administration followed the failed terrorist attempt to bring down a Northwest Airlines flight on Christmas Day 2009 as the plane approached the Detroit Airport. Although later acknowledging that the intelligence community failed to "connect the dots," the administration's initial response was to put in place guidelines that would profile all passengers coming from fourteen mostly Arab and Muslim countries.

This issue of being singled out for special screening has long been a matter of deep concern across the Arab World. In fact, in our most recent polling we found continuing displeasure with treatment meted out to Arab and Muslim immigrants and visitors to the United States. The nearly 80% negative attitudes toward these policies are almost as high as the negative ratings given to American foreign policy in the Middle East.[53] This decision to single out Muslim passengers resulted in a wave of critical editorials in even the most moderate Arab daily newspapers. One prominent pan-Arab paper decried the harassment of Muslims from fourteen countries, suggesting that it would alienate and humiliate and would not win America the support it needs from Arabs and Muslims in the War on Terrorism.[54] Another Arab newspaper said that in acting as he did, President Obama had contradicted his pledge to launch "a new beginning with the Muslim world" and has, instead, followed in the footsteps of his predecessor, George W. Bush.[55] Clearly, we still have a long way to go.

Opinions matter. This should not be surprising, especially in the West where political leaders pride themselves on remaining sensitive to public opinion and know the cost of ignoring it. Whether the public is dissatisfied with high taxes or economic collapse, corruption and a sense of entitlement in the governing party in Parliament, or the government's support for an unpopular war, political leaders know that sustaining public support is important if they want to maintain trust.

Opinions matter in the Arab World as well. Whether the United States is seen as responsible for the ouster of a respected Arab diplomat, siding with Israel against the Palestinians, imposing sanctions that humbled a once-proud people, or profiling Arab and Muslim airline passengers, the consequences can be profound.

PART 2
BEYOND SUPER MYTHS
WHO ARE THE ARABS AND WHAT DO THEY WANT?

5
SUPER MYTH ONE
THEY'RE ALL THE SAME

AFTER DECADES spent trying to better explain the Arab World to other Americans, all too often I find my efforts running up against the same mythologies and half-truths that, year after year, stubbornly maintain an alarming ability to shape our thinking about the region. I usually try to challenge these fabrications using history, my personal experience, or what Zogby International polling has revealed. But in March of 2009, the Kennedy Center—America's premier institute for culture and arts—set out to debunk these myths artfully.

Under the direction of its president, Michael Kaiser, the Kennedy Center sponsored "Arabesque," a festival of arts from across the Arab World. For three weeks, the center's halls were adorned with exhibits of Arab bridal dresses, the terrace displayed a colonnade replicating Arabic architecture, and the basement became a veritable Arab souk, selling crafts from Morocco, Iraq, and many other Arab countries.

I found "Arabesque" to be a remarkable experience and not merely for the entertainment and art it presented. To refute the claim that the Arab World is monolithic, I could point to the more than 800 artists and performers from all twenty-two Arab countries, reflecting in their performance or craft the uniqueness of their countries of origin. To those who asserted that the region was locked in the past, I could suggest attending performances by a Lebanese fusion jazz composer or a Somali hip-hop artist. And people who thought of Arabs as angry and bitter would have a hard time maintaining that position surrounded by the joyous creations of a Syrian choral group, a Moroccan Berber horn ensemble, or countless other Arab musicians, poets, painters, storytellers, calligraphers, and craftsmen.

The reality is that no productive dialogue or consistently successful enterprises between the Arab World and the West can take place without our moving past negative stereotypes and myths. With this goal in mind, I've collected five of the most pervasive and pernicious Super Myths. I intend to show how these falsehoods permeate American and Western discussions of the Arab World, and then I'll explain through polling and experience how we can recast these ideas to create a new baseline of understanding and cooperation.

My travel itineraries through the Arab World are often dictated by conferences, speeches, or polling work. But my trips also give me the opportunity to explore and better understand many wonderfully diverse Arab cities and the people who inhabit them. This is one of the great side benefits of my job. It also provides material with which to sketch out some of the immense variety of this region.

Cairo, for example, has the greatest energy of any city I've ever experienced—anywhere. Its frenetic movement and constant din make Manhattan seem tame. If I were suddenly dropped blindfolded into the middle of Cairo, I have no doubt the city's noise would give it away well before I uncovered my eyes. This is a city where people drive with their horns instead of the gas pedal; even when the traffic is in hopeless gridlock, they're still honking.

Oddly, Cairo is also the most cheerful city I've ever set foot in. Despite its loud crush of humanity, people on the street are constantly smiling and joking. In fact, the mood is extraordinary. Like anywhere, there may be complaints about politics, policies, or even personalities in power (frequently the subject of the biting humor for which Egyptians are famous). There may even be occasional demonstrations of political or social unrest, but the overall sense one gets of the place is its positive dynamism. It's amazingly energizing to be there.

Of course, this ancient city has another unavoidable characteristic best conveyed to me by Jesse Jackson. The year was 1989, and we were in Cairo together sitting on a balcony overlooking the Nile. He seemed lost in thought, so I asked, "How are you doing?"

"I was just thinking," he said. "I've been to Moscow and Paris. They're great cities. This is not just a city—it's a civilization. It's history. I'm looking at that river and thinking of all that's gone by here, and it still flows on."[1]

Jackson was right. Cairo has long and rich traditions that simply spill out onto the street. Its history isn't some dusty thing locked up in museums around the world—you feel it pulsing in the city. Walking down Cairo's streets, you find yourself surrounded by incredible French architecture mixed in with smatterings of Italian Renaissance and Baroque with a touch of Mamluk and Pharaonic thrown in for good measure. Later, you might look out the window of your hotel and see the Great Pyramids. And, though the whole city is covered in a layer of soot and exhaust, its past glory is not faded so much as transferred: the monuments of the city's past still stand, but the glory of Cairo is now housed in its dynamic people.

Other Arab cities also wear their ancient histories casually. For example, in Damascus I once walked into a stall in the city's old marketplace, the Souk Al-Hamidiyah. On one side was what appeared to be a rounded wall. Looking up through the stall's tent-like cover, I saw that it was a column, so I turned to the proprietor and asked, "What's this?"

"This is a wall," he said. "It's my shop."

He was right. It was a wall and it was his shop, but it was *also* part of the Temple of Jupiter. That's Damascus. It's the oldest continuously inhabited city in the world, so people don't make a big deal about being right next to a column that dates back millennia. Every day, residents pass by the mosque that houses the severed head of John the Baptist and the wall over which the Apostle Paul was lowered in a basket before fleeing to Jerusalem. If we dug deeper, we would most likely find that the souk merchant's shop sits on top of Hittite ruins, which no one can even see because they are covered by the ruins of the Greek and Roman cities that followed. It's all there.

By contrast, if you go to Riyadh or Abu Dhabi, you find places more like Houston or Phoenix. By this, I mean that although these cities are impressive feats of modernity with towering skyscrapers, they are more like organized commercial centers. There's a correspondingly different feel in how people relate to their surroundings. Don't get me wrong: Cairo and Beirut have their congested modern highways and numbing traffic jams on older narrow roads not meant for the twenty-first century. But these cities are famous for their street life—teeming crowds, frustrating jaywalkers, bands of young men and women out and about, and blocks of outdoor cafes. This is not the case in Riyadh, Abu Dhabi, or Dubai. These cities were designed with cars in mind. Multilane highways with overpasses, off-ramps, and service roads are all jammed with traffic.

Another totally different sensation struck me when I first arrived in Marrakesh. For one, I immediately understood why so many European artists came here to work. The sky is endless, and the rose-colored sandstone and the green landscape are incredibly vivid—all against the backdrop of the snowcapped Atlas Mountains. Every picture is a painting. For an American parallel, it's a bit like being in Santa Fe, New Mexico.

Marrakesh has its own grandeur; its cultural links to Africa give it a feeling distinct from other parts of the Arab World. Cairo and Damascus are ancient cities, mixtures of the previous French, British, Roman, Greek, Assyrian, and Egyptian civilizations. In Marrakesh, what's unique is the Berber blended with the French and the Arab.

When I return home from a trip to one or more Arab countries, I am often struck by how the variety and vitality of these cities and their people fail to be reflected in much commentary about the Arab World. In fact, the reverse is more often true: Americans and other Westerners are often fed sweeping assertions about Arabs that assume a dull, repressive, and monochromatic culture.

One of the most widely read purveyors of generalizations about Arabs is *New York Times* columnist Thomas Friedman. Friedman, a frequent commentator on the Middle East, was a strong advocate of the Iraq War, which he saw as a chance to kick-start reform in the Middle East.[2] Alas, the campaign in Iraq didn't go quite as its supporters had hoped. By the end of 2006, Friedman had figured out why the war had gone so badly, and in a remarkable *New York Times* op-ed, "Mideast Rules to Live By," he offered President Bush advice about "what to do next in Iraq" in the form of fifteen immutable rules about Arab political thought.[3]

Friedman's fifteen rules fall into four main categories. The first four axioms portray all Arabs as labyrinthine thinkers, not to be trusted in negotiations. This first category includes "What people tell you in private in the Middle East is irrelevant," and "If you can't explain something to Middle Easterners with a conspiracy theory, then don't try to explain it at all—they won't believe it."[4]

The next few rules portray Arab politics as hopelessly tending toward violence and extremism. In rule five, Friedman states, "Never lead your story out of Lebanon, Gaza or Iraq with a cease-fire; it will always be over before the next morning's paper," and rule six is "In the Middle East, the extremists go all the way, and the moderates tend to just go away." This cynical line of thinking—that change is impossible and most political outcomes in this region are mechanistically predetermined—is continued in rules seven, ten, and twelve, which states: "the Israelis will always win, and the Palestinians will always make sure they never enjoy it. Everything else is just commentary."[5]

A third category of rules suggests that "their" violence and wars are unlike "our" more enlightened Western conflicts, which tend to be over ideological differences. Instead, Friedman asserts, Arab conflicts are essentially unprincipled raw struggles for power—"Rule 8: Civil wars in the Arab world are rarely about ideas—like liberalism vs. communism. They are about which tribe gets to rule. So, yes, Iraq is having a civil war as we once did. But there is no Abe Lincoln in this war. It's the South vs. the South." This supposed tribal nature of Arab politics, in which a bad guy must win because there are no good guys, is also touched on in rules nine and thirteen.[6]

Finally, Friedman wraps up this gloomy analysis of the Arab political scene by suggesting that regional politics are guided by angry, irrational behavior: "The most underestimated emotion in Arab politics is humiliation."[7]

Friedman's message is troubling for two reasons. First, he reduces hundreds of millions of people in the Middle East to a crude negative stereotype. But, leaving aside any concerns about Friedman's lack of attention to Arab humanity and diversity, his cynical and simplistic set of rules could not help Americans—or anyone else—better deal with the situation in Iraq. According to Friedman, America and its remaining military allies in Iraq were attempting to rebuild a country in partnership with a bunch of untrustworthy, "tribal," and "extremist" Iraqis.

This bleak and unyielding view of the Middle East removes options like listening to or engaging in discussions with Iraqis—or any other Arabs—from the outset. Instead of shedding light on the real Middle East, Friedman defines all Arabs—from a soldier in Iraq to a farmer in Lebanon to a computer engineer in Abu Dhabi—as being disturbingly similar in their shortcomings. Although there has certainly been a heartbreaking recurrence of political meltdowns and armed conflicts within the Arab World, Friedman offers no specific evidence that the region is unusual in this regard—most likely because the evidence is really not there.

It is true that in the past hundred years the Arab World has seen dozens of major conflicts that spilled over into inter- or intrastate violence. However, the same period in Europe saw numerous civil wars, including those in Russia, Finland, Spain, and Greece; a decades-long Basque separatist movement; century-spanning outbreaks of violence in the Balkans and Ireland; and innumerable wars of independence and interethnic conflicts after the collapse of the Soviet Union. European political meltdowns also resulted in World Wars I and II, two of the deadliest wars of all time. So, even taking into account Europe's larger population, the Arab World doesn't seem to be more predisposed to armed conflict than Europe.

Why then does Friedman insist on explaining Arab political discord as uniquely the fault of a tribal, emotional, and irrational people? Perhaps because by stripping Middle East conflicts of their political and historical dimensions and seeing them instead as resulting from the inevitable behavior of a deeply flawed people, the West can be absolved from its role in the region, including its occupation of Iraq.

By 2006, the Iraq War had become a very bloody and expensive war. In fact, as Friedman's column came out, a real discussion about what went wrong had begun in America, Britain, and other countries, and in the United States, the Iraq Study Group was appointed to help assess the situation. But Friedman ignores that debate, instead offering advice to Bush that doubles as an excuse. "Great powers," writes Friedman in rule fourteen, "should never get involved in the politics of small tribes."[8] In other words, the only real mistake the United States and its allies made was trying to help these hopeless people.

Despite the fact that these generalizations don't help to illuminate the region where the United States and other nations have deployed hundreds of thousands of soldiers and spent hundreds of billions of dollars, these notions have persisted, appearing in high-profile books and in the comments of leading politicians.

In a lengthy December 20, 2006, interview with the Washington Post, then Secretary of State Condoleezza Rice explained the current chaos and turmoil in the Arab World not as the result of U.S.-led Western intervention, but as inevitable and even desirable. Rice sought to justify the war in Iraq, declaring, "The old Middle East was not going to stay," and adding, "Let's stop mourning the old Middle East. It was not so great, and it was not going to survive anyway."[9]

Rice's policy goals in making such an assertion were clear. In one fell swoop, she attempted to "disappear" a slew of glaring problems for her administration—including the tens of thousands of Iraqis who had died in our drive to liberate a country then embroiled in civil war. Rice knew that after years of supporting the war effort, the American public was getting restless. But instead of taking a hard look at what went wrong, she simply wrote off our increasingly messy engagement with the Arab World as the mere passing of an "old Middle East" that was "not so great" anyway.

Like Friedman, who saw the American invasion of Iraq as necessary to jump-start reform in a stagnant region, Rice relied on the mythology of a backward Middle East to explain away the failures of U.S.-led initiatives to create positive change. By reducing the Arab World from a vibrant home of 350 million people to an old and static stereotype, Rice relieved us of the need to beat our breasts with mea culpas.

Friedman and Rice are, of course, neither the first nor last to lean on this notion that the Arab World is a hopelessly backward, unchanging monolith. One of the best-traveled volumes of misinformation about the region is cultural anthropologist Raphael Patai's *The Arab Mind*.[10] Originally published in 1973, it purports to explain the Arab World to Westerners. It has been regularly reissued (most recently in 2007), and remains in use—especially among U.S. military posted in the region. Patai's book hinges on the theory that a group of people can be understood through their "personality archetype"—that there is a singular "Arab Mind." Though once a common theoretical approach (Patai, who was Jewish, also wrote a book called *The Jewish Mind*), the concept of a "personality archetype" has become widely discredited in academic circles and, increasingly, by the public at large. Patai's book is full of generalizations such as, "The all-encompassing preoccupation with sex in the Arab mind emerges clearly in two manifestations,"[11] and "Why are most Arabs, unless forced by dire necessity to earn their livelihood with 'the sweat of their brow,' so loath to undertake any work that dirties the hands?"[12] Like Friedman's fifteen rules, Patai's book steamrolls Arab diversity with statements that actually inhibit our ability to understand and listen to the people of the region.

As evidence of its continuing importance, when *The Arab Mind* was reissued in 2002, it included an introduction by Norvell De Atkine, the head of Middle East studies at the military base in Fort Bragg, North Carolina. De Atkine noted that *The Arab Mind* had informed the basis of his instruction briefing "hundreds of military teams being deployed to the Middle East."[13]

A 2003 *Newsday* article by the conservative columnist and political operative James Pinkerton also praised *The Arab Mind* for its ability to explain the Middle East to foreigners, saying: "A quarter-century-old book that I took with me to Baghdad last month helped explain what I saw when I got there."[14] Pinkerton, who was an adviser to 2008 Republican presidential candidate Mike Huckabee, goes on to explain the cultural conflict unfolding in Baghdad between the "modern" West and a "backward" Arab culture.

The problem now is that an Arab culture—much of it pre-modern in its reliance on words, much of it backward in its dependence on conspiracy theories as a substitute for reality—now finds itself cheek to cheek with

Americanism, in its technical, unsentimental belief in the bottom line. And so it's yet another battle between ancients and moderns, between poets and scientists, between romantics and rationalizers.[15]

The most high-profile acknowledgment of the continuing significance of *The Arab Mind* was demonstrated in Seymour Hersh's "The Gray Zone," which appeared in the May 24, 2004, *New Yorker*. According to a Hersh source, *The Arab Mind* served as scholarly cover for two sweeping neoconservative claims: "one, Arabs only understand force and, two, that the biggest weakness of Arabs is shame and humiliation."[16] According to Hersh's article, it was this simplistic understanding of Arabs that eventually led to the American military's programs of torture and sexual humiliation carried out on Iraqi prisoners at Abu Ghraib.[17]

Although no one suggests holding Patai, who died in 1996, personally responsible for the horrors of Abu Ghraib, it is important to understand the direct link between relying on "magic bullet" theories concerning the "Arab Mind" and our resultant diplomatic and military blunders. And yet, this distorted thinking about the Arab World lives on and not just in the anti-Arab diatribes that characterize discussions of the region on right-wing radio shows. In January 2010, the influential conservative think tank the Hudson Institute hosted an event for the release of *The Strong Horse* by Lee Smith, a Middle East correspondent for the *Weekly Standard*. Although Smith's work contains elements of Patai's cultural anthropology, his style is often closer to Friedman's brash declarations, such as, "In the Middle East, political violence is not an anomaly. It is the normal state of affairs."[18] In casting Arabs and their world as governed by immutable forces, Smith argues that the political problems of the region have little to do with conflict with Israel, the United States, or other Western interference but everything to do with a central dysfunction in the "Arab Mind."

Despite its shortcomings—like Friedman's mistakes in predicting the outcome of the Iraq War—this Super Myth remains powerful. It has repeatedly sent the United States' and other Western nations' efforts in the Arab World down the wrong track. The road to successful relations with the Middle East lies beyond cynical half-truths and outright fabrications; the path to understanding requires a deeper appreciation of the richness and diversity of the Arab World together with a recognition of the people of this region's real aspirations.

Is the Arab World dark and violence-filled? Can its culture and people be reduced to monochromatic dullness? Certainly the "Arabesque" festival would suggest this is not the case. But at Zogby International, we have another way of learning about the region. We poll Arab opinion, let Arabs speak for themselves, and then listen to what their voices tell us about their political concerns, pride in their heritage, and aspirations.

To move toward a more productive understanding of the Arab World and recognize the diversity that exists in the region, let's look at a November 2009 survey snapshot of six countries: Morocco, Egypt, Lebanon, Jordan, Saudi Arabia, and the United Arab Emirates. We can also examine citizens' responses to the question, "What do you most want the world to know about your country?"[19]

Morocco sits at the far western edge of the Arab World and is a unique mix of Arab, African, and French cultures. It has long been a tourist destination for European visitors. The country takes seriously its leadership role in the Muslim World, with its king, Mohammed VI, chairing the Organization of Islamic Conference's Jerusalem Committee. Morocco, like Egypt, also has a rapidly growing population and struggles with economic growth. But despite some obstacles, the country has a vibrant civil society and political parties that compete in elections.

Asked to explain what they want the rest of the world to know about Morocco, one-half of our respondents focused on their country's traditions and its open and tolerant culture. "We are," one said, "a country of dignity, pride and one of the most tolerant countries." Another said: "We are an old country with a great history, a kind people and great tourism." Aware of how Muslims have been stereotyped, especially following the involvement of some Moroccans in terrorist activity at home and in Europe, one-quarter of the respondents reflected a defensiveness. Wanting the world to know that not all Moroccans are terrorists, one respondent declared, "Anyone who knows us and our traditions well will discover that we are not terrorists." Another participant said: "Ours is a country of heritage, a great noble civilization known for its stability, contrary to those who think we are terrorists." A final group of Moroccans spoke of the importance of Islam and its customs and traditions in shaping their culture: "We are proud of being an Arab and Muslim country with a great history," and, "We are proud of our customs and our Islamic Arab traditions." Despite the continuing dispute to their south over control of the region known as Western Sahara, no Moroccans in our survey mentioned this issue.[20]

At the pivot point of Asia and Africa, on the southeast coast of the Mediterranean, sits Egypt, the largest Arab country and one that has long played a leadership role in intra-Arab politics. The country is proud of both its ancient history and its role in the last half century as the home of the Arab League and the locus of Arab nationalism. Despite the fact that Egypt was the first Arab country to make peace with Israel, Egyptians feel strongly about the unresolved Arab–Israeli conflict and the continued plight of the Palestinians. In the face of domestic pressures resulting from some religious extremist groups, a struggling economy, a rapidly growing population, and a highly bureaucratized and unresponsive political system, most Egyptians retain an equanimity that confounds outsiders.

When asked what they most want others to know about their country, Egyptians focused in equal proportions on four characteristics: that they are a tolerant people (for example, "our religion guarantees equity and tolerance," "we are not fanatics"); the safety, security, and stability of Egypt ("there is no place for terrorism in our country"); Egypt's central role in the Arab World ("we are the main defense for the Palestinians"); and, of course, Egypt's history and tourism industry ("we are the oldest civilization in the world, everyone should come and visit," "we are the land of the pharaohs").[21]

Lebanon is a land with great physical beauty, a rich history, and a diverse society. But it also has internal difficulties born of the sectarian-based system of governance imposed decades ago by the French. With one Christian community given a dominant governing role as France's then-reliable client and the country's Shi'a community apportioned the smallest piece of the pie, tension was built into this dysfunctional system from the outset.

After 1948, Lebanon became a refuge for more than 100,000 Palestinians fleeing their homes in what had just become Israel. Palestinians' presence has, at times, further unsettled Lebanon's situation. Unfortunately, this tension has been exploited by Lebanon's neighbors. Aggravated internal dissension led to a civil war from 1975 to 1990. Throughout the 1970s and early 1980s, Lebanon was a battleground between Palestinians and Israelis, leading to an Israeli occupation of south Lebanon. This, in turn, gave rise to Hizbullah, which has acted as both a resistance movement against the Israeli occupation and an armed militia on behalf of the Shi'a community. As a result, Lebanon has continued to be drawn into conflict with Israel and has endured three decades of armed Syrian presence. Lebanon's sects may, at times, have divergent views on critical domestic and foreign policy issues, but despite this, a strong Lebanese self-identity and love of country has taken hold among Lebanon's people.

These country-specific concerns, a result of the unique circumstances of Lebanon's development, history, and regional setting, are clearly apparent when we poll. Responses to the open-ended question, "What do you want the world to know about your country?" are instructive of what some Lebanese worry about and others take pride in. One-third of Lebanese focused on the beauty and great history of their country, speaking of its "ancient heritage," describing it as a "first-class tourist destination," or reflecting on the beauty of its "snow-capped mountains and beaches that can be enjoyed in the same day." But reflecting Lebanon's deep internal divisions, another third of respondents, still smarting from Israel's long occupation in the south and its devastating attacks, wanted the world to know of their commitment to resistance. Those surveyed said, "We are a free country that does not accept occupation and humiliation," "We are a resistance that opposes unfair occupation," and, "We keep our heads high and will not stop until we regain all of our rights."[22]

Jordan is home to remarkable Roman and Nabatean ruins. Although it is located in a tough neighborhood, Jordan has for years been an isle of stability and progress, being one of the first countries in the Middle East to promote a clean environment and consumer protection. Nevertheless, Jordanians by necessity are preoccupied with the instability generated by conflicts both to its east and west. One-third of Jordan's six million citizens are Palestinian refugees with strong familial ties to their kin living under Israeli occupation. Another 700,000 residents are recent Iraqi refugees, and their presence has created new economic pressures. It is no wonder that Jordanians of all stripes closely watch developments beyond their borders and worry about their future security.

When describing their country, Jordanians are divided almost right down the middle. Half remarked on the country's tourist attractions and historic sites, pointing out that the Kingdom of Jordan has "a great history and a noble Arab civilization" and "terrific sight-seeing in Petra, the Dead Sea and Aqaba." The other half of the population tended to focus on the unique challenges presented by the continuing Israeli–Palestinian conflict and its impact on Jordan. Some respondents said, "Our biggest issue is the Palestinian question, and their right to return to their homes," and, "We will not live in peace as long as this issue is unsolved."[23]

To Jordan's south lies the Kingdom of Saudi Arabia, home to Islam's two holiest cities: Mecca, the site of the annual pilgrimage that brings millions of Muslims to the kingdom, and Medina, where the Prophet Muhammad established the first community of believers. Saudis are, therefore, particularly proud of the pivotal role their country plays in Islam. An economic powerhouse, the country has also begun to flex its muscles politically, playing an increasingly important regional role in issues that are significant to Arabs and the broader Muslim World. But Saudi Arabia has also undergone much dramatic internal change in the past several decades: it has urbanized and, slowly but surely, is modernizing. This transformation has created social and cultural pressures that, together with a fast-growing population, are of concern to many Saudis.

When asked what they want the world to know about their country, Saudis convey the image of a stable, safe, and peaceful nation committed to Islam and its customs and traditions. Not surprisingly, over a third of the respondents focused on being "honored by God in having the two holy mosques" in Mecca and Medina. Many other respondents also spoke of Islam, either citing aspects of their religion or, with a Moroccan-like defensiveness, describing the kingdom as "a country of Islam, peace, tolerance and belief in one God," "a non-extremist country that is safe and secure," and "a Muslim country that hates terrorism and promotes peace."[24]

The United Arab Emirates (UAE) is one of the more outward-looking Arab states. It has ambitious and innovative plans to use its economic success to become a commercial, cultural, and tourist hub. The recent economic crisis in Dubai (one of the country's emirates, or states) has hit the UAE hard, shaking the confidence of some in the business community and creating a deep malaise in Dubai itself. However, the country's overall economy continues to grow and draw new investment from regional and foreign business partners. The UAE's oil-rich capital of Abu Dhabi has invested in far-reaching plans to establish itself as a cultural center, attracting Western universities (which have opened campuses in the emirate) and the Guggenheim and the Louvre (which have opened museums there), and even hosting an annual Formula 1 race. The UAE was recently elected to host the International Renewable Energy Agency, a decision the country points to with pride as evidence of its emerging global recognition. The UAE has the most diverse population of any Arab country, with its small citizen base of nationals dwarfed by the 85% of residents who are expatriates from more than 100 countries. Because of the UAE's reliance on the large expat labor force, concern with its living conditions, and its proximity to Iran and Iraq, many Emiratis worry about regional stability and the future of their country.

Perhaps because of the important roles played by tourism and expatriate workers in the country, almost 40% of UAE citizens want to assure the outside world of their country's safety and security. Some survey respondents described their home as "a peaceful country that keeps itself away from conflicts and wars" and "a secure and safe country that aims at achieving growth," and pointed out the country's "outstanding internal security system." An additional 40% spoke with pride of their economic success and tourist attractions. One respondent described the UAE as a "country with a unique mixture of Arab and Islamic customs and traditions and a tourism culture with progress in business, construction and commerce." Others focused on the UAE's "amusement parks and resorts where it is easy to relax and have fun."[25]

These are but snapshots of each of the six Arab countries in which Zogby International has regularly polled. We have surveyed others on occasion, but we chose these six for our annual surveys because they cover the three major regions of the Arab World: Morocco and Egypt from Africa; Lebanon and Jordan from the Levant; and Saudi Arabia and the UAE from the Gulf. The Arab World that emerges from our surveys is hardly a place populated by monochromatic stick figures. Rather, it is a highly nuanced region rich in detail, pointing to a simple truth: the real Arab World is more complicated than the neat caricature frequently presented by commentators, politicians, and even some academics. Cairo is not Riyadh is not Beirut is not Marrakesh. The residents of each of these cities are aware of, and proud of, the unique attributes of their countries and are deeply committed to the values of their faiths. In trying to advance our dialogue and engagement with the Arab World, it is vital that we recognize this variety among the Arabs. Only once we begin to listen to real people can we truly engage the Arab World—and stop chasing myths and shadowy rumors.

6

SUPER MYTH TWO
THERE IS NO ARAB WORLD

IN CONTRAST TO the myth of a generalized, monolithic "Arab mind" stands another myth: that the Arab World and Arab identity are nothing but fractured fictions. This myth claims that the region is so diverse and complicated that it can't really be described as a cohesive "world" and that there are no unifying threads establishing a shared identity.

Editors of the *Economist* advanced this line of thinking in "Waking From Its Sleep: A Special Report on the Arab World" (July 2009). One article in the special report dismissed Arab identity as something "slippery" that can be "put on and taken off according to taste and circumstance." It then questioned the usefulness of "the Arab World" as a concept. Because the magazine entitled this issue "A Special Report on the Arab World," the editors were forced to begrudgingly acknowledge that the term might be a "neat" way to describe the twenty-two Arabic-speaking countries of North Africa and Southwest Asia.[1] But the editors added that the idea of an Arab World is not very useful because it describes "a big and amorphous thing, and arguably not one thing at all."[2]

As our polling demonstrates, there is indeed great diversity across the Arab World. Citizens in the many Arab states do in fact maintain pride in their countries' unique histories and special features. And as we shall see later, each country's citizens have different issues that define their local political agendas. The Lebanese, for example, are concerned with their internal political divide and the threat they continue to feel from renewed conflict between Israel and Hizbullah. Jordanians focus more on the Palestinian question and the instability resulting from the continuing conflict within Iraq on Jordan's eastern border. And economic concerns mean one thing in Dubai's troubled real estate market and quite another to Egypt's poor.

Although these distinctions are legitimate, they do not negate another dynamic at work across the region: despite local differences, an underlying shared identity and a common set of concerns come through quite clearly in our polling.

Ironically enough, the *Economist* uses one of Zogby International's surveys to dismiss the importance of Arab identity.[3] In polling for the University of Maryland in April of 2009, we asked respondents in six Arab states (Morocco, Egypt, Lebanon, Jordan, Saudi Arabia, and the UAE): "Which of the following is your most important identity?" The aggregate responses were nearly evenly divided among "country of origin" (35%), "Arab" (32%), and "religion" (32%). To the magazine's editors, this apparently meant that "Arab" was not a central component of identity across the region. However, the deeper truth is that Arabs, like most people, live in a complex world with multiple pulls on their self-definition.

Surely Americans and Europeans can understand this reality. Though we may share the same currency, language, and president with millions of our fellow citizens, we are also subject to a variety of personal tugs and circumstances that help shape what sociologists call our "principal source of identity." In the United Kingdom, for example, the allegiances may come from ethnicity, religion, region, or even age. In the United States, a young African American from South Carolina, a middle-aged white Bostonian, and an Arizona retiree are likely on the surface to have little in common—differences that politicians frequently exploit. Some political analysts have even expressed the concern that this "identity problem" can, if not addressed, lead to the unraveling of a nation's fabric.[4] Odds are, though, that at the end of the day, the South Carolinian, the Bostonian, and the Arizonan are still going to define themselves, if asked, as Americans.

So it is also with Arabs. The competing tugs on identity are simply part of modern society. But the fact that one-third of respondents from six different countries representing six distinct traditions would say that their principal identity is "Arab" is quite telling, especially when we examine identity on a country-by-country basis. In our November 2009 survey we asked: "Suppose you are talking with someone from the United States. Please rate how important each of the following is in defining who you are to that American." Those responses establish that "country of origin" is the paramount self-definition, with "Arab" a strong second in every country except Morocco (where it ranks third) and the UAE (where it ranks first, possibly because one-half of our respondents were expatriate Arabs from other countries).[5] When the results are aggregated across the region, as they were in the earlier survey cited by the *Economist,* once again the "country of origin," "being Arab," and "your religion" are rated nearly evenly (see Table 6.1).

In an April 2010 survey we directly asked: "How important to you is your Arab identity?" The responses establish that it is important to three-quarters of all Lebanese and more than nine-tenths of Egyptians, Jordanians, Saudis, Palestinians, and Kuwaitis (see Table 6.2).[6] And when we asked in November 2009: "How important is Arab unity to you personally?" the responses establish that it is, in fact, important to two-thirds of Moroccans and Egyptians, three-quarters of Lebanese and Jordanians, and almost nine-tenths of Saudis and Emiratis (see Table 6.3).

But what exactly does this sense of "Arab identity " consist of? When Zogby International asked respondents to choose the most important source of "common ground between you and other Arabs," they broadly

TABLE 6.1 RANK OF IMPORTANCE FOR MEANS OF SELF-IDENTIFICATION

Suppose you are talking with someone from the United States, please rate how important each of the following is in defining who you are to that American.

	Morocco	Egypt	Lebanon	Jordan	Saudi Arabia	UAE
Family	6	6	5	6	5	4
City	5	4	3	4	3	4
Country	2	1	1	1	1	3
Religion	1	3	4	3	1	2
Arab	3	2	2	2	2	1
Social status	4	5	6	5	4	5

Source: Zogby International, *Six-Nation Arab Opinion Poll,* November 1–18, 2009. Sample size: 3,989 adults.

Note: Respondents were asked to rate the importance of each item. Rankings shown here are the order of items by the percentage of high ratings (1 indicates the strongest identity affiliation and 6 indicates the weakest).

TABLE 6.2: IMPORTANCE OF ARAB IDENTITY (in %)

How important to you is your Arab identity?

	Egypt	Lebanon	Jordan	Saudi Arabia	Kuwait	Palestine
Important	99	72	90	88	92	99.8
Not Important	2	28	10	12	8	–

Source: Zogby International, *2010 Poll of MENA Nations,* April 3–26, 2010. Sample size: 4,881.

TABLE 6.3   IMPORTANCE OF ARAB UNITY (in %)

How important is Arab unity to you personally?

	Morocco	Egypt	Lebanon	Jordan	Saudi Arabia	UAE
Important	66	68	74	76	90	87
Not important	21	13	18	16	5	4

Source: Zogby International, *Six-Nation Arab Opinion Poll*, November 1–18, 2009. Sample size: 3,989 adults.

TABLE 6.4   RANK OF SOURCES OF COMMON GROUND AMONG ARABS

What provides the greatest common ground between you and other Arabs?

	Morocco	Egypt	Lebanon	Jordan	Saudi Arabia	UAE
Language	2	2	4	5	2	2
Political concerns	1	1	1	1	3	1
History	5	5	3	2	4	3
Economy	5	4	2	4	5	5
Religion	3	3	6	2	1	4
Destiny	4	6	5	6	6	6
No common ground	—	—	—	—	—	—

Source: Zogby International, *Six-Nation Arab Opinion Poll*, November 1–18, 2009. Sample size: 3,989 adults.

Note: A rank of 1 indicates the source providing the greatest common ground with 6 indicating the source providing the least.

identified "shared political concerns" and "common language" as the two dominant factors (see Table 6.4).

Note that for Saudis, religion is the principal source of unity (for reasons relating to their unique role in Islam). Conversely, for Lebanese (owing to their deep sectarian divide) religion finishes in last place. No respondents in any of the six countries said there is "no common ground."

When we think about a shared identity, the issue of a common language immediately comes to mind. First, we have to acknowledge that speaking the same language means much more than merely sharing words and grammar. Having a common language suggests a shared history and being connected by the values and culture that are expressed by that language. Although modern Arab nationalism and political organizations like the Arab League have their roots in the early-twentieth-century resistance to colonial occupation, Arabic itself has long provided a binding force throughout the region both as the language of the Qur'an—and therefore of Islam—and as a conveyor of culture. Edward Said, the well-known Arab American writer and cultural critic, was fond of noting that he was a Christian by faith and Muslim by culture. Said recognized that Islam and the Arabic language played unifying roles in shaping his identity.

Beginning in the seventh century A.D., as the religion of Islam underwent a dramatic expansion from the Arabian Peninsula across Africa and throughout Southwest Asia, local peoples converted first to the religion and then later adopted the Arabic language. Arabic became established as the accepted tongue of governance and commerce, uniting previously distinct populations. Led by language, the idea of an Arab World took root.

Today "Arab World" describes a vast region spanning two continents, from Morocco in the west to Iraq in the east and from Syria in the north to Yemen in the south. Yet "Arab" is not a race; nor does it refer to a specific ethnicity—and, as Said noted, it includes Christians and Jews as well as Muslims. In fact, in the first half of the twentieth century, some of the most thoughtful treatises on Arab nationalism were written by Christian Arabs like George Antonius and Clovis Maqsoud. Even today, one of Morocco's most influential advisers to the Royal Court, Andre Azoulay, is an Arab Jew, as is Bahrain's current ambassador to Washington, H. E. Huda Nonoo.

Within this complex and widely diverse world are twenty-two countries, many races, and a number of fascinating religious and ethnic minority communities, each with its own unique traditions. But for the most part, these 350 million souls all share a single language and with it the common culture, shared values, and view of history that language conveys.

This is a tie that binds. In fact, it might be best to describe the region that encompasses North Africa, the Levant, and the Gulf states as the "Arabic-Speaking World" because the role of language is central to Arab identity. Thus, for example, Turks who speak Turkish are not Arabs, nor are Iranians who speak Farsi. (As our poll shows, mistaking Iran for an

Arab country is a widely held view in the United States.[7]) Like the English-speaking world, the Arabic one is home to multiple dialects as rich in local flavor as "Brooklynese," a Texan drawl, or Cockney. The region's minorities have also often preserved elements of their ancient tongues, incorporating unique vocabulary into their local slang. Nonetheless, standard Arabic used on radio, on television, and in most writing is the defining lingua franca. Hence the power of today's regionwide Arab satellite television networks like Al Jazeera, Al Arabiya, MBC, ART, LBC International, Abu Dhabi TV, and a host of others to connect Arabs with information and entertainment programming.

Another key issue in considering a unified Arab identity is whether Arabs share political concerns and how strong a role these concerns play in shaping that identity. The big answers are *yes* and *very strong*, but for the detailed picture, we go back to a 2007 survey Zogby International conducted across the Arab World. In this survey, we asked respondents a series of questions about the importance of specific political issues.[8]

In response to the question "How important is the Palestinian issue to you?" we found a universally shared concern (see Table 6.5).

More telling are the responses to the follow-up question: "Why is the Palestinian issue important to you?" Although "religious reasons" and the sense that "Palestinians are victims" generate strong responses, the sense that "Palestinians are Arabs like me" was the number-one reason given as to why this issue was so vital in every country but Jordan (where most respondents *are* Palestinian) (see Table 6.6).

Like the Palestine problem, the U.S.-led war in Iraq also weighs heavily on Arabs and tends to unite them. Four years into the war, in our 2007

TABLE 6.5   IMPORTANCE OF THE PALESTINIAN ISSUE (in %)

How important is the Palestinian issue to you?

	Morocco	Egypt	Jordan	Saudi Arabia	UAE
Important	87	97	100	97	95
Not important	13	3	—	3	3

Source: Zogby International, *Arab Views of Leadership, Identity, Institutions and Issues of Concern,* January 1–December 25, 2007. Sample size: 6,506 adults.

regional survey, we asked: "How important is the Iraqi issue to you?" In all the countries covered in our survey, the numbers were virtually identical to the ratings given to the Palestinian issue (see Table 6.7).

And, as with the Palestinian issue, we also followed up our initial question by asking those who considered the Iraqi issue important, "Why is the Iraqi issue important to you?" The responses again tracked closely with those given for the topic of Palestine. The belief that Iraqis are "Arabs like me" was the most important reason cited in Egypt, Saudi Arabia, and Morocco, with "religious reasons" dominating among Arabs in the UAE (see Table 6.8).

TABLE 6.6   WHY THE PALESTINIAN ISSUE IS IMPORTANT (in %)

Why is the Palestinian issue important to you?

	Morocco	Egypt	Jordan	Saudi Arabia	UAE
Palestinians are Arabs like me	57	50	32	40	81
Religious reasons	30	29	32	29	7
Palestinians are victims	12	20	33	30	8
Other reasons	—	1	—	—	1

Source: Zogby International, *Arab Views of Leadership, Identity, Institutions and Issues of Concern,* January 1–December 25, 2007. Sample size: 6,506 adults.

TABLE 6.7   IMPORTANCE OF THE IRAQI ISSUE (in %)

How important is the Iraqi issue to you?

	Morocco	Egypt	Jordan	Saudi Arabia	UAE
Important	88	96	100	97	89
Not important	13	4	—	3	10

Source: Zogby International, *Arab Views of Leadership, Identity, Institutions and Issues of Concern,* January 1–December 25, 2007. Sample size: 6,506 adults.

TABLE 6.8   WHY THE IRAQI ISSUE IS IMPORTANT (in %)

Why is the Iraqi issue important to you?

	Morocco	Egypt	Jordan	Saudi Arabia	UAE
Iraqis are Arabs like me	61	52	33	45	28
Religious reasons	22	28	30	26	61
Iraqis are victims	16	20	33	29	8
Other reasons	1	—	4	1	3

Source: Zogby International, *Arab Views of Leadership, Identity, Institutions and Issues of Concern,* January 1–December 25, 2007. Sample size: 6,506 adults.

For most Arabs, then, the Iraq and Palestine problems are more than just conflicts occurring within their region; they are tragedies that have befallen "people like me"—people with whom Arabs share a common language, religion, and identity. To ignore the interrelatedness of the Arab World or, as the *Economist* does in its "special report," deny that the world exists is not only intellectual folly. It's also an open invitation to bad policy and failed initiatives.

Unless we want to continually provoke hostility and resistance across such a critical part of the world, we must pay attention to the sensibilities that exist among Arabs, the history they share, the agonies they mutually suffer, and the ties that bind.

7
SUPER MYTH THREE
THE ANGRY ARAB

WHENEVER I HEAR people talking about what fire-breathers Arabs are—angry and consumed by contempt for the West and especially America—I think of the afternoon I spent in the living room of a Tunisian friend, debating his college-age nephews on politics, morality, and the United States. Like young idealists everywhere, they were intense and confident, and I later learned that they were members of a student group affiliated with the Muslim Brotherhood. Yet they also seemed quite distracted. I finally noticed that they were looking over my shoulder at the television in the next room. While arguing with me, they were also trying to watch a bawdy Italian game show.

As realizations go, this was a small one, but it pointed neatly to the perils of asserting that most Arabs have a single-minded focus on attacking America and the West generally, politically, or otherwise. Even in the case of these politicized teenagers, their sincere discontent with policies pursued by the West didn't preclude their watching a silly Italian television program. And in fact, this sort of complex, multidimensional relationship with the West is common all over the Arab World. In Jordan and Saudi Arabia, for example, the same people who voice strong criticism of American policy can be found out and about wearing jeans and LeBron James jerseys, having coffee at Starbucks, or eating at Kentucky Fried Chicken.

The supposedly monomaniacal obsession of Arabs with politics is equally overblown. Sure they care about issues affecting their region and their people, but that is not all they think about. Back in the Clinton era, I was in Kuwait researching an article on the administration's "dual containment" policy toward Iraq and Iran. Kuwait had long been square in the middle of the issue: threatened by Iran, invaded and occupied by Iraq, and finally liberated by a U.S.-led multinational military campaign. A friend of mine, a leading Kuwaiti intellectual, had invited a group of fellow academics and thinkers to meet with me at his house. They set forth their views on American policy in the region passionately and at great length, until the meeting had to be adjourned prematurely so that these serious-minded Arab thinkers could watch a World Cup qualifying match. My discussion with these men—the best and brightest of a people reputedly consumed by politics and religion—had to wait until the next day.

This was another small moment, but it was also a revealing one—evidence that Arabs, just like anybody, are a mix of values, interests, and contradictory impulses. To be sure, some Arabs think about and debate politics vigorously at times. Frequently the United States, as the biggest international operator in the region, is the subject of these discussions, and America's policies are often analyzed and debated. In the months after the 9/11 attacks, though, American front-page headlines and magazine covers often painted Arabs as driven by almost nothing but raw anger.

Of course, Americans wanted to know why 9/11 happened. Everyone around the world did. The attacks were so violent, the carnage so great, there could be no question that the perpetrators were driven by hatred. In his September 20, 2001, speech to Congress, George W. Bush raised the issue explicitly: "Americans are asking 'Why do they hate us?'" The president then went on to answer the question in chilling terms:

> They hate what they see right here in this chamber: a democratically elected government. Their leaders are self-appointed. They hate our freedoms: our freedom of religion, our freedom of speech, our freedom to vote and assemble and disagree with each other.
>
> They want to overthrow existing governments in many Muslim countries such as Egypt, Saudi Arabia and Jordan. They want to drive Israel out of the Middle East. They want to drive Christians and Jews out of vast regions of Asia and Africa.[1]

But it wasn't long before the "they" to which the president referred—the nineteen specific perpetrators and their al-Qaeda mentors—started to become a much more inclusive "they." Some suggested that the behavior of the attackers was not aberrant but characteristic of Arabs as a whole. Others found in the attack evidence that the West and Islam are not only different but inevitably headed toward a clash.

Western media reports have too often fed us mythologies and half-truths about a vengeful Arab mentality. Commentators like neoconservative Michael Ledeen spoke of "the same kind of hate that we read every day in the newspapers about what the Saudi newspapers are printing. Kill the Jews, kill the Christians, be a martyr, go to heaven, 72 virgins, the usual."[2] A Bernard Lewis piece in the *Atlantic* conjured up a unified Islamic anger predicated on historic injustices—neatly clumping together all adherents to a religion practiced by nearly one in five people on Earth.[3] More disturbing still is Lee Smith's sweeping and bigoted generalization that "the Arabs hate us not because of what we do or who we are but because of what and who we are not: Arabs."[4]

Influenced by such depictions, many in the West got used to the idea of Arabs as angry caricatures—hundreds of millions of people who go to bed hating Israel, wake up hating the American way of life, and spend their daylight hours glued to television programs that incite their passions. Many Westerners came to believe that Muslims only listen to mosque sermons that fuel their anger at the West and, if they have bile to spare, their own governments.

In early 2002, five months after the horror of 9/11, I was a guest on the television news program *Meet the Press*.[5] The Gallup organization had conducted a poll in nine Muslim countries (five of them Arab) that uncovered what appeared to be widespread antipathy toward the United States.[6] In most of the Arab countries polled, favorable attitudes about the United States were quite few. The results had shocked an already alarmed public and had become grist for the media mill. I appeared along with conservative pundit Charles Krauthammer to analyze the results.

Krauthammer's take on the survey findings was basically circular. Why does America appear so unpopular in the polls? Because Arabs hate us. Why do they hate us? Because they've been taught to hate us by the imams in their religious schools and further encouraged to hate us by Arab governments and state-controlled news outlets that are, in Krauthammer's words, "virulently anti-American, anti-Western, and anti-Semitic."[7] And why have they been taught to hate us? Because, in fact, they do hate us.

Such loopy analyses were just morphing into the conventional wisdom of the day, and, in this instance, the Gallup survey had played right into Krauthammer's hands. But I knew the story was far more complicated than that. Using the resources of Zogby International, my brother John and I set out to find the deeper truth with an in-depth, multination Arab poll.

It turns out that as the world's only superpower, "America" means many things to many people in a variety of contexts. As we have seen dramatically in recent years, American policies directly affect the lives of tens of millions of people throughout the Middle East. America is also an economic colossus, consuming the region's natural resources and, in this age of globalized commerce and information, promoting and selling products worldwide.

Our study attempted to measure how Arabs felt about the many ways that America manifested itself in their region and touched their lives. By going beyond simply asking about favorable and unfavorable attitudes toward "America," we also attempted to determine whether Arab adults differentiated between their feelings toward the American people and culture on one side and American policy in the Middle East on the other.

After conducting face-to-face interviews in March 2002 throughout five Arab nations—Egypt, Saudi Arabia, Lebanon, Kuwait, and the United Arab Emirates (UAE)—we found that those polled expressed a high regard for many aspects of America's broader cultural contributions.[8] For example, when questioned about American science and technology, many Arabs were favorable, and the positive majorities were frequently overwhelming. Likewise, majorities in all countries were also favorably inclined toward America's democracy and freedom. American movies and television as well as education and products were also well received by majorities in all countries.

Contrary to the negative claims of pundits like Krauthammer, we found that Arabs actually *liked* many things about America. But it wasn't American values or people that had caused the image of the United States to crater. America's overall ranking sank because of the incredibly low marks Arabs gave to U.S. policy toward Arab nations generally and Palestinians specifically (see Table 7.1).

Nearly nine out of ten respondents in every Arab nation gave a negative rating to the U.S. handling of the Palestinian conflict—an issue viewed uniformly as "the most important" or "a very important" concern facing the Arab World today. In other words, if we need to have a headline claiming that Arabs hate something, then it would be more accurate to say, "Arabs Hate U.S. Policy Toward Their Region"—although that probably won't sell as many newspapers.

We presented the results of our "Impressions of America" poll at a press conference on April 11, 2002. After I explained that "America" was not hated but that American policy did create negative attitudes among Arabs and Muslims, a reporter asked me to summarize our results.

TABLE 7.1   ARAB ATTITUDES TOWARD U.S. VALUES, PRODUCTS, AND POLICIES (in %)

Aspect of America	Saudi Arabia Fav/Unfav	Lebanon Fav/Unfav	UAE Fav/Unfav	Egypt Fav/Unfav	Kuwait Fav/Unfav
Overall opinion of the United States*	12/87	26/70	11/87	15/76	41/48
Science and technology	71/26	82/16	81/14	78/11	86/12
Freedom and democracy	52/44	58/40	50/44	53/38	58/39
People	43/51	63/33	43/42	35/47	50/38
Movies and TV	54/42	64/35	64/32	53/40	54/44
Policy toward Arabs	8/88	9/86	15/76	4/86	5/88
Policy toward Palestinians	5/90	6/89	10/83	3/89	2/94
Policy toward terrorism	30/57	30/65	37/48	18/67	30/62

Source: Zogby International, *The Ten-Nation Impressions of America Poll*, March 4–April 3, 2002. Conducted face-to-face interviews in ten nations. Only data for the Arab nations covered in this part of the poll are shown here. Sample sizes: Saudi Arabia (700), Lebanon (500), UAE (500), Egypt (700), Kuwait (500).

Note: Favorable includes both "very favorable" and "somewhat favorable" responses. Unfavorable includes both "very unfavorable" and "somewhat unfavorable" responses. Percentages do not add to 100% as numbers were rounded, and the percentage responding "not familiar" or "not sure" has not been included.

* Data related to "overall" opinions for 2002 are from James J. Zogby, *What Arabs Think: Values, Beliefs and Concerns* (Utica, NY: Zogby International/The Arab Thought Foundation, 2002).

I boiled down our polling to four words: "It's the policy, stupid."[9] And it still is. Which suggests that instead of asking, "Why do they hate us?" we should be asking, "How can we create a broader base of support across the Middle East to ensure that those who would do us harm are permanently isolated and defeated?" That way we starve the resentments on which terrorists feed.

Our 2002 polling found a receptive audience. My brother and I addressed the Department of State, testified before Congress, and lectured on the results before distinguished audiences across the United States. People listened, and many sympathized, but we were still unable to dislodge the idea that Arab resentment of America was the inevitable result of some sort of "clash of civilizations."

As with the Super Myths of a monolithic or a nonexistent Arab World, accepting that "All Arabs Are Angry" and "All Arabs Hate Us" was oddly comforting to the uninformed; it absolved our political leaders from worrying about plummeting approval ratings in the region. If America hadn't really created the gap separating us from the Arab World, how could our policy makers be held responsible for this negative opinion? And if the Arab hatred of the West was effectively permanent and immutable—if we were never going to win their hearts and minds—why bother to even try? As U.S. engagement increased with the Middle East, far too many of our government officials simply refused to acknowledge the negative effect of American policies in the region.

Watching the Bush administration's inconsistent approach to public diplomacy and outreach was equally frustrating. Although President Bush himself talked about the need for Arab, Arab American, and Muslim support to combat extremism and reminded Americans that Islam is not the enemy, the president simultaneously initiated the roundup and deportation of thousands of Arab and Muslim immigrants. President Bush also failed to denounce anti-Muslim statements made by leading administration officials like Attorney General John Ashcroft.[10] All of this deepened the already worrying divide between us and the Arab World. As a result, the Bush administration ultimately failed to recruit needed support across the region. Then, in 2003, we invaded Iraq—an operation that further alienated Arabs from America.

In 2004, two years after our initial poll, we found that overall favorable ratings for the United States had declined—dramatically in some cases. Even more disturbing was the fact that Arab attitudes toward American values, people, and products had also turned negative in many Arab countries (see Table 7.2 on pages 88–89).[11]

This overall decline in Arab approval of America was still being driven by extremely unfavorable views of U.S. policy, especially now that the invasion of Iraq had thrown grease on the fire. In 2002, Arab attitudes about American involvement in the Israeli–Palestinian conflict were already extremely negative, but in 2004 these opinions were eclipsed by an *even greater* Arab rejection of U.S. policy toward Iraq. In Morocco, Saudi Arabia, and Egypt, for example, America's Iraq policy earned a less than 1% favorable rating. In Jordan it received a 2% rating, and in Lebanon and the UAE, only 4% of the public approved of U.S. policy in Iraq.

In responses given to open-ended questions, the role that American policy played in this growing Arab disenchantment became even more clear. When asked to identify the "first thought that comes to mind," the "best and worst things [they] could say about America," and "what America should do to change its image in the Arab World," most of the respondents focused on policy issues. "Stop supporting Israel," "Change your Middle East policy," and "Stop killing Arabs" were among the most common responses.[12]

By 2006, when we once again polled these attitudes, the Iraq War was in its third year, U.S. engagement with the region was largely unchanged since our previous surveying, and Arab opinion toward America was still in freefall. For example, our polling found that overall favorable attitudes toward the United States had plummeted in Morocco and Jordan, moving from the mid-30% range in 2005 to single digits in 2006.[13]

The numbers were bad enough in general, but what ought to have been of special concern to U.S. leaders was the "hardening" of the negatives. In Egypt and Saudi Arabia, the United States already had extremely low favorable ratings: 14% and 12%, respectively. These didn't change, but there was a notable movement from "unfavorable" attitudes to "very unfavorable."

Another aspect of these hardening attitudes was that Arab appreciation for American elements unrelated to policy began to slip. Back in 2002, we found that overall negative views were a function of frustration with U.S. policy. Nonetheless, as noted earlier, Arabs still liked "American freedom and democracy," "American people," and "American products" and culture. Not so in 2006. The steady drip of unpopular policies eroded once favorable perceptions of American people, products, and values. Now only U.S. education received mostly favorable ratings in all Arab countries. Attitudes toward "American freedom and democracy" declined sharply across the board, and "American products" received net favorable ratings only in Lebanon.

The story these poll numbers were telling us was echoed in a random encounter I had on a Riyadh–London flight in 2003. I fell into conversation with a fifty-year-old Palestinian businessman named Mahmood. I was continuing on to Washington; he was transferring to Boston—a city he described as the closest place to home. Mahmood was born in a refugee camp in Lebanon, and his career was in Saudi Arabia, but he said his heart would always be in Boston. It was in this U.S. city that he had spent his formative years and gone to school, and it was where his two adult sons now lived with their families.

But because Mahmood had not been to the United States since 9/11, he was also nervous about his trip. The stories he'd heard about harassment and harsh treatment at the airports had initially kept him away. "I love your country," Mahmood said. "It's easy to love. But I don't understand your policies."

Eventually our discussion shifted to business, and Mahmood made a related and intriguing observation: "Compare Japan, Germany, China, and the U.S. All of them are major exporters of products. But there's a difference.

TABLE 7.2 ATTITUDES TOWARD AMERICA AND ITS PEOPLE, PRODUCTS, AND CULTURE: 2002/2004/2009 (in %)

Aspect of America		Morocco[c]			Egypt			Lebanon		
		2002	2004	2009	2002	2004	2009	2002	2004	2009
Overall opinion of the United States[a]	Favorable	38	11	55	15	4	30	26	20	23
	Unfavorable	61	88	41	76	95	64	70	69	75
Freedom and democracy	Favorable	na	53	55	53	56	53	58	41	38
	Unfavorable	na	41	36	38	41	39	40	56	62
People	Favorable	na	59	49	35	60	41	63	39	58
	Unfavorable	na	29	35	47	39	47	33	58	35
Movies and TV	Favorable	na	60	46	53	38	57	64	30	60
	Unfavorable	na	37	42	40	59	36	35	66	40
Products	Favorable	na	73	57	50	57	58	72	39	73
	Unfavorable	na	24	31	45	46	33	25	57	27
Education	Favorable	na	61	61	68	32	54	81	38	74
	Unfavorable	na	16	24	17	23	30	16	54	19
Policy toward Palestinians	Favorable	na	3	34	3	1	19	6	4	7
	Unfavorable	na	93	69	89	94	76	89	90	93
Iraq policy[b]	Favorable	na	1	11	na	<1	17	na	4	6
	Unfavorable	na	98	82	na	92	78	na	93	91

Aspect of America		Jordan[c]			Saudi Arabia			UAE		
		2002	2004	2009	2002	2004	2009	2002	2004	2009
Overall opinion of the United States[a]	Favorable	34	15	25	12	4	41	11	14	21
	Unfavorable	61	78	74	87	94	59	87	72	69
Freedom and democracy	Favorable	na	57	49	52	39	81	50	39	18
	Unfavorable	na	40	47	44	60	18	44	53	82
People	Favorable	na	52	70	43	28	88	43	46	46
	Unfavorable	na	39	27	51	64	15	42	35	34
Movies and TV	Favorable	na	56	69	54	35	67	64	54	46
	Unfavorable	na	41	31	42	60	33	32	43	52
Products	Favorable	na	61	85	53	37	81	68	63	65
	Unfavorable	na	35	13	44	59	18	27	34	22
Education	Favorable	na	59	81	58	12	90	79	63	60
	Unfavorable	na	29	10	35	74	9	13	23	24
Policy toward Palestinians	Favorable	na	7	4	5	3	13	10	5	14
	Unfavorable	na	89	95	90	95	86	83	90	85
Iraq policy[b]	Favorable	na	2	12	na	1	12	na	4	17
	Unfavorable	na	78	86	na	97	88	na	91	83

Source: Zogby International, *Impressions of America*, April, 2002. Sample size for the countries listed here: 2,400 adults

Zogby International, *Impressions of America*, June, 2004. Sample size: 3,286 adults

Zogby International, *Six-Nation Arab Opinion Poll*, November 1–18, 2009. Sample size: 3,989 adults

[a]Data related to "overall opinions for 2002 are from: James J. Zogby, *What Arabs Think: Values, Beliefs and Concerns* (Utica, NY: Zogby International/The Arab Thought Foundation, 2002). Sample size for countries listed here: 3,000 adults.

[b]Attitudes on U.S. policy toward Iraq not asked in 2002.

[c]Attitudes on "Freedom and democracy," "People," "Movies and TV," "Products," "Education," and "Policy toward Palestinians" not asked in Morocco and Jordan in 2002.

Note: Favorable includes both "very favorable" and "somewhat favorable" responses. Unfavorable includes both "very unfavorable" and "somewhat unfavorable" responses. Percentages do not add to 100% as numbers were rounded, and the percentage responding "not familiar" or "not sure" has not been included. Where "na" appears, question was not asked in that year.

Japan, Germany, and China export only products. America exports its culture. Even with your products and your franchises, you sell a little bit of the American way of life. That's what makes your products so desirable and unique."[14]

According to our poll numbers, Mahmood was not alone in these sentiments. The Middle East policies pursued by the Bush administration were compromising our people, our ability to conduct business, and our relationships with Arab allies.

On another occasion, a Lebanese friend of mine described the general Arab mood as "not a rejection of America, but a feeling of being rejected by America—not hatred of America, but feeling hated by America. There is a longing to be accepted and respected by America and the clear sense we are not. You can say we feel like jilted lovers."[15]

Another thing I find remarkable about the myth of the angry Arab is how closely it has become associated with the Qatar-based Al Jazeera cable news. Fox News Channel's Bill O'Reilly, for one, has called Al Jazeera "a propaganda network that's bent on encouraging violence and sympathetic to terrorists."[16] To be sure, Arab television-viewing habits can tell us a great deal about Arab needs, concerns, and attitudes toward the world in which they live. But the notion that millions of Arabs are glued to Al Jazeera all day is primarily a successful product of its own public-relations campaign.

Since 2000 Zogby International has been surveying Arab viewing behavior, measuring hour-by-hour program preferences over a seven-day period. What we have found is that Arabs, like their American counterparts, watch television primarily for fun and to relax.

Among those shows that have gained enormous popularity across the Arab World is *Freej,* a program on Dubai TV. During the month of Ramadan in 2007 and 2008, *Freej* was the highest-rated show in the Gulf region, and it is neither political nor angry.[17] Influenced by the U.S. sitcom *The Golden Girls, Freej* is an animated feature about four traditional grandmothers living in old Dubai and their humorous encounters with modernity.

Like most people, Arabs also use their TV remotes a lot, switching from one network to another. In our most recent survey, we asked, "When you sit down at night to watch television, which type of programs are you most likely to watch?" In the most populous Arab countries—Egypt and Saudi Arabia—movies were the top preference; in Morocco, it was soap operas and dramas. Overall, news programs finished third, but "watching the news" does not automatically mean Al Jazeera or other Arab satellite news networks. In Lebanon, Egypt, Morocco, and Saudi Arabia, it meant local news programs.[18] Many Arabs tend to watch their home-country networks just as Americans watch their own local news in far larger numbers than the higher-profile national cable news (see Table 7.3).

In times of crisis, of course, Arabs do watch satellite news networks. But here, too, we found differences in viewing habits. Al Jazeera may be the "most watched" network for news because, like Fox News or CNN, it features regular, up-to-the-minute reporting. But because Arabs can be quite discerning, Al Jazeera is not always rated the "most trusted" news source.

And contrary to the frequent assertion that young Arabs have learned to hate the United States by watching inflammatory television, we found that in every Arab country polled, the youngest groups (18–29 years of age) were substantially more positive about American products, people, and values than other age groups. Indeed, youth itself appears to be a key factor; negativity grew with age. The same trend also held true for those with satellite TV and Internet access. Those with the most access were the most positive toward American freedom and democracy, American movies and television, American-made products, and American education.[19]

TABLE 7.3   RANK OF TELEVISION PROGRAM TYPES VIEWED

When you sit down at night to watch television, which type of programs are you most likely to watch?

	Morocco	Egypt	Lebanon	Jordan	Saudi Arabia	UAE
Movies	3	1	2	2	1	3
Soap operas and dramas	1	2	3	3	3	6
News	7	3	1	1	2	1
Reality shows	6	5	5	5	6	5
Music and entertainment	2	6	4	4	7	2
Game shows	4	8	8	7	8	4
Sports	8	4	6	6	4	8
Religious shows	4	7	7	8	5	7

Source: Zogby International, *Poll for Arab Broadcast Forum, Abu Dhabi, UAE,* March 11–26, 2008. Sample size: 4,046 adults.

Note: Respondents were asked to rank the types of programs in order of their preference with 1 being the highest preferred and 8 being the lowest (of the options available).

In short, with increased exposure, negativity tends to dissipate. This leads to an obvious conclusion: instead of continuing to feed the myth that Arabs hate us, we ought to be cultivating the affection of those most inclined to see the West in a positive light—the young, the educated, and the well traveled. These are the people who will be the Arab World's next generation of leaders. That's the future. That's also the challenge. And the sooner we in the West rise to it, the better all of us will be.

In the spring of 2008, I went on a speaking trip in the Middle East. While addressing and meeting with hundreds of journalists, students, and academics, I was struck by how closely elite opinion in the Arab World was following the U.S. elections. In many instances, these Arab opinion shapers were paying more attention to our election than many Americans were. I received very specific and technical questions about the Middle East positions of each of the three remaining candidates (Hillary Clinton, Barack Obama, and John McCain). But I also fielded questions about the role of superdelegates, whether delegations from Michigan and Florida would be seated at the Democratic National Convention, and whether Americans were really ready to elect an African American with a Muslim parent.

The audiences I addressed clearly saw the American election as critical to their lives. The Bush years had taken a toll across the Middle East, and many Arabs were gripped by a sense that they had lost control of their futures. They had been forced to watch the unraveling of Iraq, the destructive neglect of Palestine and Lebanon, and the emboldening of extremists and Iran. Now in its final year in office, the Bush administration was threatening to unleash dynamics that could spill over into new conflicts.

In many ways the Arabs with whom I spoke viewed the upcoming U.S. presidential election as their own, with a mixture of hope and trepidation. "I studied in the U.S. I loved and learned from your country," one colleague said to me. "But you've given peace a bad name, democracy a bad name—what else will you destroy?"

On another occasion, I asked a noted Egyptian intellectual who he hoped would win the 2008 election and whether he believed change was possible. He did not want to give his opinions because, he said, "I've been disappointed too many times before by events in America. At this point I don't want to hope again."

Yet, despite a grim era in which Arab and American blood was shed daily and communication between Arabs and Americans became more difficult, many of these people still wanted to believe that America was not the country they saw acting out across the region. Instead of hating America, they wanted desperately to believe in us and hoped that America would come back.

The Obama administration swept into power in early 2009 with enormous expectations riding on its shoulders. But even without major changes in Middle East policy, Obama's election, name, race, and efforts at public diplomacy—including an interview with Arab media; his historic speech in Cairo; and his intent to close Guantanamo, end torture, and exit Iraq—have made regional opinion toward the United States tick upward. With the Obama administration only weeks old, 51% of respondents reported that they were hopeful about U.S. policy in the Middle East.[20]

Subsequent polling has shown that despite a stalled Middle East peace process, the failure to close Guantanamo on schedule, and what some Arabs feel has been the failure of the Obama administration to translate the rhetoric of the Cairo speech into real change, initial optimism has dimmed but not yet dissipated. What's more, this optimism has helped boost Arab attitudes toward American values, people, and products. As we saw earlier, in Table 7.2, by 2004, Arab opinions about almost everything American were in the tank and remained low in subsequent surveys in 2006 and 2008. Then, in our 2009 polling, the rebound was in many cases dramatic.

On the issues of greatest specific importance to Arabs—whether the Obama years will bring improved relationships with the Arab World and, critically, a resolution to the Israeli–Palestinian conflict—opinion is still forming. Arabs are understandably wary, having been disappointed too many times in the past. But as Table 7.4 shows, in early 2009, they were

TABLE 7.4   WILL OBAMA BRING CHANGE TO U.S. FOREIGN POLICY? (% answering "yes")

Will Obama bring change to . . . ?

	Morocco	Egypt	Lebanon	Jordan	Saudi Arabia	UAE
U.S.–Arab relations	36	53	43	53	78	57
Israeli–Palestinian conflict	35	42	24	39	62	13

Source: Zogby International, *Arab Opinions on President Obama's First 100 Days,* 2009.

not without hope (though, as we shall see in chapter 13, that hope may be fading).

What these numbers tell us is that although many Arabs are still upset with aspects of U.S. policy in the region, the idea of the eternally angry Arab is a fiction. This tired myth exists only in the rarified environment of talk-show punditry and hermetically sealed policy debate. Optimism of the sort described by our surveys doesn't happen when anger is everywhere; it could not take root in a field of hatred. When we lay this canard to rest, we can begin to see much more clearly the real challenges that the United States and the West in general face in the Arab World.

8

SUPER MYTH FOUR
THE LENS OF ISLAM

IN 1994, DURING THE heyday of the Oslo peace process, world-renowned Israeli hairstylist and activist Vidal Sassoon invited me to address a major symposium on anti-Semitism sponsored by Hebrew University. In hopes of opening a dialogue on what I saw as a growing concern, I presented a paper called "Anti-Semitism and the Other Anti-Semitism," in which I pointed out that, historically, the prejudices against Jews and Arabs have been a linked phenomenon.

Today, we tend to think of anti-Semitism as an exclusively anti-Jewish prejudice. But Arabs are themselves Semites, Arabic is categorized as a Semitic language, and for centuries the European mind grouped Jews and Arabs together as distinct but similarly worrisome threats to the Christian West. Because Jews lived among them, some Europeans perceived Jews as an "internal threat." Arabs and Muslims, on the other hand, were confronted as an "external danger." Despite this inside/outside distinction, both groups were clearly identified as "problems," and their wealth, power, and even their corporate identities were seen as potentially damaging to the West. Jews and Arabs both were "unlike us." Both were commonly vilified and caricatured.

At times, these perceived similarities have been presented in horrible but fascinating ways. For example, many of the anti-Jewish political cartoons from pre-Nazi Germany and Tsarist Russia are virtually identical to more recent American cartoons denigrating Arabs. Older caricatures are often of Jewish bankers or revolutionaries, and the more "modern" ones take on oil sheikhs or Arab Muslim terrorists. But the physical properties are strikingly similar: obese torsos, exaggerated noses, bloodthirsty expressions, and on and on. "Jewish money" segued into "Arab petro-dollars," and "Jewish subver-sives/revolutionaries" morphed into "Muslim terrorists." Both groups were seen as using their "undeserved wealth" to buy up and threaten "our way of life."[1]

Cartoons were only the leading edge of this more broadly interpreted anti-Semitism. In speeches, newspaper columns, learned books, and back-alley gossip, both Arabs and Jews were portrayed as alien and hostile, ac-cused of not sharing Western values and being prone to conspiracy. For Jews, this systematic dehumanization laid the groundwork for the brutal violence they faced in Europe—centuries of anti-Jewish pogroms culmi-nating in the horror of the Holocaust. And now, with Arabs and Muslims so often negatively stereotyped or vilified in the West, is it any wonder that this has become a matter of concern in the Middle East?

Almost two decades ago, the noted conservative American intellectual William Buckley warned, "We are going to have to take explicit notice of the incompatibility of our own culture and that of the fundamentalist Mo-hammedan" before further suggesting that we "organize our immigration laws with some reference to this."[2] Buckley was writing in the 1990s, but there is a distinct echo from *Mitteleuropa*'s history of the 1920s and '30s.

Likewise, in a review of Robert Spencer's 2008 book *Stealth Jihad,* for-mer CIA director R. James Woolsey Jr. wrote, "Robert Spencer makes a solid case that the major threat to our way of life does not come solely from those radical Islamists who embrace violence and terrorism. It also comes from those who do not accept that they must live side-by-side on a basis of equality with those of other faiths in a civil society."[3] Woolsey does not indicate how we identify these people, but he certainly leaves the door open for an ever-widening suspicion of all practicing Muslims and Islamic groups.

The scholarship behind these attacks was clearly flawed and biased. Indeed, "scholarship" hardly seems to be the right word. Yet just as me-dieval Christians once held all Jews culpable for Christ's death, so present-day "scholars" have time and again advanced one-sided interpretations of Islam that cast Muslims as a fundamental threat to Western civilization. British author and former editor of the *New Statesman* Paul Johnson claimed in *National Review* that "Islam is an imperialist religion, more so than Chris-tianity has ever been, and in contrast to Judaism."[4] Like other such claims, Johnson's assertion about the inherent militancy of Islam relied on out-of-context or heavily edited quotes from the Qur'an. As with the Torah or the New Testament, passages can be selected from the Qur'an to support innumerable contrary claims. Likewise, if the moral standards used to harshly judge the historical record of Muslim empires were uniformly applied to European Christian empires—Russia, Spain, Britain, and France—they would reveal similar past failings.

The Super Myth that Arabs are blinded by intolerant religious beliefs appeals to a broad coalition of pro-Israel advocates who find it helpful to portray the majority of Arabs as untrustworthy radicals. Many neoconservatives, fundamentalist Christians, and foreign-policy hawks view the existence of a Muslim menace as a convenient replacement for the Soviet Union. With the dissolution of our old Cold War rival, the hawks were adrift—they needed a new threat to rail against and to justify arguments for increased vigilance and an ever-fatter defense budget.[5] For this purpose, Islam and "the Arabs" are ready-made targets: Muslims are foreign and not well understood, abundant negative stereotypes already exist, and they are the enemy of our Cold War ally Israel. The campaign against Islam had already cast a negative shadow on the religion and its adherents long before the attacks of 9/11, but when "they" attacked "us," it was off to the races.

To be sure, 9/11 more than justified American attempts to neutralize actual threats like al-Qaeda. Almost from the beginning, though, labels like "Arab," "Muslim," and "Islamic" were judged sufficient grounds for official suspicion and, too often, action. In fact, many of the Department of Justice's early post-9/11 efforts cast such a wide net that thousands of Arab and Muslim immigrants were unfairly subjected to interrogation, detention, and even deportation. The results were devastating: lives ruined, families broken up, and trust destroyed.

Of the dozens of such cases with which I became personally involved, two stand out—the Kesbeh family from Houston, Texas, and the Hamoui family from Seattle, Washington. In both instances, the fathers had come to the United States in 1991 seeking political asylum. Both had large families that included American-born children who were, thus, citizens. Both men had become successful and were contributing members of their respective communities. Following 9/11, both had their pending asylum requests denied, and without explanation they were arrested and held for deportation. Both men were detained for months, and despite receiving strong congressional support were deported along with their entire families—who were given the choice of having their family bond permanently severed or being deported with their husband and father.

The net impact of these roundups of Arab and Muslim immigrants, the extensive use of infiltrators and other forms of surveillance, and law-enforcement profiling took a toll on these communities. A December 2009 *New York Times* article reported on a worrisome breakdown in trust between the FBI and some cooperative American Muslim groups who felt besieged by surveillance and constant scrutiny. David Schanzer, an expert on terrorism and homeland security at Duke University, described the frayed relationship as a national-security issue: "It's absolutely vital that the F.B.I. and the Muslim-American community clear the air and figure out how to work together."[6]

Meanwhile, the Cold Warriors of an earlier war were busy morphing an old threat into a new one. The historian Bernard Lewis, for example, wrote a piece for the *Atlantic* called "Second Acts," in which he observed:

> The better part of my life was dominated by two great struggles—the first against Nazism, the second against Bolshevism. In both of these, after long and bitter conflict, we were victorious. Both were a curse to their own peoples, as well as a threat to the world, and for those peoples, defeat was a liberation. Today we confront a third totalitarian perversion, this time of Islam—a challenge in some ways similar, in some different.[7]

In a series of speeches that covered much of the same terrain, in 2005 President Bush attempted to win back waning public support for the war in Iraq by speaking of the global threat of Islamic extremism. Again, past wars were the model. Conflating Iran's regime, al-Qaeda, and the insurgency in Iraq, the president construed a monolithic threat, using images and language right out of Ronald Reagan's 1960s speeches about communist ambitions to dominate the world. Then, in an August 2006 press conference held at his ranch in Crawford, Texas, the president upped the ante even further, reaching all the way back to World War II and its run-up when he referred to an "Islamo-fascism" ideology that was "real and profound."[8]

Maybe the worst effect of this intellectual effort to define Muslims and Arabs as the fundamental threat to the West has been the way it has lowered the bar for demagogues like Pat Robertson, a prominent leader of the fundamentalist Christian, right-wing movement in America.

At the end of 2009, for example, Robertson went so far as to deny Islam its religious roots: "It's not a religion, it's a political system, it's a violent political system bent on the overthrow of the governments of the world and world domination. . . . I think we should treat it as such, and treat its adherents as such, as we would members of the Communist Party, or members of some fascist group."[9] When many leading American Christians, Muslims, and Jews demanded that Robertson apologize, the televangelist's response to those appeals was almost as shocking as his original statement. Robertson was not only unresponsive but emphatic in affirming his intolerance and bigotry toward Islam.

Robertson might be easier to dismiss as a kook and yesterday's news if Republican candidates for high office didn't actively solicit his support. Bob McDonnell, for example, a law-school graduate of the Robertson-founded Regent University and a current board member at the school, was elected governor of Virginia in November 2009 with political and financial backing from Robertson and his family, who together contributed $40,000 to McDonnell's campaign.[10]

Although the competition is stiff, Virginia, once the "Cradle of Presidents," might today deserve the title "Cradle of Anti-Muslim Bigotry." In a 2006 letter to Virginia constituents, then Congressman Virgil Goode almost seemed to be channeling Pat Robertson in a rant about newly elected Congressman Keith Ellison, who, as a Muslim, had decided to take the oath of office using the Qur'an. Goode wrote:

> I do not subscribe to using the Koran in any way. [I]f American citizens don't wake up and adopt the Virgil Goode position on immigration, there will likely be many more Muslims elected to office and demanding the use of the Koran. . . . I fear that in the next century we will have many more Muslims in the United States if we do not adopt the strict immigration policies that I believe are necessary to preserve the values and beliefs traditional to the United States of America and to prevent our resources from being swamped.[11]

Although it's odd enough that a Virginia congressman would expend so much vitriol on a newly elected colleague from the Fifth District of Minnesota, Goode's diatribe was all the more bizarre when you consider the subject of his anger. Keith Ellison is not a recent immigrant. He's an African American who can trace his American ancestry back to the 1700s. In other words, stricter immigration would have had *absolutely no effect* on Ellison's citizenship and subsequent election to Congress. Further, Ellison is no anomaly: the largest component group of American Muslims is African American converts, not Arab immigrants.

This distasteful smearing of a world religion and its followers continued unabated through the most recent presidential election in the United

States. In 2008, an independent group supporting the McCain campaign was involved in the massive distribution of an anti-Muslim "documentary" called *Obsession: Radical Islam's War Against the West*. Mailed free to 28 million households in battleground states, the documentary was also screened at some thirty college campuses nationwide and distributed as a paid advertisement through seventy newspapers. *The New York Times*, for example, delivered approximately 145,000 of the DVDs as an insert in its national edition.[12] Although it was prominently and favorably featured on CNN and Fox News and was called "the most important movie of our lifetime"[13] by Glenn Beck, it is in fact an act of incitement against Islam. One of the newspaper publishers who refused to carry the ad—Robin Saul of the *News & Record* of Greensboro, North Carolina—characterized the documentary simply as "fear-mongering and divisive."[14]

Though this gambit clearly failed, the spirit behind it lives on whenever pundits use the Middle East's supposed religious fanaticism to explain why Arabs are "so different" from us, why the Arab World is so hard to understand, and why its politics tend toward extremism. Why search for the right answer when an easy one is so close at hand?

The question we need to ask is what role does religion play in the life of real Arabs, not conjured ones? From the outset, I should mention that not all Arabs are Muslim—or even particularly religious. In fact, weekly mosque attendance rates in the Arab World closely parallel church attendance rates in the United States. It's also worth noting that the second-largest religion in the region is Christianity, and there are sizable Christian communities in Lebanon (my own family among them) and Egypt. That said, our polling did show quite clearly that, overall, religion is important in the Arab World and does inform Arabs' values, though not in the singular way the mythmakers would have it.

We've already seen in earlier chapters that Arab television viewers prefer movies, soap operas, reality shows, and sporting events to religious programming (Table 7.3). Asked why Palestine and Iraq are important issues, respondents in almost every country surveyed (with the exception of Jordan) ranked religious ties to those trouble spots well below the fact that Palestinians and Iraqis are "Arabs like me" (Tables 6.6 and 6.8). This was also true when we inquired about the principal source of Arab unity (Table 6.4). Even when we asked respondents how they would identify themselves to someone from America, respondents in most Arab countries chose their country or being Arab over their religious ties (Table 6.1).

Except for a radical few—and the same could be said of the United States in particular and the West as a whole—religion is not the sole lens through which Arabs view the world or the sole dictator of their actions. As with most people, Arabs find their values through their religion, and when you shut out the shrill voices that surround the subject and drill a little deeper, you find that Arab and American values are strikingly similar.

When we asked back in 2002, "What is most important to you?" the most significant difference that appeared between the answers given by Arabs and Americans had to do with the importance of religion. American respondents put religion near the bottom of their list (seventh out of eight personal-life categories), and Arabs put it third, after the quality of their work and family (see Table 8.1). On the surface, Arabs and Americans would appear to have differing priorities with regard to religion.

However, when we compared Arabs with Americans who were regular churchgoers, the rank order of values was quite similar. Both "religious" Americans and Arabs care about their faith and listen to their preachers, but they care just as much about the economy, jobs, education, and the well-being of their families.

The similarities and differences were equally instructive when we asked both Americans and Arabs to prioritize the values they taught their children. For both groups, the top three values—"self-respect," "good health and

TABLE 8.1   RANK OF IMPORTANCE OF PERSONAL CONCERNS TO ARABS AND AMERICANS

How important to you are each of the following concerns?

Value	Arab rank	American rank
Quality of work	1	2
Family	2	1
Religion	3	7
Job security	4	5
Marriage	5	4
Friends	6	3
Foreign policy	7	6
Leisure time	8	8

Source: James J. Zogby, *What Arabs Think: Values, Beliefs and Concerns* (Utica, NY: Zogby International/The Arab Thought Foundation, 2002).

Note: Respondents were asked to rate the importance of each concern. Rankings are based on the percentages of respondents who rated concerns as of high importance.

hygiene," and "responsibility"—were the same, as were five of the top six. Once again, religion was higher in importance for Arabs than Americans, but it was still in seventh place (out of twelve) for Arabs. And although I was at first struck by the low rank that Arabs gave to "creativity" and "tolerance for others," I couldn't help but notice that Americans also ranked both near the bottom (see Table 8.2).

Is this the portrait of a people blinded by faith, committed to extremism, and hell-bent on some secret (or not-so-secret) plot to rule the world? Obviously not. That myth is no more accurate than the one painted of Jews by Nazi Germany propagandists or the one created about Russians by Western fearmongers during the Cold War. We have largely moved beyond those two dangerously blinding stereotypes. Now it's time to move beyond the one about Arabs as well and start listening to what Arabs themselves say about their values. And in Barack Obama, America appears to have a president finally willing to do just that.

From the beginning, President Obama made an effort to open a door to new understanding between the United States and the Arab and Muslim

TABLE 8.2   RANK OF IMPORTANCE OF VALUES TO TEACH CHILDREN: ARABS AND AMERICANS

How important is it to teach each of the following values to children?

Value	Arab rank	American rank
Self-respect	1	2
Good health and hygiene	2	3
Responsibility	3	1
Respect for elders	4	5
Achieve a better life	5	8
Self-reliance	6	4
Religion/faith	7	12
Serious work habits	8	6
Obedience	9	11
Creativity	10	9
Tolerance for others	11	10
Respect for authority	12	7

Source: James J. Zogby, *What Arabs Think: Values, Beliefs and Concerns* (Utica, NY: Zogby International/The Arab Thought Foundation, 2002).

Note: Respondents were asked to rate the importance of each concern. Rankings are based on the percentages of respondents who rated concerns as of high importance.

Worlds. On his first day in office, he called a number of key Middle Eastern leaders, promising to reengage American diplomacy and seek a resolution to the Arab–Israeli conflict. Then on day two, as a sign of his resolve,
he announced the appointment of a respected statesman, former Senator
George Mitchell, as his special envoy to the Middle East peace process. On
the third day, the president sat for his first television interview—and did so
with an Arab satellite network, Al Arabiya.

In his interview with Al Arabiya, Obama repeatedly asserted both his
intent to listen and the need for bilateral communication between the
Arab and Western worlds. "My job," he said, "is to communicate to the
American people that the Muslim world is filled with extraordinary people
who simply want to live their lives and see their children live better lives.
My job to the Muslim world is to communicate that the Americans are not
your enemy."[15]

It didn't take the U.S. Congress long to remind the new president how
difficult his job would be. Shortly after the president's Al Arabiya interview, Senator John Kerry, the new chairman of the Senate Foreign Relations Committee, convened a hearing called "Engaging with Muslim
Communities Around the World"[16]—an obvious effort to bring Obama's
message home to Capitol Hill. In an equally obvious move to stifle any attempt to turn the page on Arab–American relations, Senator John Kyl, a
Republican from Arizona, countered by hosting the notorious anti-Muslim propagandist Geert Wilders at a Senate reception held at the exact
same time as Kerry's hearing. Wilders, a Dutch Parliament member, is
under indictment in his own country for incitement of hate. Among other
quotes, Wilders is credited with saying, "Islam is not a religion; it's the ideology of a retarded culture."[17] Wilders also has called the Qur'an a "fascist"
book and has tried to have it banned in the Netherlands because it "incites
hatred and killing."[18] John Kyl's Senate reception, it seems, was not
arranged to celebrate freedom of religion or of speech.

One election and a new president cannot, by themselves, change the ac-
cumulated impact of decades of abuse and neglect. Nor has President
Obama, for all his efforts, succeeded in quieting those intent on widening
the divide between the Arab World and America. Following the president's
speech at Cairo University on June 4, 2009, I debated Liz Cheney and former Senator George Allen, who were both harsh in their criticism of the
president's remarks. As noted earlier, in talking points Republican opera-
tives had prepared for them, Cheney and Allen accused the president of
what they called "moral equivalence" (meaning that he equated his concern

for the Palestinians with the traditional American support for Israelis) and "apologizing" for our policies in Iraq and Iran.[19]

When asked by one interviewer whether I thought that the president's speech would succeed in opening a door in the Arab and Muslim Worlds, I responded, "I think he'll change the hearts and minds of people in the Muslim world. I question whether or not he'll be able to change the hearts and minds of American conservatives."[20] In the short run, it may indeed be easier and more comfortable to keep that door closed than to expend the effort needed for understanding. But our sustainable long-term security, peace, and prosperity will be in serious jeopardy until we yank that door open and see Islam for what it really is.

In Obama's own words from his Cairo address, "So long as our relationship is defined by our differences, we will empower those who sow hatred rather than peace, those who promote conflict rather than the cooperation that can help all of our people achieve justice and prosperity. And this cycle of suspicion and discord must end."[21]

9
SUPER MYTH FIVE
IMMUTABILITY, OR
THE FROZEN CAMEL

MANY YEARS AGO, I came across an Arabic poem describing a camel running across the desert. Suddenly, the camel freezes in mid-stride. First, it looks back in fear at what it was running from, and then it stares forward, also in fear at the unknown that is its destination.

Though the poem dates back to pre-Islamic times, that scene serves as a perfect literary analogy for the feelings that define any people or society caught up in a process of rapid social change. Such was true in Western Europe during the Industrial Revolution, in post–World War II America, and in Eastern Europe after the fall of communism. And it is true in the Arab World today—caught midway between tradition and modernity.

The aptness of the camel metaphor struck me almost the moment I landed in Riyadh, during my first visit to the Gulf Arab states almost three decades ago. That camel—frozen between the past and future—has been on my mind through every subsequent visit.

Up until the 1950s, Riyadh had been a small city of about 100,000 people. By the time I first arrived there in 1980, the city had grown to well over a million, exploding outward to its current population of about 4.5 million. Driving through the city on my first trip, I felt like I was traversing a massive construction site, the horizon stacked with cranes and the sights and sounds of buildings going up everywhere.

I returned the following year to attend a conference in the mountainous resort community of Ta'if, an area west of Riyadh famed as the oasis visited by the prophet Muhammad. The conference had been organized by a group of Saudi businessmen—part of their chamber of commerce—

and government officials. Many of those involved, I learned, were jok-ingly referred to as the "USC Mafia," named for the University of South-ern California, one of the first American schools to admit large numbers of Saudi students. The "Mafia" consisted of a small group of young men who in the 1960s had earned their PhDs in the United States and then come home to build their country. They built and modernized ministries, wrote labor and commercial codes, and organized the chamber of com-merce, a vibrant institution of tens of thousands of Saudi businessmen and businesswomen.

The group was helping to move Saudi society incrementally toward modernity, and as I learned at that conference, these men were absolute marvels. Their talk was of urban planning, labor law, and how to reconcile tradition with modernity and move forward. They were literally building their city and the structure of governance from the ground up. Everything in Saudi Arabia, it seemed in their company, was happening on a grand, massively dynamic scale.

At one point, I sat in a room where Syrian, Lebanese, Gulf Arab, and African Arab professionals were hammering out business deals. One sub-ject under discussion was an innovative business plan to raise beef cattle on the grass fields of Sudan and then export the meat to other countries in the Arab World. Almost everyone was involved in the most intricate details. As physically different as their home countries were, this was their under-lying unity: they were businessmen and knew how to talk and work with each other. Commerce was the engine driving their ambitious efforts.

The scale of their ambitions was unlike anything else I had experi-enced previously in the region. I ended up feeling much the same way when I first visited Abu Dhabi, also in 1980. I've seen pictures from the 1950s that show it as a coastal encampment for the mere 10,000 people who lived there. By 1980, the city had grown to 200,000 people. This city, too, was bursting with commercial energy, civic vision, and a desire to create something unique in the world, even if it had to be built to an as-tounding degree on reclaimed land.

With a current population of around 1.5 million people, Abu Dhabi is smaller than modern Riyadh and also better organized. Even with its in-credibly rapid growth, Abu Dhabi has benefited from very precise building codes. It's a remarkably green city, despite being on the desert's edge. Sheikh Zayed, the visionary behind the city, planted 233 million trees and built an internal park system, all of which are irrigated with reclaimed water.

During my 1980 visit, I took a picture of a camel-crossing sign. The crossing was on the two-lane road that connected Dubai and Abu Dhabi, the major population centers of the United Arab Emirates (UAE). If you look closely at the photo, you can actually see camels walking across the road. Today that road is a massive highway—six lanes each way. Needless to say, the camels don't cross anymore.

Although the sometimes hyper-ambitious and dramatic developments in Dubai caught the imagination of many in the West—the world's tallest building, an indoor ski slope, and the creation of an island residential and resort community in the shape of a massive palm tree—some now realize that this unchecked growth was unsustainable. Abu Dhabi, on the other hand, has pursued a more studied development on its way to becoming a world-class city and tourist destination. Abu Dhabi not only hosts satellite branches of the Guggenheim and the Louvre, it is also now the home of prestigious international universities like the Sorbonne and New York University. Both Abu Dhabi and Dubai have opened media, Internet, and health centers that have become magnets for Arab entrepreneurs, journalists, and investors regionwide.

Even though they may borrow and benefit from the West, these Arab modernizers in the UAE and other Arab Gulf countries are profoundly protective of their traditions and culture. They are changing of their own volition, at their own pace, and in their own way.

These developments in Riyadh and Abu Dhabi are commercial and structural transformations on an amazing scale, and yet this dynamism is not reflected in contemporary Western thinking about the region. As we observed in Chapter 3, U.S. textbooks have done their part in spreading the myth that the Arab World is stuck in the past by relying too heavily on depictions of Bedouins and camels in descriptions of the modern Arab World. And because the prevailing view in the West is that unless change comes dressed in Western garb it will not come at all, too often real progress being made is missed.

One of the more prominent voices articulating this view of the inability of the Arab World to advance on its own is Bernard Lewis, the British American Orientalist and a professor at Princeton University. Lewis argues that change, when it has occurred in the Middle East, has been "initiated by past European rulers."[1] Echoing Lewis is Danielle Pletka, a conservative foreign-policy scholar at the American Enterprise Institute. She writes that although change in the Arab World must come from within, "it is demonstrably false to assert that such change can come without outside pressure. . . . The West must hold open the door."[2]

Quite simply, their point is that this region is hopelessly stuck unless the West pushes or, in the case of the Iraq War, shakes and then molds these Arabs into the future. This latter view has often been espoused by Thomas Friedman of the *New York Times*. According to Friedman, "the forces against change are powerful" in "this ossified region," but he credits "the Bush team" for opening "a hole in the wall of Arab autocracy" using the bulldozer of the Iraq War.[3]

The Arab World's rapid transformation may or may not mirror or owe its lineage to the West, but the change is nonetheless real and profound. Of course, there are the surface changes that are easy to spot and often entirely recognizable to Western eyes as well. In 2007, I traveled to Jeddah to attend the Jeddah Economic Forum, the Saudi kingdom's premier gathering of regional and business elites. The event was staffed by young women—business students at Effat College. Women were not present at the Ta'if business conference I attended some three decades earlier, but Saudi businesswomen have delivered keynote addresses at the Jeddah forum in recent years. Following the forum, I traveled from Jeddah to Riyadh. The next day I was drinking coffee in the lobby of that city's Four Seasons Hotel. The hotel is part of a massive mall complex, with Saks Fifth Avenue on one floor and Marks & Spencer on the next. Across the street sits a McDonald's; on the other side is a Pizza Hut. Walking through the mall, I passed boys in jeans and baseball hats and girls with *abayas* (robes) open, showing off fashionable jeans. They were having fun at the mall— much like teenagers in the United States. But these same boys and girls will, at home, in social gatherings, or at prayer, comfortably don their traditional garb: white *thobes* (robes) and *ghutra* (headdresses) for men; and black *abayas*, the *hijab* (head veil), and *niqab* (face veil) for women. These teenagers move effortlessly from one style to the other, as if to claim both for their own.

Outside the mall, the scene was almost as recognizable. Men and women were hustling to work, and others were shopping. The kids who had been parading in the mall were spilling out on their way to school. I could have found much the same scene wandering around my own city of Washington, DC. To be sure, these were surface changes, but they were indicative of a deeper opening of society, reflecting a more nuanced transformation. As in many other countries, the scale of this rapidly evolving, modern urban life had made it impossible to do business as per centuries-old traditions.

For example, it is commonplace for the king or any major prince to meet with the public in a *majlis,* a large gathering at his residence or office. At these weekly sessions, as many as 500 people will come to present their petitions or requests for favors to meet special needs. One group might want land for a school. Someone might need an operation for his son. Others still might seek help closing a business deal. The king or prince will promise to take care of them personally. The practice of the *majlis* continues, and indeed it is a fundamental part of what is understood as the ruling family's "social contract" with the people. However, in Saudi Arabia today, the weight of modern society is tilting in another direction. Personal appeals are still granted, but the king and princes increasingly adhere to zoning rules or business regulations. The structure of relationships has changed in the past half century, increasingly rationalizing both the social and economic orders.

Change is never easy, and the more rapidly it comes, the more likely it is to tear at the social fabric. In America and across the Western world, the acceleration of change has given birth to religious fundamentalists, "angry white voters," and, particularly in Europe, neo-nationalist and populist movements. Threatened by a loss of control and an erosion of what was comfortable and secure, many vent their discontent at what they identify as the source of this threat: big government, immigration, gays, undocumented workers, or just "them."

So it should not be surprising when we look at the Middle East—where change has been so rapid, dramatic, and transformative—that similar fundamentalist phenomena have been playing out. As with our own Western extremists, this Arab variation opposes change and promises security and fulfillment by a return to tradition and a mythical past.

Like the West, too, the Arab World has had to cope with this rapid transformation while also dealing with a global recession and sometimes troubling demographics. Saudi Arabia is a case in point. Demographic projections indicate significant growth of the Saudi labor force in the coming decade. This will no doubt place enormous stress on the nation, requiring the creation of more than three million jobs in the next ten years—brisk growth that cannot be met solely by a dramatic expansion of the public sector, at least not without severely straining government resources.

What's truly telling, though, is not the scope of this challenge but the fact that Saudi government officials and business leaders have moved so aggressively to deal with it. As I write, five massive new industrial cities are being built, and the government has invested well over $100 billion in a fund to spur private-sector growth. When completed, these new projects and communities are designed to generate millions of new jobs, mostly in the private sector.

Changes are also being pushed through the Saudi educational system. From the king, the message has been clear: young men and women alike must be imbued with a greater sense that advancement can occur with ambition, hard work, and skill. Social attitudes in Saudi Arabia and across the Arab World are undergoing transition. On the issue of women in the workplace, for example, 91% of Arab respondents say it is acceptable for women to work "to find a fulfilling career"; in Saudi Arabia, it's 85%. "Should women have equal rights?"—80% of all Arabs agree, with 76% of Saudis concurring.[4]

Even some of the most commonly cited examples of Arab intransigence to change are, on closer examination, something quite different. In 2002, the United Nations Development Program and the Arab Fund for Economic and Social Development issued the first of a series of highly critical Arab Human Development Reports (AHDR).[5] The AHDR outlined areas where the Arab World, in general, was lagging behind other emerging areas in the world—for example, Southeast Asia and India. Specifically, the reports cited deficits within the Arab World in the areas of freedom, women's rights, and knowledge, noting that "lasting reform in the Arab World must come from within."[6] The AHDR was met by a chorus of "we told you so's" by Arab bashers in the United States. But what these commentators were ignoring was that these reports were written by Arabs for Arabs. The AHDR received wide acclaim across the Arab World. In fact, the AHDR were not, as they were perceived in the West, a mere catalogue of complaints; rather, they were meant to be a roadmap to future progress.

A September 17, 2009, article in the *New York Times* captured this spirit of change:

> In just a few decades petrodollars and modernity have whipsawed Arab states in the Persian Gulf, elevating living standards while eroding practices that have defined identity for generations. Fishing and pearl diving have been replaced by petrochemicals and financial services. English has

challenged Arabic as the language of business. Traditional crafts have become novelties. What little architecture of the past existed has often been bulldozed to make way for the glass and steel skylines of the present.[7]

The article went on to focus on the efforts of some people, including a female minister of culture, to maintain Bahrain's ancient burial mounds in the midst of all this social and economic upheaval. Examples of this same concern with protecting heritage while moving headlong into the future can be found in all the Gulf states.

Zogby International's recent polling across the Middle East has found an Arab World generally coping well with the powerful forces of change sweeping across it. Arabs, our surveys show, look more to the future than to the past and want nothing more than the opportunity to raise their families and live productive, healthy lives. Especially among the middle classes, many are optimistic about upward mobility for themselves and their children.[8]

In 1980, in the closing days of the U.S. presidential election, Ronald Reagan was still trailing then President Jimmy Carter, who was running for reelection. It was a troubled time in America, and with one question Ronald Reagan turned the tide of that election. He urged Americans before they cast their vote to ask themselves: "Are you better off than you were four years ago?"[9] Since then, politicians have regularly asked that same question to get a sense of the mood of the election.

We have been asking that question of Arabs for a decade now. We have also expanded upon the Reagan question, asking it in three different ways to determine not only the satisfaction of our respondents with their current situation, but also their long- and short-term optimism or pessimism about the future. We ask: "Are you better off/worse off than you were four years ago?"; "Will you be better off/worse off four years from now?"; and "Will your children be better off/worse off than you are?"

Over the years, we've tracked trends in each of the polled countries as citizens in these nations have reacted to both domestic and regional developments. In most cases, optimism and satisfaction levels have remained quite high in the Gulf countries. But in Lebanon, Jordan, and Egypt, the ebb and flow of events of the past decade—the Iraq War and three bloody conflicts in the West Bank, Gaza, and Lebanon—have taken a toll. In 2006, for example, Lebanese and Jordanians were quite depressed. However, when we last polled in late 2009, there was an uptick in those countries' optimism scores—with only the UAE's numbers plummeting, largely because of the shock of the economic crisis that hit Dubai (see Table 9.1). Nevertheless, overall there is a general mood of relative satisfaction and optimism about the future that compares favorably with "better off/worse off" ratios in the United States.[10]

TABLE 9.1   OPTIMISM AND SATISFACTION IN SIX ARAB COUNTRIES: 2009 (in %)

	Morocco	Egypt	Lebanon	Jordan	Saudi Arabia	UAE
Better/worse off than you were four years ago?	41/19	39/24	38/22	41/18	59/15	30/21
Will you be better/worse off four years from now?	51/13	39/20	41/18	47/13	55/5	32/21
Will your children be better/worse off than you?	46/15	40/23	52/19	40/14	63/5	43/10

Source: Zogby International, Six-Nation Arab Opinion Poll, November 1–18, 2009. Sample size: 3,989 adults.

Note: Percentages above denote better/worse.

True, the pace of Arab social progress does not always conform to Western standards or expectations. As Table 9.2 shows, advancing democracy, increasing political debate, and liberating the role of women in society are, at best, of moderate interest to many Arabs asked to rank the importance of specific issues. But to deny that change is taking place simply because it's not the change we want in the West is, at best, laziness and, at worst, malicious. If we are actually interested in playing a role in advancing Arab society, we have to keep our eyes and ears open to what truly is—and what is really wanted.

Overall, the top-ranked issues were improving health care, expanding employment opportunities, improving the education system, and resolving the Israeli–Palestinian conflict. But country-by-country experiences play a role, too. Note, for example, the heightened concern in Lebanon and Morocco with combating terrorism and extremism, or how, in Egypt, Lebanon, and Jordan, fighting corruption and nepotism are high on the list.

This is life as it's lived on the ground in the Arab World, not as it is imagined by Western reformers and policy makers. And this same ground-level view is clearly reflected when we ask Arabs from these countries which of these same reform issues the United States can be most helpful in addressing (see Table 9.3 on page 116).

When asked which issues the United States could be most helpful in addressing, most Arabs put resolving the Israeli–Palestinian conflict high on their list, since that is an issue the United States is uniquely positioned to address. They also give priority to capacity-building efforts: expanding employment and improving health care and education. Nowhere high on the list in any country is the desire to see the United States meddling in their internal affairs by promoting political reforms.

What's the bottom line? Arabs across the Middle East are not so much rigid traditionalists as they are resistant to change solely on American terms. They simply follow their own unique paths forward. That's hardly radical. Just imagine how receptive Americans would be to British offers to bring down per capita U.S. handgun deaths or to a Japanese proposal to reform America's health care system. Likewise, although many Americans might support advancing women's rights throughout the Arab World, it only makes sense to first check that Arab women actually *want* the changes we seek to bring about, or want our involvement in their lives.

Understanding where our help and assistance is requested not only makes sense; it also assures that our time and money will be much better spent and can create conditions for future cooperation on reform. But that requires listening.

TABLE 9.2 IMPORTANCE OF ISSUES FACING COUNTRY

On a scale from 1 to 5, where 1 is "most important" and 5 is "least important," how important are the following issues facing your country today?

Expanding employment opportunities	*Improving the health care system*	*Increasing rights for women*
Combating extremism and terrorism	*Resolving the Israeli-Palestinian conflict*	*Lack of political debate on important issues*
Political or governmental reform	*Protecting personal and civil rights*	*Advancing democracy*
Ending corruption and nepotism	*Improving the education system*	

Rank	Morocco	Egypt	Lebanon	Jordan	Saudi Arabia	United Arab Emirates
1	Health care	Health care	Employment	Israel–Palestine	Health care	Education
2	Employment	Employment	Terrorism and extremism	Education	Employment	Israel–Palestine
3	Education	Education	Israel–Palestine	Corruption and nepotism	Israel–Palestine	Health care
4	Terrorism and extremism	Corruption and nepotism	Corruption and nepotism	Employment	Education	Employment
5	Corruption and nepotism	Terrorism and extremism	Reform	Health care	Terrorism and extremism	Protecting civil rights
6	Protecting civil rights	Israel–Palestine	Health care	Advancing democracy	Corruption and nepotism	Women
7	Israel–Palestine	Protecting civil rights	Protecting civil rights	Protecting civil rights	Advancing democracy	Corruption and nepotism

(continues)

TABLE 9.2 IMPORTANCE OF ISSUES FACING COUNTRY (CONTINUED)

On a scale from 1 to 5, where 1 is "most important" and 5 is "least important," how important are the following issues facing your country today?

Expanding employment opportunities
Combating extremism and terrorism
Political or governmental reform
Ending corruption and nepotism

Improving the health care system
Resolving the Israeli-Palestinian conflict
Protecting personal and civil rights
Improving the education system

Increasing rights for women
Lack of political debate on important issues
Advancing democracy

Rank	Morocco	Egypt	Lebanon	Jordan	Saudi Arabia	United Arab Emirates
8	Advancing democracy	Advancing democracy	Advancing democracy	Terrorism and extremism	Protecting civil rights	Terrorism and extremism
9	Lack of political debate	Reform	Education	Reform	Women	Reform
10	Women	Women	Lack of political debate	Women	Reform	Advancing democracy
11	Reform	Lack of political debate	Women	Lack of political debate	Lack of political debate	Lack of political debate

Source: Zogby International, *Six-Nation Arab Opinion Poll,* November 1–18, 2009. Sample size: 3,989 adults.

Note: Rankings reflect the issues that received the highest number of "1" and "2" responses combined.

TABLE 9.3 REFORM ISSUES WITH WHICH THE UNITED STATES CAN BE HELPFUL

Which of the following issues can the United States be most helpful in addressing?

Expanding employment opportunities
Combating extremism and terrorism
Political or governmental reform
Ending corruption and nepotism

Improving the health care system
Resolving the Israeli-Palestinian conflict
Protecting personal and civil rights
Improving the education system

Increasing rights for women
Lack of political debate on important issues
Advancing democracy

Rank	Morocco	Egypt	Lebanon	Jordan	Saudi Arabia	United Arab Emirates
1	Employment	Employment	Israel–Palestine	Israel–Palestine	Israel–Palestine	Israel–Palestine
2	Education	Education	Terrorism and extremism	Education	Employment	Education
3	Health care	Israel–Palestine	Health care	Employment	Education	Health care
4	Israel–Palestine	Health care	Employment	Health care	Health care	Employment

Source: Zogby International, *Six-Nation Arab Opinion Poll,* November 1–18, 2009. Sample size: 3,989 adults.

Note: Ranks are based on percentages.

PART 3

WHY IT MATTERS
BLUNDERS, FAILURES, AND FALLOUT

10
IRAQ
HISTORY CUTS LIKE A KNIFE

IN THE SUMMER OF 2005, I had lunch with Karen Hughes. A long-time President George W. Bush confidant and communications adviser dating back to the president's days as governor of Texas, Hughes had recently taken over as undersecretary of state for public diplomacy and public affairs—the same position that had befuddled Charlotte Beers. Though we were not of the same political persuasion, I respected Hughes and was intrigued by her decision to come out of retirement to take on this admittedly difficult job. She was known to be tough and smart, and she no doubt wanted Bush to succeed in his second term.

Hughes also assumed the role of undersecretary with a huge reservoir of personal trust with the president. In an October 2000 press conference, when then presidential candidate Bush was struggling to explain away potentially damaging revelations about an arrest for driving while inebriated, Hughes seized control and literally pushed her candidate out of the line of fire. Because of their close relationship forged in moments like that, I allowed myself the faintest glimmer of hope that if Hughes could be convinced of the need to reexamine our approach to diplomacy, then some changes might occur.

Over lunch at the State Department, Hughes and I discussed her upcoming trip to the Middle East. She asked me the same question each of her predecessors had asked: "What should I do first?"

Once again, my response was, "Listen."

Because she was going to Saudi Arabia, I also shared some of the lessons I had taken away from a June 2003 stay in Riyadh. I was in the country as a guest of U.S. Ambassador Bob Jordan, who had arranged for me to be a guest speaker at an embassy luncheon with some fifty prominent Saudi business leaders, including some of my old "USC Mafia" friends.

I wanted these Saudis to fully understand the impact 9/11 was having on the U.S.–Saudi relationship, so I focused my remarks on reliving those horrible days as I had experienced them. I spoke about both the widespread fear and anger following the attacks and the outpouring of support for Arab and Muslim Americans after the initial backlash. Finally, I warned that the image of Saudi Arabia was suffering in part because the Saudis were doing so little to challenge the negative campaign being waged against them. My audience was full of Saudis who knew America and cared about the future of our relationship; I urged them to do more.

Both Ambassador Jordan and I were struck by his guests' reaction. "No one spoke to us this way before," one said—because the United States had been too busy talking *at* Saudis and not *with* them.[1] Based on this experience, I suggested to Hughes that she not make a policy address. "Secretary Rice can do that," I pointed out, referring to the secretary of state. "You can do something different." Speak from the heart, I told her, and ask questions to let them know you are listening.

I also told Hughes how, during the question-and-answer session that followed my remarks at the 2003 luncheon, the top issues raised were problems securing visas to the United States and the difficulties many Saudis were experiencing upon entry to our country. Many of these people had studied in the United States, were involved in partnerships with American businesses, or had children studying in colleges and universities across the country; they all had stories to tell about problems they or their relatives had encountered trying to visit America. I suggested that if Hughes wanted to have a real listening tour, she should visit the U.S. embassy in Riyadh and talk to people applying to visit, study, or do business in America. I suggested Hughes ask these people why they want to come, ask what problems they might be having getting a visa, and let them know she was listening. Such an effort would be seen as a powerful and respectful gesture that could open doors to new understanding.

My advice was simple but apparently not easy to follow. When Hughes embarked on what was billed as a listening tour of the Arab and Muslim Worlds, she could not stop herself from lecturing. During a talk with female students in Jeddah, for example, Hughes expressed her desire that women would "fully participate in society."[2] She pressed especially hard on the issue of women driving—a topic that is simply not a top priority among women in Saudi Arabia.

Inevitably, Hughes's comments were received by her audience as patronizing and a negative comparison between Arab women's role and the role of women in American society. In response; a Saudi woman spoke up, saying, "The general image of the Arab woman is that she isn't happy. . . . Well, we're all pretty happy."[3] The exchange created an initial bad impression of Hughes in the region, once again reinforcing the notion that we were "talking at" and not "talking with" Arabs. Like her predecessors, Hughes's inability to put listening first—on a listening tour, no less—undermined her considerable talents.

Karen Hughes's tenure as undersecretary of state for public diplomacy and public affairs did have some bright spots, including efforts to reorganize how U.S. assistance was being distributed to support diplomacy in the Arab World. I had shared Zogby International's polling data with Hughes, pointing out that the United States was mistakenly focusing too much of our aid on the very areas where Arabs were telling us they didn't want our help, and not enough on the capacity-building areas where Arabs *did* want our help: education, health care, and expanding employment opportunity. Hughes did seem to listen to this, and the shift toward more demand-driven assistance that began during the second Bush term has happily continued into the Obama administration. But this significant step in the right direction was largely lost as the United States plunged forward in the Arab World with a tin ear for policy and an overweening and misplaced pride in our "successes."

I last talked with Hughes the week that she stepped down from her position. We met for coffee at the Hay-Adams Hotel, across the park from the White House. She had just penned an op-ed in the *Washington Post* boasting that we were "winning" in the Muslim World because a new poll showed al-Qaeda's disapproval rating in Afghanistan and Iraq was up to 90%.[4] I told her that unfortunately recent polls across the region were demonstrating that America's disapproval ratings were also between 82% and 91%. I cautioned her against declaring victory, because if we listened to what these numbers were saying, her observation was only partially right: "Al-Qaeda might be losing, and that's a good thing, but that's not the same thing as America winning."[5]

Why aren't we winning? In this part of the book, I focus on five specific theaters—four in the Middle East (Iraq, Lebanon, Saudi Arabia, and Palestine) and one at home (the situation of Arab Americans)—to show how a stubborn ignorance has imperiled Arab as well as American interests in the last decades. We'll begin with Iraq.

By the end of 2006, only the deluded could pretend that things had gone well in Iraq. Assured by media pundits of a hero's welcome by "cheering" and "grateful" Iraqis, American soldiers were instead greeted by a determined and increasingly bloody resistance. A war originally sold to the American people as quick, cheap, and easy had consumed hundreds of billions of dollars and already taken the lives of more than 3,000 U.S. soldiers as well as tens of thousands of Iraqi civilians. Staring at the chasm between the promises made by war advocates and the sobering realities, Congress finally ordered a full-scale review.

The bipartisan, blue-ribbon Iraq Study Group (ISG) was created to review U.S. conduct during the war and to recommend a way forward. Headed by two of America's most esteemed statesmen, former Secretary of State James Baker and former Chairman of the House Committee on Foreign Affairs Lee Hamilton, the ISG eventually issued a report that was a relative rarity: a comprehensive review of a U.S. policy failure in the Arab World. The panel also issued numerous and detailed recommendations based on interviews with leaders and analysts worldwide.[6]

Despite this novel and exhaustive approach, what emerged from the ISG's findings was disturbingly familiar. In page after page, the Iraq War was revealed not to be an isolated anomaly but a well-worn collection of U.S. policy failures and shortcomings in the region writ large. Many of the findings supported a single idea: we were paying a very high price for our forays into a region about which we understood precious little.

In this sense, the yawning gap between the liberation promised and the occupation delivered was nothing more and nothing less than the gulf that had long separated Americans and the Arab World. However, this time the stakes were higher, with more than 150,000 troops in harm's way, hundreds of billions of dollars spent, thousands of lives lost, and U.S. prestige damaged. No one could say how long it would take to rebuild Iraq, a deeply fractured country facing conflict for years to come. There is no clearer example of how decades of ignorance about the Arab World—whether passive or engineered—have created havoc across the region than this tragic enterprise in Iraq. And the way the ISG was received only serves to highlight the ongoing refusal of policy makers to listen and learn. Except this time, the voices that Washington would not heed were those of its finest statesmen and foreign-policy experts.

During the months preceding its release, the ISG Report was much anticipated. When published, however, its findings and recommendations were largely ignored. In the end, the U.S. Congress played politics with the ISG Report, and the Bush administration cherry-picked the parts it liked, pushing aside the rest. But burying the truth will not kill it.

In the run-up to the Iraq War, the noise machine was on high, cranking up expectations for a massively successful military campaign. White House spokespeople told Americans the fighting would be over in a few weeks, U.S. soldiers would be greeted as liberators, the war would cost America $1 to $2 billion before Iraqi oil production would pay for the rest, and Iraq's new democracy would be a "beacon for the new Middle East."[7] Throughout the media universe, commentators echoed these boasts, regularly churning out outrageous claims on par with Iraqi leader Saddam Hussein's pre–Gulf War warning that that conflict would be the "mother of all battles."

Before the invasion began, for example, Fox News's most popular host, Bill O'Reilly, wagered "the best dinner in the gaslight district of San Diego that military action will not last more than a week."[8] A similarly euphoric (and ultimately equally misleading) statement by Bill Kristol, a prominent conservative columnist and founder and editor of the *Weekly Standard,* soon followed: "There is a certain amount of pop psychology in America that the Shi'a can't get along with the Sunni. . . . There's almost no evidence of that at all."[9] Finally, journalist Fred Barnes, another Fox News host, chimed in, saying, "The war was the hard part. . . . And it gets easier. I mean, setting up a democracy is hard, but not as hard as winning a war."[10]

As Washington geared up for an increasingly inevitable war, I found myself 400 miles to the south—as the Batten Professor of Public Policy at North Carolina's Davidson College. For the first time in twenty-five years, I wasn't part of the talk-show rat race. Instead, from the quiet of Davidson's campus, I found that these events, seen from outside the noise machine, were both surreal and incredibly valuable. Instead of dispensing disposable quotes in three-and-a-half-minute segments, I was able to reflect on Arab history and to place everything playing out in the Middle East in this broader context.

Caught up in the ferocious present tense of debate, we all can forget the importance of history—a fact I was reminded of whenever I opened the newspaper or switched on a television. For too many reporters and political commentators, history begins the day they receive their assignment. Not knowing the history or culture of the Middle East, they either ignore the context of the events they are covering or accept, as given, the interpretation provided by U.S. officials—a dynamic only heightened by our collective ignorance about the region.

As a result, most American media coverage of the Iraq War was missing any sort of context. This was a massive disservice to an anxious American population, especially when they were debating life and death in a distant and foreign land. It's true that no one could predict *exactly* what might happen once the United States and its allies entered Iraq. But simply applying historical and local perspective to the blather then jamming the airwaves could have given us all a much better idea of the disasters to come. In fact, history could have provided a sort of early warning system three years *before* the Iraq Study Group became necessary.

For example, O'Reilly's claim about a "one-week" war ignored the difference between quick, well-delineated military objectives and the occupation of a nation—a distinction spelled out in countless military histories. Three years later, U.S. military action was still well under way, with the body count growing on both sides. Likewise, Kristol's dismissal of sectarian rifts ignored an entire recent history in which the Hussein-allied, minority Sunni had repressed Iraq's majority Shi'a population. Three years later, Americans were all too familiar with the phrases "Sunni Triangle" and "Shi'a militia," Iraq was poised on the edge of civil war, and many U.S. commentators were calling for a division of the country along religious and ethnic lines. Finally, Barnes's declaration that building a democracy would be relatively easy not only sidestepped decades of muddled colonial interventions in the region, it also ignored the recent past of his own Republican Party. In the 1990s, many leading conservatives and Republican politicians had strongly argued against such "nation-building" efforts. Although sometimes worthy, they are incredibly difficult, expensive, and time-consuming, and in any case, require at least a modicum of knowledge about the nation being "built." Three years later, many Americans were just hoping to salvage some sort of nonhostile, semifunctional state in Iraq—not build an open, Western-style democracy.

Obviously, three historically illiterate claims were not responsible for the messy occupation that resulted, but they do serve as an introduction to the nearly fact-free environment in which the war was launched. The simple truth was that, in the run-up to the invasion of Iraq, most Americans knew virtually nothing about the country. In March of 2003, for example, *National Geographic* released the results of a survey testing the general knowledge of young Americans. Among their findings: only 13%

of Americans between the ages of 18 and 34—the very same young men and women who would be asked to fight in foreign wars—could locate Iraq on a map.[11]

This lack of basic knowledge allowed war advocates to operate within the flexible parameters of a knowledge-free zone—an advantage they pressed fully. With few voices challenging them, pro-war pundits and analysts became instant "experts" when the cameras rolled. Instead of informing the public, these media personalities and network regulars usually just regurgitated the pronouncements ground out by the White House or Pentagon public-relations shops. Operating as echo chambers for administration talking points, these commentators enjoyed carte blanche in detailing the ultimately nonexistent Iraqi threat to America, creating a dangerously mistaken "conventional wisdom."

As a result, by early 2003, talking heads like O'Reilly, Kristol, and Barnes were far from alone in their overheated invasion fantasies. Absent any reality check from this country's largely history-free journalists, cowed Congress, and bullied intelligence agencies, America drifted further away from the reality awaiting us in Iraq.

With the war drums beating, I tried to encourage a debate over the wisdom of rushing into Iraq. Before the February 2003 meeting of the Democratic National Committee, Illinois Congressman Jesse Jackson Jr. and I announced our intention to introduce a resolution urging "President Bush to continue to pursue diplomatic efforts to achieve disarmament of Iraq, to clearly define for the American people and Congress the objectives, costs, consequences, terms and length of commitment envisioned by any U.S. engagement or action in Iraq, and to continue to operate in the context of and seek the full support of the United Nations in any effort to resolve the current crisis in Iraq."[12]

I also wrote an op-ed titled "Unanswered Questions," which appeared in the *Baltimore Sun*.[13] I knew from polling and my personal contacts with Democrats across the country that the overwhelming majority (68%) disapproved of this rush to war.[14] Jackson and I both felt that a genuine debate should occur on this critical issue of national importance. Party officials, though, felt otherwise. I was permitted to present my motion at an executive committee meeting and argue my case, but then I had to sit silently while the chair ruled that no discussion or vote would be allowed.

From Davidson, I made another effort to pierce the rolling fog that preceded this war. Thanks to Abu Dhabi TV, I was able to offer a direct exchange between my students and a group of their peers in Baghdad. On March 12, 2003—less than a week before the bombing of Iraq began— when the large screen in Davidson's student union went live with the image of a hundred Iraqi students, a hush came over my audience. "It was so hard," one student recalled, "to see their faces. We knew that within days the bombs would be falling, and there we were looking at them and talking to them."[15]

As the Davidson students actively debated this war—with some sharply critical of the Bush administration—a number of students were troubled by the fact that the Iraqi students would not criticize their own government and its policies. After pursuing this topic through a number of questions, I asked the U.S. students whether they believed that their Iraqi counterparts were being truthful in their expressions of support for the positions of their government. The vote was overwhelmingly negative.

In response, one frustrated young Iraqi woman noted, "Yes, there are things we want to change. . . . But right now we're focusing on major changes. We're focusing on stopping a war; we're focusing on surviving through a blockade. It's just like when the tragedy of 9/11 happened, you stopped criticizing the government; you stopped criticizing everything in general. It was a crisis, and that's exactly what we have now."[16]

Later, another Baghdad student mocked what she called the "joke" she had heard about Iraqis greeting U.S. soldiers with flowers. She instead gave the chilling warning that if even one American entered Iraq, "We will fight you."[17] Overall, in fact, these Iraqi students did not give the impression that they would be waving the stars and stripes as American soldiers marched by. Though neither Ba'athist nor anti-American (some fondly recalled visits to the United States), most of these students simply wanted to prevent the bombardment of their country. What's more, they saw Americans as invaders—before the U.S.-led forces had even arrived.

Two months later, after the U.S.-led forces had heavily bombed Baghdad and deposed Saddam Hussein, my students and I reconnected with the University of Baghdad via satellite for a follow-up dialogue—under radically different circumstances. The same U.S. students participated, but with their country in chaos, the Iraqi students had mostly dispersed. Without phone or mail service, and with major security problems throughout the country, Abu Dhabi TV worked tirelessly to assemble a representative audience of Iraqi students and citizens.

It quickly became clear that the Iraqis were angry at U.S. actions in their country. Although a number expressed their relief that the regime of

Saddam Hussein had been toppled, when asked whether they viewed the U.S. campaign as a war of liberation or occupation, almost 90% indicated that they saw the United States as an occupier.

A principal source of Iraqi ire was the chaos that prevailed in their country. These Iraqis were deeply troubled by the widespread looting, which a number of participants accused the Americans of allowing or even encouraging. They were equally frustrated by the lack of security, the absence of basic services like running water and electric power, and the destruction of the city's infrastructure. Among the typical responses were these: "If the Americans had really intended to liberate us, they should have planned for the aftermath of the war like they planned for the war itself." "Why did they protect the oil but not the museum and the hospital?" "Why after all this time, do we still not have electricity?"[18]

When one Davidson student reminded the Iraqis that they were now free and therefore could speak their minds, one Baghdad participant shot back: "Who said that we didn't before? At least then, when we had such a discussion, the secret police were listening. Who is listening now? No one is hearing us."[19] Iraqis were now free not only to criticize the toppled regime but their "liberators" as well.

A former CIA official attended this second dialogue. She provided my students with some context and asked probing questions. After hearing the Iraqis speak, she said in an aside to me, "I hope someone in Washington is watching. There is a lot for us to learn."[20]

Unfortunately they were not watching, or if they were, they weren't paying attention to what the Iraqis were saying. If someone had been listening, they might have better understood the extensive problems U.S.-led forces would have in gaining the support of the Iraqi population—and where effort was needed to deal with the growing resistance. Clearheaded analysts would also have gathered that the U.S. military had entered not just the country of Iraq but its history as well. For better or worse, America now had a role in Iraq's future: we were the "new regime." From that day forward, Iraqis would judge America's actions through the prism of Iraq's past—about which we knew almost nothing.

The idea that a people's history provides a context for future events is not particularly novel. During the Cold War, for example, many Americans knew that because Russia had for centuries been invaded through Eastern Europe, the Soviet Union would prioritize a buffer zone in that area. The West didn't have to accept the Soviet occupation of Eastern Europe, and it was right that we did not, given the price it exacted on the many nations held captive as a result. But dealing with our Cold War adversary mandated that we understand the historical dynamic at work. The opposite approach—engaging a country without gaining a sense of its past—is dangerous and foolish.

Certainly, after talking with ordinary Iraqis for two hours, my students already had a respect for the power of local historical context. As a result, they understood Iraqi distrust of the occupation better than America's insulated political leaders. Indeed, without the kind of ground-level exposure that comes from listening, disastrous misunderstandings were virtually assured once the invasion began. Americans and Iraqis, people from two completely distinct historical realities, could watch the exact same events unfolding, but understand them completely differently. This kind of "double vision" was precisely the confounding dynamic that began unfolding in March of 2003, undermining our efforts there.

To American eyes, the famous yet staged footage of U.S. soldiers toppling Saddam Hussein's statue was an uplifting scene, reminiscent of the fall of the Soviet Union over a decade earlier. Surely, American troops would now be greeted as liberators—the "cakewalk" some U.S. commentators had predicted.

To Iraqis, though, the storyline was not so cut-and-dried. To them and to many other Arabs, Baghdad, the city the United States bombed so intensely prior to a ground invasion, was an ancient and fabled city—a place of grandeur, wealth, and learning, the historical seat of the great caliphs. Baghdad had been sacked before—by the Mongols, who torched the city's magnificent libraries in the twelfth century—and occupied more recently by the British. Now, while Americans saw a city liberated, Iraqis saw the treasures of Arab Islamic civilization again being attacked and looted, an impression made far worse by the initial failure of allied military forces to protect the city's museums and art centers. To Iraqis, America wasn't a modern Prometheus with the gift of freedom; the U.S. soldiers were simply the new Mongols.

Interestingly, as the occupation faltered and encountered a full-fledged resistance, Americans suddenly faced events that could not be controlled and that media spin could not explain away. Now it was our turn to make sense of Iraq using the American historical prism: was this another Vietnam? True, one war was fought in tropical Asian jungles using napalm and Huey helicopters to combat a communist insurgency, while the other saw Humvees driving in sunbaked cities as U.S. soldiers battled a variety of religious and nationalist militias. Yet despite these differences, the Vietnam War was still the reference point because of the enormous scar it had left on America's historical memory. This is the power of history's lens: Iraq was clearly not Vietnam, but in trying to understand an increasingly bloody insurgency, we immediately compared it to Vietnam. (And indeed this prism continues to be utilized: Vietnam is today the principal reference point for our skirmishes against the Taliban in the snowcapped mountains of Afghanistan.)

Ultimately, it was America's lack of knowledge about Iraq that set the stage for the delusional claims of the punditry, the lack of historical understanding, and all the other bumbling that followed. Policy makers initially took advantage of this ignorance in pressing the case for war now infamous for its holes and politicized "intelligence." Media commentators share significant blame as well. Although President Bush's "Mission Accomplished" speech is today derided for its hubris, that was not the view at the time. "He looked like an alternatively commander in chief, rock star, movie star and one of the guys," said CNN's Lou Dobbs.[21] The following day Gwen Ifill of PBS News offered this description: "The war winds down, politics heats up. . . . Picture perfect. Part Spider-man, part Tom Cruise, part Ronald Reagan. The president seizes the moment on an aircraft carrier in the Pacific."[22]

But once the war unraveled, the general lack of knowledge and ignorance of realities we had thought didn't matter proved fatal. In themselves, these failures were nothing new—they had been well documented for decades. What *was* different about the Iraq War was that this stark ignorance was now creating front-page news, ranging from pro-war advocates' delusional claims to articles chronicling our inability to successfully adapt once things in Iraq started going downhill.

Worse still—and maybe more preventable than our ignorance about Iraq— was the profound shortfall of practical skills needed for our engagement with the Iraqi people. After the fall of Baghdad, the virtual absence of Arabic speakers quickly became a pressing issue both for coalition soldiers and the fledgling U.S. bureaucracy. As the Iraq Study Group reported, few Americans could actually speak to Iraqis—the people whose country we were presumably putting back together.[23] Not only did the provisional government have to physically sequester itself behind the heavily fortified walls of the Green Zone, but the roughly 1,000 people working at the U.S. embassy faced a massive language barrier as well. Only a handful were fluent in Arabic, and just a few dozen had any knowledge of the language at all.

This communication breakdown wasn't limited to the floundering U.S. bureaucracy. Members of the ISG were reportedly amazed to find that, despite our spending billions on Iraq in 2006, more wasn't being done to try "to understand the people who fabricate, plant and explode [the] roadside bombs" that were killing U.S. soldiers.[24] Because knowledge of Arab history and culture and Arabic language skills were so rare, few American military units had someone who could read captured documents or simply understand people on the street.

Reading these reports, I found it hard not to think of the concurrent efforts to shutter the Khalil Gibran International Academy in New York or the disturbingly low number of U.S. university students in advanced Arabic language courses. It was exactly this type of hostility to, or lack of emphasis on, Arabic language instruction that made it difficult to produce diplomats and soldiers who could speak to the people of the Arab World. Simply put, years of neglect combined with efforts to actively suppress teaching Arab history and culture left the United States ill-prepared for an ever-deepening engagement in the region.

Having a better grasp of Iraq's past would also have meant understanding that, for many Iraqis and other Arabs, Saddam Hussein's bloody, eight-year war with Iran in the 1980s was largely supported by other Arab states who feared Iran's Shi'a "revolutionary fundamentalism." Hussein was a brutal dictator, to be sure, but post-Saddam, many Arabs were concerned that Iraq's Shi'a majority might lead the country to become an Iran-allied state. Indeed, as our in-country polling showed, this was a virtual article of faith to a large majority of Iraqi Sunni Arabs. But U.S. military actors in Iraq and American policy makers back in Washington seemed to either ignore or completely misplay this history. Iran was identified by President Bush as a member of the "Axis of Evil" more than a year before the invasion of Iraq, but those were just words. America's subsequent actions have served only to increase Iran's heft in the region.

Here's what we know now: our polling shows that significant majorities of both Arabs and Americans want U.S. forces to leave Iraq—arguing that the American presence provokes the insurgency and worsens the situation for the Iraqi people.[25] As late as May 2009, when we asked Arabs across the region "if Iraqis were better off or worse off after the war," only 6% of Arabs said "better off," with 72% saying "worse off."[26] We have also historically found widespread hostility across the Arab World to *both* U.S. and Iranian roles in Iraq. In each of the five countries polled, substantial majorities gave negative ratings to the roles played by the United States in Iraq, with Iran faring only slightly better (see Table 10.1).

TABLE 10.1 U.S. AND IRANIAN ROLES IN IRAQ (in %)

U.S. role in Iraq	Egypt	Lebanon	Jordan	Saudi Arabia	UAE
Positive	15	21	3	31	25
Negative	83	76	96	68	70

Iranian role in Iraq	Egypt	Lebanon	Jordan	Saudi Arabia	UAE
Positive	37	36	19	19	14
Negative	56	59	73	78	71

Source: Zogby International, *"Four Years Later" Five-Nation Poll,* February 26–March 10, 2007. Poll taken in Egypt, Lebanon, Jordan, Saudi Arabia, and UAE. Sample size: 3,400 adults.

*Percentages are rounded and do not include responses of "not sure." As a result they may not add up to 100%.

But this desire for a Western exit from Iraq was coupled with the fear that, should coalition forces leave prematurely, the country could disintegrate into a civil war that would further destabilize the region, encouraging Iran (see Table 10.2).[27]

As a result, there is a deep ambivalence found not only in our polls across the Arab World but also in conversations with Iraqis. On the one hand, they want Americans to leave. On the other, they fear the consequences of an abrupt U.S. departure.

TABLE 10.2 GREATEST WORRY ABOUT IRAQ (in %)

	Egypt	Lebanon	Jordan	Saudi Arabia	UAE
U.S. permanent occupation	38	15	47	23	16
Iraq splits into three parts	12	16	14	16	8
Iran	10	10	5	20	16
Iraqi civil war	39	57	33	39	53

Source: Zogby International, *"Four Years Later" Five-Nation Poll,* February 26–March 10, 2007. Poll taken in Egypt, Lebanon, Jordan, Saudi Arabia, and UAE. Sample size: 3,400 adults.

This was brought home to me in May 2007 when Abu Dhabi TV once again provided me the opportunity to host a conversation between students at Davidson College and the University of Baghdad. Throughout the ninety minutes we spent together via satellite, the U.S. students were captivated by the stories they heard and the frustrations expressed by their Iraqi counterparts. The most powerful testimony came from one young Iraqi woman who captured the ambivalence in a single sentence: "We need help—don't leave us," she begged, "but you must leave as soon as possible."[28]

At the beginning of the satellite discussion, I asked the Davidson students whether they were for or against the United States remaining in Iraq. Most wanted the United States to leave. At the end of the session, I asked the same question. This time, however, most felt the United States had a responsibility to remain. One Davidson student came up to me after the show and said, "It's so frustrating that the political debate here in the United States doesn't include what we heard today. Democrats want to leave now, and Republicans want to stay and 'win,' but neither side is listening to what the Iraqis need."[29]

Despite the persistence of sectarian fissures that were exposed in the 2010 national elections, there is an agenda on which most Iraqis agree. In an April 2010 survey, when asked to prioritize their country's most pressing needs, Iraqis from all sects and in all regions overwhelmingly identified "achieving national unity" as the most important goal. Following that they listed, in order: improving the economy and increasing employment; political reform; and ending corruption.[30]

Listening to what Iraqis want and working with them to help achieve these goals is the responsible way forward.

In September 2006, U.S. Senator Trent Lott spoke frankly to the media about his frustration with events in Iraq. "It's hard for Americans, all of us, including me, to understand what's wrong with these people," said Lott. "Why do they kill people of other religions because of religion? Why do they hate the Israelis and despise their right to exist? Why do they hate each other? Why do Sunnis kill Shiites? How do they tell the difference? They all look the same to me."[31]

Lott's horrifying display of ignorance was the voice of a nation in disarray. Lott wasn't just an American senator but a member of the Senate Intelligence Committee emerging from a briefing with President Bush. America had been in Iraq for more than three years at the time, but Lott sounded like he'd just heard of the place.

As a result of their long and frustrating engagement with Iraq, many Americans became at least peripherally interested in a country about which they had known almost nothing when we invaded in 2003. But as we found in our most recent poll, most Americans still lack a clear idea of even the geographic setting of Iraq (see Table 10.3).

As important as a knowledge of geography is, it is only the starting point of understanding. History creates context, and communication allows us to learn what we don't know; both have been tragically lacking in our Iraq engagement. The Iraq Study Group acknowledged as much with one of its key recommendations: to establish a regional contact group that would help to create a security framework and support efforts at promoting internal reconciliation.

Now, with all of America's coalition partners having left Iraq and the U.S. public looking forward to the departure of the nation's forces at the end of 2011, historical perspective once again is on the table. Will policy makers remember in shaping future policy and practice that all of Iraq's neighbors have legitimate concerns about that country's future and stability? And that all these bordering countries will, to some degree, attempt to engage in Iraqi affairs in an effort to protect their interests? Some, like Kuwait and Saudi Arabia, have been directly harmed by Iraq in the past. Iran fought a long and costly war with Iraq; Turkey, Iran, and Syria share with Iraq the need to address legitimate Kurdish concerns; Syria and Jordan have borne the burden of sheltering Iraq's refugees; and the rest of the countries of the Arabian Peninsula are wary lest the continued instability in Iraq spill over, threatening regional security. The fact is that all of these

TABLE 10.3   AMERICANS ABLE TO IDENTIFY COUNTRIES BORDERING IRAQ (in %)

Countries	Americans able to identify
Kuwait	47
Saudi Arabia	35
Turkey	29
Jordan	25
Syria	23
Pakistan*	28

Source: Zogby International, *Poll of American Voters,* November 30–December 8, 2009. Sample size: 1,006 adults.

* Pakistan does not border Iraq but was still selected.

concerns are woven together in the history of Iraq, the story of America's presence there, and the challenge of extricating ourselves from the situation we have done so much to create.

During the 2008 U.S. presidential primaries, although many in the Democratic Party's leadership were favoring a quick withdrawal from Iraq, Barack Obama distinguished himself from the pack, declaring that he favored a "responsible departure." If the departure is to be responsible, much work remains to be done to help heal Iraq's deep sectarian rift and to create the ISG's long delayed "contact group" that would involve Iraq's neighbors in a collective effort to create a regional security framework. It is not too late to listen and learn from the lessons of Iraq's history. Ultimately, success or failure will be determined not by the date set for the departure of U.S. soldiers but by whether, drawing on the lessons of history, America makes the right choices and does the right things between now and that date.

11
LEBANON
HEARING HALF THE STORY

ON FEBRUARY 14, 2005, a massive explosion ripped through the motorcade of Lebanese Prime Minister Rafiq Hariri, killing him and twenty-one of his associates. Within days, hundreds of thousands of Lebanese had taken to the streets both to mourn Hariri and demand the implementation of his political goals, including the end of Syria's military occupation of Lebanon. This spontaneous display of sorrow, anger, and patriotism was given several names, including the "Cedar Revolution," and later the "March 14th Coalition" after the date of massive demonstrations in the center of Beirut.

Because the Cedar Revolution was seen as a struggle for self-determination, it was also heralded internationally. In the United States, conservatives touted the movement as clear evidence of American success in spreading democracy throughout the region. About three weeks after Hariri's assassination, I was on the cable news show *Hardball* discussing the events in Lebanon with host Chris Matthews, former Pentagon official Ken Adelman, and David Ignatius of the *Washington Post*.[1] Ignatius had just returned from Lebanon and was glowing in his praise for the Cedar Revolution. Both he and Adelman were convinced that the movement had been inspired by the "success" of the Iraq War and represented, in Ignatius's words, "a new generation rising everywhere in the Middle East, [including] all Lebanese, across confessional lines."[2]

Eager to see a silver lining in the increasingly messy Iraq War, President Bush agreed. That same day, March 8, 2005, Bush spoke at the National Defense University, celebrating what he called "the advance of freedom." After listing the "successes" in Afghanistan and Iraq, he cited Lebanon as clear evidence of yet another victory.[3]

I wasn't so sure.

I had visited Hariri often on my trips to Lebanon and found him to be a visionary committed to rebuilding his beloved country. Like many others, I mourned the loss of his leadership and was moved by the demands of his followers. I supported their goals of ending the Syrian occupation of Lebanon and bringing to justice those responsible for the assassination of Hariri. However, in a country as complex as Lebanon, I didn't think that interpreting the subsequent outpouring of protest was so easy. There was more going on than the neat, unified "march toward democracy" spin that most American commentators were using to explain events in Lebanon.

For starters, the Cedarists, as they were also known, were not the only group organizing mass demonstrations in the wake of Hariri's death. In my office, as one television showed President Bush's speech heralding the "advance of freedom," another was tuned to Al Jazeera, which was covering a massive, Hizbullah-led counterdemonstration being held simultaneously in downtown Beirut. Like the pro-Hariri marches, this pro-Syria rally also stretched on for miles, with hundreds of thousands of protestors denouncing the United States. Clearly, Hariri's death had unleashed more than one dynamic in a country with a complicated and deeply troubled recent history.

In this same time period, Zogby International had released a new poll of Lebanese opinion that revealed a profound division on the critical matter of whom the Lebanese held responsible for Hariri's assassination. Our polling showed that about one-half of the Christian Maronite community felt that opposition Lebanese or Syrian authorities were involved in Hariri's death. Among Hariri's own Sunni community and the Orthodox Christians, equal numbers suspected Syria/Lebanon and the United States/Israel as the culprits. Meanwhile, only 14% of Shi'a Lebanese pointed the accusing finger in Syria's direction, and more than 70% claimed that either Israel or the United States was responsible.[4]

Our polling was publicly available, but no one on *Hardball* seemed concerned by the fact that perhaps 40% of Lebanon blamed the United States or Israel for Hariri's death. To do so would have directly contradicted the notion, promoted by the Bush Administration and political commentators, that the Lebanese people had been inspired by America's overthrow of Saddam Hussein and recent Iraqi elections.

In fact, it seemed as if an active American effort was under way to repackage the tumultuous events unfolding in Lebanon. The name "Cedar

Revolution," for example, was not coined by Lebanese patriots (though a cedar tree is featured on the Lebanese flag) but by Paula Dobriansky, a U.S. undersecretary of state.[5] The movement was initially known in Lebanon as the "Independence Intifada." *Intifada* is Arabic for "shaking off," but in an effort to create distance from the Palestinian intifada, the State Department preferred to speak glowingly of the de-Arabized "Cedar Revolution." This phrase had the added advantage of reminding Americans of Eastern European pro-democracy movements like Ukraine's Orange Revolution and the Czech Republic's Velvet Revolution. This neat branding of the pro-Hariri demonstrations, though, would soon prove misleading: Lebanon was not the Czech Republic. Until we understood Lebanon's complex history, we were only getting part of the story.

In part because of its unique position in the eastern Mediterranean, Lebanon is the most religiously diverse country in the Arab World. Sunni and Shi'a Muslims can each claim roughly 30% of the population. Most of the remainder is Christian, with Maronites the largest subgroup. In an attempt to mitigate the differences among these sects, Lebanese politics is organized under a power-sharing, "confessional" political system. This arrangement was a product of post–World War I French rule that allocated various political positions to different religious groups. Under this pact, the Lebanese president must be Maronite, the prime minister must be Sunni, and the president of the National Assembly is always Shi'a—with the Greek Orthodox and Druze populations given lesser roles. Other positions of influence and the distribution of resources followed from this model.

Historically, this pact has been moderately successful, with periods of peaceful coexistence among these communities. However, changing demographics—particularly Shi'a population growth vis-à-vis the Maronites without a resultant expansion of political power—have rankled many Shi'a. These internal rifts have been exacerbated by external pressures, including Israel's 1948 expulsion of hundreds of thousands of Palestinians (100,000 of whom settled into refugee camps in Lebanon where their population continued to grow apace) and political and military meddling by Syria, Israel, the United States, and, more recently, Iran. By the 1970s, these outside influences weighed heavily on Lebanon's delicate demographic balancing act. In 1975, these stresses finally plunged the country into a fifteen-year civil war, the end of which left Israel occupying the south of Lebanon, with Syria politically dominant in the rest of the country, having established an armed presence there.

American commentators like Ignatius and Adelman seemed to have ignored this history in interpreting the events of 2005, but I had experienced these growing societal fissures firsthand during my 1978 and 1979 visits to Lebanon in the midst of the civil war.

After one trip—in which I interviewed a group of recently released Palestinian prisoners who had been tortured during their long incarceration in Israeli prisons—I found myself increasingly uncomfortable with the disintegrating situation within the country. When I tried to explain to my Maronite Lebanese relatives why I was going to the Palestinian camps, they would wonder why I would want to visit "them." When I got to the camps, I would be forced to turn over my passport to a fourteen-year-old Palestinian youngster, menacingly armed with a Kalashnikov, who would mutter at my obviously Christian name. There was a strong sense, communicated in many different ways, that Christian Lebanese shouldn't be working with or even talking to Muslim Palestinians and vice versa. For my efforts, the best I got were comments like, "You just don't understand . . . ," or, "Well, you're not bad for a Christian." This enormous tension in Lebanon back then made me think that my energies could be better focused from outside the country.

It was during this same civil war that Rafiq Hariri had returned to Lebanon. Born to a modest Sunni family, Hariri had become a multibillionaire as the preferred contractor of the Saudi royal family during the 1970s—a period of explosive growth in both Saudi construction and global oil prices. Though he could have remained in comfortable exile in Saudi Arabia, he chose to return to Lebanon during the war-torn 1980s. Once in his homeland, Hariri began spending large amounts of his fortune on educational and charitable institutions.

The 1980s in Lebanon were bleak to say the least, but Hariri's massive philanthropic presence was one of the few bright spots. When I finally came back to visit Lebanon in 1991, I was overwhelmed by the absolute horror of seeing Beirut completely destroyed. Still more painful was the reality that, even with the massive Israeli bombardment and invasion of the city in 1982, the Lebanese had done much of this to themselves. I remember talking to a friend of mine, a female doctor in Beirut, about these still-fresh wounds. "You know," she said, "you Lebanese Americans may be the last people who think of all of Lebanon. The civil war did a lot of damage. Everybody still thinks Lebanon, everybody still talks Lebanon, but the picture they get in their mind is of their party or their region—they don't even see the other party or travel to other regions of our small country. You, on the other hand, still want to see and feel the whole country."[6]

Eventually, Hariri's charitable work led him into politics. I met him soon after he was elected prime minister in 1992 and got to know a man who was larger than life and incredibly passionate about rebuilding the ancient and now rubble-strewn city of Beirut.

One day my cousin Jack and I visited Hariri in his Beirut office.[7] My cousin was a traffic safety expert, and Hariri, a broad man with bushy eyebrows, wanted to know what he thought of Beirut's roads. My cousin's first reaction was a laugh.

"What are you thinking?" Hariri asked.

"In Cairo, they paint the lines on the street, and yet they are ignored," said my cousin. "But I have to hand it to you—knowing that people aren't going to pay attention anyway, you saved the paint."

Hariri chuckled a little bit. Over the years we developed a good, honest rapport. But it was also clear that he wanted to make the roads, and everything else, work. Hariri loved all of Lebanon, but Beirut was always its crown jewel. Every time I'd return, the first question he'd ask me is, "What do you think of your city now?"

One time I told him about the complaints I'd heard from some Lebanese that he spent so much time and money rebuilding Beirut that nothing was reaching other areas. Hariri quickly responded, "We are spending money out there, but if the heart doesn't beat, the country can't live—so the city comes first. It has to."[8]

Another day, when we were having lunch at his extraordinary home up on a hill overlooking the city, I said to him, "Just do me one favor. Leave one block the way it was and put a sign over it warning people that this kind of destruction easily could happen again."

Hariri looked at me for a second and then said, "That's interesting, but I don't think it's going to happen."[9]

After Hariri's death, I wrote a tribute saying there's no need to build a monument to him. "His monument already exists—it's called Beirut." So it was bitterly ironic that a man who had expended the last several decades of his life trying to push Lebanon away from the memory of war-torn ruins had died in a bombing that cratered another Beirut street.

In one sense, Hariri's death wasn't in vain. His enormous efforts to move the country back toward peaceful growth had made him a figure celebrated by many Lebanese across sectarian lines. After his assassination, Hariri achieved icon-like status. Our polling showed that substantial majorities of Lebanese from every group were "angered," "sad," or "shocked" by his killing. Large groups from each of Lebanon's communities also said that even though they previously did not support Hariri's "vision for Lebanon," they now did and would even vote for candidates who were "close to former Prime Minister Hariri" in the upcoming parliamentary elections.[10]

The problem with icons is that they often shine so brightly they can be seen from several different directions—and their legacy interpreted in divergent ways. Our polling had already shown that many of the Lebanese demonstrating in the streets couldn't agree on whether to blame Syria or the United States and Israel for Hariri's death. But this was just the beginning of the disagreements.

Even though the Lebanese were largely united in mourning Hariri, sectarian rifts still plagued the country. Polling results revealed what Zogby International had anticipated and the competing demonstrations made manifest—Lebanon was deeply divided, with attitudes on most issues split right down the middle. For example, although almost two in five Maronites and Druze believed that Hariri's assassination would lead to a Syrian withdrawal, as it eventually did, only 7% of Shi'a agreed.[11] Almost 60% of Shi'a, on the other hand, now worried that in the wake of the assassination, measures would be taken that would result in a deterioration of Lebanese security, an attitude shared by only about 15% of Maronites and Druze.[12]

Not surprisingly, these divergent communities also couldn't agree on how best to proceed with securing Lebanon. Only Maronites saw a Syrian withdrawal as a key measure—roughly half agreed with this solution—but just one-third of Shi'a and Sunnis and fewer than one-fourth of Greek Orthodox concurred. This disparity was also reflected in overall attitudes toward whether the United States or Syria was playing a positive role in Lebanon, with a significant split between the Maronite and Shi'a communities (see Table 11.1).

TABLE 11.1   SUPPORT FOR THE UNITED STATES AND SYRIA BY LEBANESE SECTARIAN GROUPS

		Maronite (%)	Sunni (%)	Shi'a (%)
United States	Support	67	20	7
	Oppose	31	80	93
Syria	Support	15	34	54
	Oppose	84	65	42

Source: Zogby International, Lebanon Poll, April 7–14, 2005. Sample size: 1,250 adults.

In contrast, many Lebanese—in particular Orthodox Christians, Sunni, and Shi'a—saw the solution to their nation's security in "reinforcement and deployment of the Lebanese army and security forces all over Lebanon." And although 60% of Druze saw the disarming of Lebanon's militias as necessary for the country's future, only about one in six Maronites, and even fewer Sunni Muslims, agreed. Not surprisingly, no Shi'a assented, because the "disarming" provision of United Nations Security Council Resolution 1559 specifically had the Shi'a group Hizbullah in mind (see Table 11.2).

Almost immediately, our polling painted a picture of a country perhaps united in grief, but in complete discord about how to react and proceed. Commentators like Ignatius and Adelman were right to label the demonstrations important, but that observation was the easy part. All the questions about how best to move a fractured Lebanon forward remained unanswered. I cautioned that before we began celebrating falling dominos—much less claiming credit for them—it was important to know where they might fall and what might come afterward.

Although many Western pundits were not commenting on—or didn't even realize—the still delicate nature of national politics in the post-Hariri world, the Lebanese themselves were certainly aware. In July 2005, following a complete Syrian withdrawal of uniformed soldiers, newly elected Prime Minister Fouad Siniora shocked many in the West by naming Hizbullah ministers to several positions in his cabinet.

TABLE 11.2   DISARMING OF HIZBULLAH

Should Hizbullah be disarmed?

	All (%)	Maronite (%)	Sunni (%)	Shi'a (%)
Disagree	41	8	31	79
Only if Hizbullah agrees	31	57	28	6
Agree	6	18	3	—
Agree if peace exists	18	17	28	14

Source: Zogby International/Information International, *Lebanon Poll*, April 7–14, 2005. Sample size: 1,250 adults.

Siniora's goal was clear enough. To be truly "unified," his government had to provide adequate representation to the country's Shi'a minority, nearly a third of the population. And the Shi'a, long isolated from political power and bitter over Israel's extended occupation of Lebanon's south, had been largely driven into Hizbullah's arms. Siniora understood the risk of letting Hizbullah inside the government, but his gambit was that a big-tent approach would give all major religious groups a say—and a stake—in Lebanon's future (see Table 11.3).

The move was bold, but the ghost of Lebanon's divided past continued to haunt the country. In July of 2006, Hizbullah killed and kidnapped several Israeli soldiers, a provocation denounced by Siniora and a majority of the Lebanese government's cabinet. A subsequent, massive Israeli bombing campaign severely damaged Lebanon's infrastructure, including the newly renamed Rafiq Hariri Airport in Beirut. The conflict was over within a month, but it left roughly 160 Israelis and 1,400 Lebanese dead—and another internal political meltdown brewing.

Unfortunately, the United States had an ongoing role in exacerbating this conflict. American commentators and policy makers were, understandably, enthusiastic about the Siniora government. But their tendency to play ideological favorites—offering support to Siniora, while refusing to acknowledge American support for Israel and America's silence in the face of the massive destruction resulting from Israel's 2006 assault on Lebanon—had strengthened Hizbullah's hand and weakened moderates and the U.S. position in Lebanon. All of this contributed to making a bad situation worse. Instead of helping Siniora move toward reform and reconciliation in the postwar period, America pushed toward confrontation.

Then, just as had happened in the 1970s, external players encouraged both sides to harden their stances. The United States and other Western

TABLE 11.3   NATIONAL UNITY

Do you support or oppose a national unity government including Hizbullah?

	All (%)	Maronite (%)	Sunni (%)	Shi'a (%)
Support	76	70	77	79
Oppose	12	17	12	12

Source: Zogby International/Information International, *Lebanon Poll*, April 7–14, 2005. Sample size: 1,250 adults.

nations rallied behind Siniora, as Iran and Syria offered encouragement and financing to Hizbullah. Feeling increasingly invulnerable and righteous, each side claimed for itself absolute and exclusive legitimacy. Each purported to represent the majority will, denigrating opponents as "mere puppets" under foreign influence. And each asserted that the other was engaged in a "coup."

Had the United States lent support to the Siniora government while also pushing to reform Lebanon's outmoded political system—something that had broad support across sectarian lines—we might have found a useful spot in the middle of the shouting. There was also consensus we could have built on, such as the desperate need to expand the economy, creating jobs and opportunities that would enable Lebanon's young to remain in the country of their birth—all issues that our polling showed had widespread appeal among all Lebanese. Instead, by reducing itself to "a side" in Lebanon's internal partisan conflict, the United States diminished its role and became a part of Lebanon's problem, not a pathway to a solution.

At the time, I wrote a paper for a congressional briefing encouraging a fundamental shift in policy toward Lebanon. Its confessional system needed to be reformed in recognition of the country's changed demography, with attention to securing the rights of all religious communities. Also the central government required strengthening and the Lebanese army needed to be trained, equipped, and empowered to expand its role to all parts of the country. This had to be done with the recognition that there can be no armed groups—including Hizbullah—outside of a truly representative government's control. I also urged Lebanon's leadership and their international backers—including the United States—to recognize that the country was a tinderbox and everybody was still playing with matches.

In November 2006, the Siniora government faced a massive setback as all Hizbullah-linked ministers stepped down from their posts. They objected to a U.N. investigation into both the assassination of Rafiq Hariri and the continuing murders of many Hariri supporters and the press. Tensions heightened, and Siniora's outreach fell apart. The next month, the Shi'a group led street mobilizations against the government that effectively shut down parliament and placed the prime minister's office under siege. By early the following year, these protests had spilled over into violence. Throughout 2007, Lebanon was the scene of more internal bloodshed and government paralysis. The next year was no better: in May of 2008, in a move that gave many Lebanese flashbacks of their long civil war, Hizbullah resorted to arms against the government, sparking still more domestic strife. With the United States unable to play a constructive role in finding a way out of the impasse, it fell to the government of Qatar, acting on behalf of the Arab League, to negotiate a solution that would stabilize the country until the 2009 elections.

When national parliamentary elections were held in May 2009, the March 14th Coalition parties, led by Rafiq Hariri's son Saad Hariri, won a majority of seats. Because the younger Hariri was seen as pro-Western and headed up a coalition that opposed a Hizbullah-led group, the election was heralded in America as an endorsement of our values and efforts in the region. But given Lebanon's fractured polity, real problems remained. For example, because the seats are portioned out by district, Saad Hariri's coalition won a clear majority in the new parliament. Even though Hizbullah-led opposition candidates won fewer seats, they did win more votes overall. As a result, Hizbullah insisted that their voice be included in the next cabinet. To secure approval for a new government, the younger Hariri eventually had to patch together a national unity cabinet, including Hizbullah elements, just as Siniora had before him.

Despite the persistence of these political problems, it is important to note that the Lebanese are positive and energized. As our May 2009 polling shows, the public is satisfied with the direction of their country and optimistic about the future (see Table 9.1). This was the first time in the decade we saw positive numbers in Lebanon. It is a promising development upon which the government can build.

What is also new and promising is the convergence of views among Lebanon's many sects. In April 2010, when we asked Lebanese to identify "the most pressing priorities facing the country" all groups, across the board, agreed on the same three top priorities: improving the economy and increasing employment; protecting national independence; and achieving national unity. This agenda unites Lebanese and can provide a way forward.[13]

In encouraging and supporting the Saad Hariri government, which I believe is the right thing to do, U.S. policy makers need to keep in mind both the lessons of recent history and the complex nature of Lebanon's consensus-based politics. When sectarian rifts revealed themselves after 2005, I kept hearing people on both sides of the conflict, as well as policy makers and commentators in Washington, echoing the old proverb: "Things must get worse before they can get better." This viewpoint ignored the reality that "things," if carelessly and thoughtlessly aggravated, most often *only* get worse. More relevant, I suggested, would be to pay attention to an old Lebanese adage: "No victor, no vanquished."

Lebanese politics remain based on the need for delicate compromise. The lesson that should have been learned by now is that blindly playing sides without understanding a country's history and listening to the concerns of all its people can be a dangerous game.

12
SAUDI ARABIA
THEIR REFORM, NOT OURS

THE MAJLIS AL-SHURA, the Saudi parliament's main building, is housed inside Riyadh's massive Al-Yamamah Palace complex. From the outside, it is a large white structure with a single dome in the middle. Inside, walls shine with gold flourish in the ornate Italian style popular in the region. However, the actual meeting room looks just like a Western parliamentary chamber: the appointed members of the legislature sit at desks in the round, and speakers stand in a well surrounded by a profusion of distinguished, dark colors and stained wood.

In 2004, I visited with members of the Majlis al-Shura while working with several U.S. policy analysts, assessing attitudes toward reform in Saudi Arabia. The American group had prepared questions for a diverse group of Saudi intellectuals, policy makers, and opinion shapers. At the time of my trip, promoting democracy in the Arab World was all the rage in the United States. Indeed, it had become a veritable cottage industry, with serious and not-so-serious analysts and ideologues all getting in on the act. Not a month went by without another forum held or paper published on the topic. Pushing Middle Eastern democracy had also become a new fallback position for justifying the Iraq War, as the initial goals like finding weapons of mass destruction had disappeared. And there were liberals and conservatives alike who argued, without any empirical evidence, that the region's ills and its "anger at the West" could be blamed, quite simply, on an absence of democracy.

In the United States, "advancing democracy" was also the one foreign-policy issue on which the Bush administration and its critics fully agreed. Yet, bipartisan appeal aside, this was also a subject on which both sides were frequently dead wrong. In general, expanding citizen rights and participation are goals well worth embracing. However, as my meeting with leading Saudi lawmakers would suggest, when the United States pursues these objectives without understanding that a big concept like "reform" can mean a lot of different things, we end up doing more harm than good.

The first group we met during that trip in 2004 was led by Dr. Abdulrahman al-Zamil—a dynamic member of the parliament and an extraordinary figure in Saudi Arabia's history. One of the "USC Mafia," he had spent decades in government posts, helping to write laws and codes, organize ministry operations, and create civil society structures. In his sixties, al-Zamil retired from public service to devote his energy to building the family business. His company became one of the most successful enterprises in the country, measured in terms of earnings from exports, and was publicly traded on the Saudi stock exchange. A few years later, he was called back into government service as a member of the Majlis. Ever the fighter, he continued to advocate for change.

Just days before our meeting, in fact, al-Zamil had led a successful challenge against the Transportation Ministry's request for increased road taxes. He based his rejection on the government's lack of fiscal transparency and accountability. His public questioning of and challenge to the minister appearing before the Majlis was carried live on Saudi 3, the kingdom's equivalent to C-SPAN. Before our encounter began, a number of his friends who had gathered to join our discussion teased that he had become a celebrity—that his challenge had inspired viewers and had boosted the public's confidence in the Majlis. This, in my lexicon, was the definition of a "reformer."

As our meeting began, al-Zamil was asked what he thought of President Bush's new U.S. policy to promote Arab democratic reform. He quickly erupted: "We do not want your reform. We don't need it!"[1]

It would be easy to read al-Zamil's response as knee-jerk anti-Americanism, but there were more subtle lessons to be drawn from this adamant "No!" At the time of our interview, Arab public opinion of American values was being steadily dragged down by the war in Iraq, the torture scandal at Abu Ghraib prison, the disturbingly prolonged incarceration of Arabs at Guantanamo Bay, and other serious questions about U.S. policy in the region. Although Americans might still have imagined U.S. society as a model for reform, many Arabs had come to disagree. Further conversation with al-Zamil revealed that the buzzwords in the question that prompted his impassioned rejection were not "democratic" or "reform" but rather

"President Bush" and "U.S. policy." This was not a rebuke of reform, per se—or even of America.

The point is this: when offering foreign citizens help in improving their country, it's important to first understand how they view yours. Saudi Arabia has a long-standing and generally positive relationship with the United States. Likewise, al-Zamil and many other members of the Majlis had been educated in the United States and were friendly with many Americans. But they still had no interest in reform offered by a U.S. administration associated with the war in Iraq, Abu Ghraib, and Guantanamo Bay. At the time, American democracy seemed a lot like damaged goods to many Arabs.

One of America's foremost blunders has been the persistent belief that the United States—all on its own, and simply by invoking its name and history—can be the agent of a democratic transformation in the Arab World. Behind this assumption is the naïve notion that all Arabs see the United States as freedom's champion, a transference from the days of the Cold War when many in Eastern Europe did, in fact, look to the United States to help liberate them from Soviet domination. Although it's true that many in the Arab World admire aspects of American life, U.S. policy in the region has increasingly undermined Arab attitudes toward America as a global model. Indeed, in 2004, the year of my visit with Majlis al-Shura members in Saudi Arabia, Zogby International had polled in five Arab nations with the question: "How helpful can the U.S. be in supporting democracy in your country?" We got an overwhelmingly negative response in every country but Lebanon, where there was a deep sectarian divide on this issue (see Table 12.1).

Following the exchange with al-Zamil, the next day we met another group of Majlis members to hear their views on the same reform issues. The first Majlis member of this group to respond to the same questions about President Bush's democracy agenda was a reformer of a different stripe. A lawyer and educator by training, he had long provided a challenging voice within Saudi society. Though soft-spoken, he was both brilliant and intense.

Unlike his colleagues, he enthusiastically embraced President Bush's reform program. But when pressed to elaborate, he shocked my U.S. associates with his explanation. Bush's call for reform was helpful, he explained, because it *weakened* the Arab governments that had for many decades been allied with the United States and relied on American support. The price those governments had paid was dear. They muted their criticism of U.S.

TABLE 12.1 POSITIVE EVALUATION OF U.S. HELP ON ISSUES AFFECTING THE ARAB WORLD

When asked to evaluate the effectiveness of U.S. assistance on each issue, the percentage of respondents indicating that U.S. help would be positive was as follows:

	Morocco	Jordan	Lebanon	Saudi Arabia	United Arab Emirates)
Supporting democracy in your country	10	17	46	1	7
Resolving the Israeli–Palestinian conflict	58	44	62	32	43

Source: Zogby International, "Arabs Want Reform, U.S. Help in Solving Israeli–Palestinian Crisis," December 6, 2004. Based on poll taken November 6–24, 2004. Sample size: 2,600 adults.

support for Israel and exploitation of Arab weaknesses. He continued, saying that as a result of having taken this path, these governments had lost their legitimacy and stood humiliated in the Arab and Muslim Worlds. With reform, the people's will would dramatically change policies throughout the region, end U.S. interference, and produce the opportunity to create a unified Arab and Muslim response to the challenge posed to the region by both the United States and Israel.

This Majlis member's reaction revealed a secondary cost of unpopular U.S. strategy in the region: not only do these policies make advocating democracy harder for Americans; they put all political actors associated with the United States in a precarious position. Witness, for example, the ill-fated support America gave to Fatah in the 2006 Palestinian legislative election. Hamas, Fatah's rival party, exploited for its advantage the revelation that the United States had provided indirect funding to support Fatah candidates. Democracy was perhaps served—but as a tool wielded against the United States and its interests. Far from helpful, America's political embrace had proved a burden that, in this case, Fatah could not bear. The lesson here was clear: when you roil a region, turn it against you, and then advocate an election, the side that ends up winning may not be the one you favor.

In seeking to expand democracy in the Middle East, U.S. policy makers need to realize, first, that many Arabs do not regard Americans as the democracy experts we assume ourselves to be. Second, Arab democratic governments, should they emerge, may not be as we hoped.

Rightfully, Americans put a lot of faith in the power of democracy, but before encouraging reform, it is imperative to understand how Arabs view America and its policies in their region. As my 2004 interviews with the members of the Saudi parliament suggested, imagining that our plan for democratic transformation would deliver some sort of universal cure for the Middle East—or would be eagerly received—overlooks a much more complex political terrain.

For many years, the relationship between anti-U.S. extremism and America's Arab allies has been misunderstood. U.S. policy, *not Arab autocracy*, is the seedbed of anti-American sentiment. Arab governments put themselves most at risk precisely when they support American policies unpopular with their own people. When it comes to Arab public opinion, America has proven much more likely to weigh down our allies than bolster them.

In fact, as Shibley Telhami—the University of Maryland's Anwar Sadat Chair for Population, Development, and Peace—noted at the advent of the Iraq War, a likely consequence of that conflict would not be the advance of democracy in the Middle East, but its contraction. With Arab anger at the United States predictably increasing, and Arab governments close to America facing domestic pressure, Telhami postulated that those governments would be less inclined to open up their political systems.[2] The seven years since the start of the Iraq War have shown just how prophetic he was. Governments like Jordan's that had been making progress toward democratic participation have felt compelled to put a hold on forward movement. During the same period, Lebanon, Palestine, and Egypt held elections in which hard-liners won victories and were strengthened. As a result, other governments in the region that had been contemplating making democratic reforms decided to freeze their efforts.

As a corollary, extremist movements including al-Qaeda have targeted Saudi Arabia, Egypt, and Jordan not because of their lack of democracy but because of their relationship with the United States. In a perverse way, when the United States advocates pro-democracy initiatives in the Arab World, we most often end up undercutting our own allies.

In 2005, I was attending the World Economic Forum at a Dead Sea resort when U.S. Principal Deputy Assistant Secretary of State Liz Cheney began her remarks with a dramatic confession: for the last sixty years, U.S. policy in the Middle East has been a betrayal of our values.[3] There was a gasp in the audience; people thought she was going to acknowledge that U.S. policy had been unbalanced, that we hadn't been fair in dealing with the Arab–Israeli conflict. Instead, she took shots at America's Arab allies, apologizing for the fact that the United States had supported dictators and monarchs and not encouraged democracy. Cheney may merely have been test-marketing this line in the Arab World, preparing the ground for Secretary of State Condoleezza Rice's major address one month later in Cairo developing the same theme. But if this was an exercise in "testing a message," neither Cheney nor Rice apparently paid attention to how badly it was received.

It was, in fact, quite stunning. Here was a U.S. official—the vice president's daughter—in Jordan undercutting its king, a man who had often put himself at risk to be a steadfast U.S. ally. A year later, with the Middle East roiled by a U.S.-led war in Iraq and Israeli attacks on Gaza, U.S. popularity in Jordan was down to a scant 5%.[4] Nevertheless, when President Bush flew to Amman to meet Iraqi Prime Minister Nouri al-Maliki, he was greeted at the airport by Jordan's King Abdullah. The series of events led me to wonder, "Does George Bush know how great a risk this king is taking to display his friendship at this time?"

This exact same contradiction had been brought home to me a few years earlier in a phone conversation with an adviser to then Crown Prince Abdullah of Saudi Arabia. The caller, a longtime friend, had telephoned late on election night to inquire whether or not John Kerry had won the presidency. "It's still too close to call," I told him, "but I was certain you would want George Bush to win. He supports you, while John Kerry has been very critical of the kingdom."

His response surprised me: "It's better for us, in my opinion, to have a U.S. president who dislikes us, than to have a U.S. president who pursues policies that lead our people to dislike your country."[5] Once again, unpopular U.S. policy had made it extremely difficult for our allies to remain friendly with us, creating odd and paradoxical allegiances.

Policy makers in the United States and elsewhere in the West are fond of arguing that democracy by itself is the antidote to extremism and anti-Western sentiment.[6] Proponents of this theory contend that even crudely imposed transformations that at least appear democratic will lead people to put away their grievances and focus on building a new order.

Again, quite the opposite is true. As we have seen in several elections throughout the Arab World, populations roiled by anger and a sense of injustice are not grateful simply to have an open election. In fact, the freer the election, the greater the opportunity that this hostile public sentiment will emerge victorious. In recent years this anger has often, although not exclusively, been directed at the United States and our allies.

The United States experienced this same phenomenon more than forty years ago during a period of domestic democratic expansion. During the mid- to late 1960s, as African Americans were demanding long-denied rights, largely black, inner-city neighborhoods kept exploding with deadly riots summer after summer. President Lyndon Johnson, the man who led the passage of the landmark civil rights legislation, was initially angry and confused but eventually understood this outrage. "When you put your foot on a man's neck and hold him down for three hundred years, and then you let him up," figured Johnson, "what's he going to do? He's going to knock your block off."[7]

Likewise, in some Arab countries, the period immediately following freer elections was not a period of settling down but of settling scores. This clearly was the case with the 2006 Hamas victory in Palestine and the continued popularity of Hizbullah among some groups in Lebanon. And it is also true of gains won by some sectarian extremists in Iraq.

Yet another nonempirical assumption sometimes used to promote democratic reform in the Arab World is that democracies don't make wars. However, this notion is a tough sell in a region that lived through Israel's 1956 and 1967 wars. In the wake of the 2003 U.S. "war of choice" in Iraq, most Arabs regard this claim as laughable.

U.S. efforts at democracy promotion, so solidly supported in America, can weigh themselves down and even be counterproductive if their advocates don't have a clear understanding of Arab opinions toward reform, democracy, and America itself. None of this negates the importance of expanding freedom and opportunity in the Arab World, but such growth takes root when the seeds are planted from within, not from without. Arab academics, professionals, and business leaders have shown that they can provide significant input in decision making if they are given the chance. Arab youth need to be given hope for their ideas and aspirations. Citizens and noncitizens alike need to know that their rights will be protected and their views respected. All that works best when we recognize that democratic transformation is a process grounded in history, requiring social and cultural prerequisites. Assuming that the West is serious about prioritizing real reform and democracy promotion, we need to factor Arab opinion into future policy decisions.

Saudi attitudes are not overwhelmingly anti-American. Like many Arabs, Saudis strongly disagreed with many Bush administration policies. But as we've seen, our polling soon after Barack Obama's election showed widespread support for the new American president. Nowhere was that support greater than in Saudi Arabia, where four in five respondents gave Obama a positive rating.[8] Likewise, the several high-profile diplomatic gestures toward the Middle East that marked the new president's first weeks in office were met with high approval among Saudis: 79% said Obama's actions had left them hopeful about U.S. policy in the region. Poll numbers that stratospheric never last forever, but the more support that the president and his policies can garner in Saudi Arabia, the easier it will be to expand democratic participation in the kingdom without fear of an anti-American backlash. Ultimately, Saudis and other Arabs do want change, but the progress they seek is different from that being promoted by the more ambitious plans of Western governments. What our surveys of Arab opinion consistently reveal is that the most critical first steps to be taken are to grow Arab economies and improve the quality of life and essential services.[9] Finally, Arab opinion, as shown in our polling, seems to be saying that internal political affairs are just that—internal.

Given this apparent rejection of outside interference in domestic political matters, it would be more useful for Western supporters of Arab reform to find ways to assist infrastructure development and the expansion of trade and investment in order to promote economic growth. Successful economic and educational development would lead to the political changes sought by reformers without incurring resentment or resistance. Reform, in any case, must be demand-driven and not imposed from outside. This, as I will develop in the final section, appears to be the direction favored by the Obama administration. From the president's June 4, 2009, address at the University of Cairo to Secretary of State Clinton's remarks at Morocco's "Forum for the Future" in November 2009, the Obama administration is pursuing a less ideological and more realistic approach to reform. Democracy remains a goal, but not one that can be promoted without attention to local needs and conditions. Instead, the focus is on promoting human rights, improving education, supporting civil society organizations, and expanding employment opportunities. These are areas in which Arabs want and need U.S. assistance. And positive growth in these matters is a prerequisite to a broader and sustainable reform agenda.

In terms of major political issues, there is just one issue in which Arab opinion consistently wants positive U.S. involvement: a peaceful resolution of the Israeli–Palestinian conflict (see Table 12.1). If the United States were to deliver in this area, it just might enhance American credibility and pave the way for a more active—and successful—U.S. role in advancing other reform issues.

13

PALESTINE
A WOUND IN THE HEART

IN DECEMBER 2008, after three years of exchanging provocations, rockets, and artillery shells, the Israeli military and Palestinian fighters living in the Gaza Strip began a sadly familiar sequence of events. Following a series of exchanges of cross-border violence, Hamas, the *de facto* government in Gaza, declared the end of a five-month-long partial ceasefire and intensified rocket strikes on southern Israel. Israeli armed forces then began a wave of air strikes on Palestinian police stations, government buildings, and civilian structures. This relentless bombing campaign was followed by a massive ground invasion. By the war's end roughly a month later in January 2009, more than 1,300 Palestinians and 13 Israelis were dead—a 100-to-1 ratio—and hundreds of thousands of Gazans were without homes and basic utilities like water and electricity.

The different ways in which Arabs and viewers of Western media experienced this conflict was indicative of a larger split. Because Israel had denied Western journalists access to the war zone, most Westerners followed these events from a distance. The nightly news broadcasts typically featured correspondents standing at a vantage point outside Gaza while smoke from bombing raids billowed in the background. These journalists' reports consisted mostly of what Israeli military briefers told them was happening.

In stark contrast, Arab television networks had correspondents or other observers in Gaza, giving vivid eyewitness accounts of the horrors of the assault. One reporter described the situation faced by the outgunned captive Palestinians with a distinctly American expression: "This isn't a war; it's a turkey shoot!"[1] All this time, food and medicine were in short supply because of the continuing hostility and the prolonged Israeli enforced closure of Gaza.

Arabs watched all this and wept in quiet rage. One of them was a junior minister in an Arab Gulf country, who called me in the midst of the offensive, overwhelmed by a feeling of powerlessness. Western-educated, decidedly pro-American, and no fan of Hamas, the minister was deeply troubled. "I need to do something, especially for the children, to stop this, to help. But I feel so useless."[2]

The minister captured Arab feelings about Palestine in a nutshell. When Zogby International polls across the Middle East, we find the Palestinian issue consistently among the top three concerns. Time and again, Arabs tell us, and demonstrate with their actions, that Palestine is more than a political question. It is, rather, a very personal concern, experienced by Arabs much as American Jews felt the suffering of their European counterparts during World War II. There is no Holocaust—a word reserved for the killing of six million innocents—in Palestine, but there is the same pain, the same identification, the same feelings of vulnerability and futility, and even the same guilt over the continuing suffering of people with whom Arabs identify. For Arabs, Palestine—its history and the agony of its people—is the wound that will not heal.

In America, resolving the Arab–Israeli conflict is considered an important issue: U.S. presidents dating back to Nixon have all agreed a lasting peace is central to regional stability. But most Americans have never understood the visceral, personal Palestinian sense of dispossession or how their loss resonates in the broader Arab World. For America to fulfill a meaningful role in repairing this rift, we must peer beneath the contentious surface of reprisal and retribution. We need to grasp the powerful, competing histories that feed this ongoing tragedy.

In 2005, I addressed what was for me an unusual audience: forty Israeli generals and colonels in Washington for a seminar on public policy at the National Defense University.[3] I had spoken to Arab audiences, challenging them to understand the Jewish–Israeli story, the reality of Jewish feelings of vulnerability, and the undeniably important role the Holocaust had played in shaping this story. Now, I had a rare opportunity to challenge an Israeli audience—military leaders, no less—to understand the Palestinian and Arab narrative. In particular, I wanted them to understand the roles that losing Palestine and the continuing plight of the Palestinian people have played in defining an Arab sense of having lost control of their history.

I reminded these Israelis that although the story of their nation's birth focused on Britain's Balfour Declaration, which pledged support for a Jewish homeland, the Palestinian narrative of dispossession emphasized the betrayal by Britain and France of their commitments to the Arabs.

The British mandate of Palestine brought a massive influx of Jews, who viewed themselves as Zionist pioneers, but who were seen by the Arabs as foreign agents of dislocation and insecurity. During the next two decades, Arabs rebelled time and again against both the new immigrants and the British authorities, agreeing to a truce in 1939 on the condition that the British control Jewish immigration and recognize legitimate Arab concerns.

During this same period, before and after World War I, the other nations of the Levant succeeded in gaining some degree of independence—all except Palestine. Then, with the Zionist victory in 1948 that created Israel, came the expulsion of more than 650,000 Arabs from Palestine, further compounding the Arab sense of loss and vulnerability. To Arabs, the establishment of a Jewish homeland in what had for centuries been Arab territory was the *Nakba,* or "the disaster." Even Arabs geographically removed from the scene commonly described the Palestinian loss as "a wound in our heart"—a deep cut that still has not healed.

This narrative split hadn't stopped with the creation of Israel, I told the generals. Rather, it has been widening continuously over the last sixty years. Many Israelis saw the 1967 Six-Day War, the confiscation of Palestinian lands to build Jewish settlements, the demolition of Palestinian homes, and the jailing and expulsion of Palestinian political leaders as measures justified by security concerns. However, most Israelis didn't realize that this expanding repression aggravated not only Palestinians, but many Arabs, who experienced these same events as reminders of the denial of their rights and their own vulnerability.

I related all this to my Israeli audience, not expecting to win converts but to push them to recognize the Arab narrative and to open a dialogue. Afterward, there were a few tough questioners, but some in the group appeared open to views that challenged their thinking—not everyone, though.

I was describing how "losing control of their history" had played a critical role in defining the Palestinian psyche when an aggravated man in the audience challenged my assessment. He argued that what I had to offer were nothing but "nice words" and that the reason for the problem was solely Palestinian failings. The Israeli officer blamed the origin of the conflict on Yassir Arafat, the Palestinian refusal to recognize the Jewish state, and the Palestinians' penchant for violence.

I replied that he could, if he wished, blame Palestinians and deny their reality, but the price for such denial was great. Refusing to acknowledge the history and the grievances of the "other" with whom Israel was in conflict was both delusional and insensitive. Worse, it would be a recipe for further conflict, incurring not only Palestinian wrath but enmity throughout the region, prolonging the bloody conflict.

The exchange was testy, at best, but as my questioner spoke, I noted others in the audience wincing or shaking their heads in disagreement. When I responded, others were nodding in understanding and agreement. I took this as a positive sign and a clear indication that narratives can be shared and understood, even by Israeli military officers whose job it is to fight against Palestinians struggling to define their competing narrative. At the session's end, several of the attendees gave me their cards and asked to receive my weekly column and to remain in contact. Some have.

For this decades-old conflict to have a peaceful resolution, the region's competing narratives must be shared and respected. More Israelis and Americans must understand and acknowledge the role that Israel, with U.S. and other Western support, has played in the disenfranchisement of the Palestinians. Likewise, Arabs in general and Palestinians in particular must gain a deeper appreciation for the roles that history and Arab behavior have played in fueling the vulnerability that defines the Jewish psyche.

Critical historical experiences are extremely powerful, but they are not rare. Every people—tribes, clans, cultural or religious groups, and nations—has had such defining moments, ones that gave shape and meaning to their past and future. Often, these moments are experienced as a loss of control over history, as was the case for American Southerners, for example, during post–Civil War Reconstruction, or Eastern Europeans behind the Iron Curtain. For Palestinians, this watershed event was the 1948 founding of Israel, the date when they became either refugees or foreigners in their own land.

But Palestinians aren't alone in their story of victimhood. Jews, too, tell a compelling story of bigotry and pogroms culminating in the Holocaust. Thus, bombs in a Jerusalem market or Tel Aviv nightclub, or rockets falling on Sderot do more than claim innocent lives and spread fear. These horrors also play out in the Jewish consciousness against the backdrop of the last century of suffering. They resonate in much the same way that an assault on Gaza or a house demolition in Jerusalem unfolds in the Palestinian and Arab psyche—reinforcing their vulnerability. By not acknowledging the importance of the other side's history, Arabs and Israelis alike fail to understand how their current behavior serves to validate that history.

Any successful Western participation in the Arab–Israeli conflict must grasp the significance of these pivotal moments. Unfortunately, just as Western coverage of the January 2009 Israeli offensive was filtered through Israeli military briefers, so Americans and Europeans have from the very beginning tended to view the creation of Israel through our own literature and entertainment media. One such example is the profound and lasting impact made by Leon Uris's 1958 bestselling novel, *Exodus,* and the 1960 movie of the same name. The film starred Paul Newman as Ari Ben Canaan, a rebellious Jewish former army officer who faces down the British navy and leads his people to the promised land.[4]

Stories have circulated for years that Uris's two years of on-site research for the book were funded by a New York public-relations executive named Edward Gottlieb, who was looking for ways to improve Israel's image in the West.[5] Whether or not that is so, *Exodus* does paint an intensely sympathetic portrait of hardworking Israeli settlers whose dreams of land and freedom were opposed by the natives—a story that, not coincidentally, echoes old American ideals of hardscrabble homesteaders battling "savage" Native Americans.

American audiences also would have read Uris's novel and seen the movie in the context of the horror of the Holocaust and in the broader context of the Bible. This framing of the story serves to equate the founding of Israel not only with Western atonement but also with biblical fulfillment. In fact, both the book and its film adaptation were so successful that they have defined, even for succeeding generations who have not heard of Leon Uris, the parameters of the Arab–Israeli conflict. It became "locked in place," so to speak, and part of our Western culture to define the Israelis as pioneers who "share our values." In the West, the Palestinian story of dispossession does not resonate with our history or religious experience in the same way. Not only do we not know much Middle Eastern history, but Israeli interests have long understood how crucial it is to define the entire history of their nation's founding in Western terms—including the story of the Palestinians as seen through the lens of Israel.

Because Israel recognized the importance of telling us their stories and because the Palestinians have, to this day, never mounted a successful, sustained campaign to explain their history, the Israelis are still able to define how Westerners understand the conflict. To be certain, since its modern founding, Israel has also maintained an overwhelming military superiority over any potential enemies in the region and has not been afraid to use these forces. But the most important battle has been the one for narrative control.

Initially, Israel wanted to be seen as a nation of hard workers, modernizing the Middle East and making a supposedly barren desert bloom with life as they fought to secure their future against backward, one-dimensional Arabs. This collection of crude stereotypes was but an elaboration of Zionism's most important early leader Chaim Weizmann's famed 1930s description of the conflict: "[O]n the one side, the forces of destruction, the forces of the desert . . . and on the other side, the forces of civilization and building. It is the old one of the desert against civilization."[6] In the 1970s, though, as the conflict between Palestinians and Israelis intensified, Israel needed more narrative management, and a broader strategy emerged.

In the late 1970s, the Israeli right wing, under the guidance of a young Benjamin Netanyahu, organized a media campaign designed to define the Palestinians as "terrorists" and agents of the Soviet Union. This strategy was brilliantly documented by a young U.S. researcher, Philip Paull, who showed how Netanyahu, by playing the anti-Soviet card, was able to bring together sympathetic U.S. columnists and politicians to design and implement a systematic operation to distort the Palestinian image.[7] Knowing that the field was open to their efforts—because the Palestinians would not contest them—Netanyahu and his American allies succeeded.

The negative stereotypes they projected achieved their goal of defining the Palestinian reality and desensitizing Americans and Europeans to the suffering of Palestinians, who weren't seen as real people but "objects," be they "terrorists" or mere body counts. All this helped lay the propaganda groundwork for the devastating 1982 invasion of Lebanon and the effort to make the Palestine Liberation Organization illegal in the United States. Although the Israelis' military superiority created favorable conditions on the ground, their ability to frame the conflict as that of a "civilized nation" defending itself against "savage terror" allowed them to take these actions relatively unimpeded.

Meanwhile the Palestinians, because they failed to comprehend the nature of this campaign, never engaged in a counterstrategy, relying instead on hollow political appeals to "international legitimacy" and the like. What Palestinians did not understand was that the critical political and information battles being waged were not over the definition of abstract concepts like "justice." The fights were about the story of who the Palestinians were as a people. This is the conflict the Palestinians have continually lost—and that they continue to lose today. If you can succeed in delegitimizing and dehumanizing your opponent, as the Israelis have done, then your opponent is left powerless and unable to make an effective claim to justice. This lesson was brought home to me almost three decades ago by then Mayor of Nazareth Tawfiq Zayyad. That ancient city, most famous as the biblical childhood home of Jesus, is today located in northern Israel and home to a large Palestinian Arab population, who are citizens of Israel.

Zayyad was well known throughout the Arab World for his compelling poetry of Palestinian memories and aspirations. He was also down to earth and could be quite funny. My first meeting with Zayyad came in 1975 at New York's JFK Airport. He was part of a group of Israeli Arab leaders who had come to the United States for a speaking tour. In greeting one of them—an older, distinguished intellectual—I mentioned that I had read his writings and learned from them. Then, turning to Zayyad, I added: "I wrote a chapter of my dissertation about you."

Zayyad poked his colleague laughing, "You see. You he reads; me he writes about!"

Five years later, Zayyad was back on another tour. Everywhere he went, he challenged the counterproductive use of violence by Palestinian groups. One of the events was a fundraising function sponsored by a local Palestinian American organization. The occasion was billed as a "celebration of Palestinian folklore" and featured a Palestinian dance troupe, traditional dress, and poetry. At one point in the program, a group of child dancers came onstage in khaki military dress carrying wooden guns, and Zayyad became quite distressed. He turned to me and said, "This is not our culture or our tradition. This, tragically, is what has been forced on us. It is not to be celebrated."[8]

Zayyad himself was well versed in an older tradition of Palestinian storytelling—one that conveyed the people's attachment to their land and a desire to restore their now dispersed, dismembered nation and to maintain their identity and traditions. I had been introduced to that same world in the mid-1970s by Zayyad's own poetry and by the work of other poets such as Ibrahim and Fadwa Tuqan, Mahmoud Darwish, and Sameh al-Qasim. I also discovered painters like Kamal Boulatta and Ismail Shamout. These Palestinian artists had used their hope as a raw material to give a collective voice to the dreams and stories of their people. Their work also demanded recognition so that others might come to appreciate what the Palestinians had lost—and respect their right to justice.

Now, after nearly four decades of heartbreak and violence, what troubles me is how much of this work is lost or ignored. The stories are rarely told, their poetry has not been widely available for years, and the paintings are not shown. A new generation wishing to learn about Palestine must instead make do with news reports or political rants.

When I see thousands of young men in Gaza demonstrating, angry fists jabbing the air, or hear the charged rhetoric of Hamas's leadership, I think of Zayyad's admonition against celebrating violence. It is no secret why these young people are fuming. Since the mid-1990s, youth unemployment in Gaza has been between 50% and 80%. With Israel controlling Gaza's borders and restricting movement of labor as well as imports and exports, Palestinians remain trapped in poverty in one of the most densely populated places on Earth. Under these conditions, the younger generations grow irate and ripe for radicalization. But understanding can never excuse violence that has taken victims on all sides.

The tragedy, though, goes deeper than that. Preyed upon by Hamas's hard-line leadership, these young Palestinians have lost their dreams, their poetry, and their hope—and in the end have taken a path that confirms, for many in the West, the crude stereotypes of Palestinian terrorists that were the staple of the Israeli narrative.

In 2005, Israel unilaterally vacated Gaza, refusing to work with the Palestinian Authority to ensure an orderly transfer. The Israelis rejected U.S. Secretary of State Condoleezza Rice's calls that they negotiate their withdrawal with Palestinian President Mahmoud Abbas and develop a post-withdrawal framework. Rice wanted an agreement to govern the movement of goods and services in and out of Gaza, allowing the Palestinian Authority to move their police and other agencies of governance into the Strip. The Israelis insisted instead on a unilateral withdrawal. And even though Rice was able to press the Israelis to agree to a post-withdrawal economic framework, it was never implemented. With Israel out and Gaza sealed off from the outside world, what remained was a reservation of poverty and anger. Because the Palestinian Authority was not present to provide economic and political benefits, and was denied the ability to move between Gaza and the West Bank, it should be little wonder that Hamas became the ascendant power in Gaza.

After winning legislative elections in January 2006, Hamas made terrible decisions—choosing actions that could have been scripted by Netanyahu's terrorist propaganda team in the late 1970s. Instead of reining in the violence, Hamas allowed it to continue. Instead of assessing the balance of power, calculating the needs of their people, and embarking on a political path toward empowerment, Hamas stubbornly maintained a rejectionist posture more fitting to a marginalized opposition party than to a government. As a result, they continuously forfeited needed international aid and support, squandering the fruits of their victory.

It is bad enough that Hamas chose to ignore history's lesson to "never pick a fight you can't win" and instead persisted in provocations certain to increase the already unbearable hardships endured by the Palestinian people. But by playing the role of the unrepentant terrorist, Hamas has essentially fought on the Israeli side of the narrative struggle. That's part of the tragedy of modern Palestine, but it's also part of the tragedy of modern Israel. Israelis live next door to a people they, for the most part, are not allowed to see or understand.

That's literally true in the case of the West Bank wall and barrier—in places a thirty-foot-high concrete divider—that now stretches over hundreds of miles. It snakes in and out of Palestinian lands, cutting some villages in half. Most telling are the segments of the Israeli side of the wall painted to resemble flowers and grass—a pastoral landscape that pointedly omits the Palestinian towns immediately on the other side. The barrier shields the settlers from seeing or even imagining the very people that they have dispossessed.

But the fact that Israelis can't see or understand their Palestinian neighbors is also true in a more figurative sense. This was brought home to me by a June 2009 article in the New York Times describing the struggles of young classical musicians in Gaza and the lack of awareness among the neighboring Israelis that any Palestinians might be creating art and music. The article quoted Noam Ben-Zeev, a music critic for the liberal Israeli daily Haaretz: "We cannot perceive them as people who have their own cultural lives."[9]

Israel's clear military advantage has not spared the region a multiplicity of wars—in 1948, 1956, 1967, 1973, 1978, 1982, 2006, and 2008–2009, not to mention almost continuous raids and reprisals. Just as countries bordering the Pacific Ocean's Ring of Fire suffer a disproportionate number of fatal earthquakes, Palestine and Israel sit atop a rift created by these two competing narratives.

Even with all these setbacks, there are signs that some Palestinians are seeking to reclaim their nation's story and to project it in a more positive way. There is, for example, Palestinian Prime Minister Salam Fayyad's ambitious two-year plan, *Palestine: Ending the Occupation, Establishing the State*. This framework calls for Palestinians to build economic, political, and security institutions within the West Bank to incubate a Palestinian state in preparation for the end of the Israeli occupation. Fayyad has been bold in advancing his program, taking it to the prestigious international gathering of the World Economic Forum in Switzerland as well as to Israel's most important annual policy conference at Herzliya. There is also the growing phenomenon of nonviolent demonstrations against the Israeli wall that runs through the West Bank. Some of these protests have drawn Israeli peace activists and other Western supporters. Certain protesters have been creative in their efforts to project a Palestinian message, with some Palestinians painting themselves blue, casting themselves as members of the Na'vi tribe from the film *Avatar*. These Palestinians make the case that, like the Na'vi, they are indigenous people engaged in legitimate resistance to oppression.

In the face of the continued denial of Palestinian rights, the fissures from conflict run deep throughout the Arab World. Many Arabs living thousands of miles from Palestine—and far from any immediate Israeli threat—claim the Palestinians' story as their own. We've already seen polls suggesting how important the Arab–Israeli conflict is in geopolitical terms, but simply asking, "How important is the Palestinian issue to you personally" shows just how deep support for the Palestinians goes. Two out of three Moroccans said it was important, and that was the lowest level of support among Arab populations polled. Most countries gave support of 85% or higher (see Table 13.1).

This issue has profound personal resonance because of the shared Arabic identity with Palestinians. But on a more political level, Arabs also view the Palestinian issue as the "greatest obstacle to peace and stability in the Middle East." In other words, majorities in almost every country polled see the resolution of the Arab–Israeli conflict as the linchpin to a brighter political future (see Table 13.2).

Given the paramount importance of this issue, it is heartening—and indeed almost amazing—that ongoing frustrations with U.S.-backed Israeli policies don't prevent Arabs from supporting a peaceful, two-state solu-

TABLE 13.1   IMPORTANCE OF THE PALESTINIAN ISSUE (in %)

Using a scale from 1 to 5, where 1 is not important and 5 is extremely important,
please tell me how important the Palestinian issue is to you personally.

	Morocco	Egypt	Lebanon	Jordan	Saudi Arabia	UAE
Important	66	76	88	90	88	85
Not important	19	12	7	4	12	2

Source: Zogby International, *Six-Nation Arab Opinion Poll*, November 1–18, 2009. Sample size: 3,989 adults.

Note: "Important" is the aggregation of responses of 4 and 5. "Not important" is the aggregation of responses of 1 and 2. Percentages do not add to 100% because numbers were rounded, and the percentage responding "not sure" (3 on the scale) has not been included.

TABLE 13.2   GREATEST OBSTACLES TO PEACE AND STABILITY IN THE MIDDLE EAST (in %)

Of the following, what do you believe is the greatest obstacle to peace and stability in
the Middle East?

	Morocco	Egypt	Lebanon	Jordan	Saudi Arabia	UAE
U.S. interference in the Middle East	38	37	10	9	40	10
Lack of democracy	3	5	11	15	7	7
Economic inequality	4	3	11	4	6	11
Israeli–Palestinian conflict	53	54	58	69	47	59
Iran	1	<1	7	2	1	12
Religion	<1	1	2	1	—	2
Not sure	1	1	2	1	—	—

Source: Zogby International, *Arab Opinions on President Obama's First 100 Days: A Six-Nation Survey*, April 21–May 11, 2009. Sample size: 4,087 adults.

Note: Percentages do not add up to 100% because numbers were rounded.

tion. However, as our polling shows, many remain unconvinced that Israel is inclined to accept such an outcome (see Table 13.3).

Likewise, despite more than sixty years of almost continuous conflict and disappointment, many Arabs remain hopeful that they will see peace in their lifetime (see Table 13.4).

TABLE 13.3   PREPARED FOR PEACE? (in %)

Which of the following statements is closer to your view?

1. *I am prepared for a just and comprehensive peace with Israel if Israel is willing to return all of the territories occupied in the 1967 war including East Jerusalem, and the Arab governments should put more effort into this.*
2. *I am prepared for a just and comprehensive peace with Israel if Israel is willing to return all of the territories occupied in the 1967 war including East Jerusalem, but I don't believe the Israelis will ever give up these territories peacefully.*
3. *Even if the Israelis return all of the territories occupied in 1967 peacefully, the Arabs should continue to fight Israel no matter what the outcome.*

	Morocco	Egypt	Lebanon	Jordan	Saudi Arabia	UAE
(1) Prepared ... and	14	14	34	36	37	10
(2) Prepared ... but	49	52	47	49	44	70
(3) No	6	8	18	13	18	8
(4) Not sure	22	14	2	2	1	12

Source: Zogby International, *Six-Nation Arab Opinion Poll*, November 1–18, 2009. Sample size: 3,989 adults.

TABLE 13.4   HOW LIKELY IS PEACE IN YOUR LIFETIME? (in %)

How likely do you think it is that there will be peace in the region in your lifetime?

	Morocco	Egypt	Lebanon	Jordan	Saudi Arabia	UAE
Very likely	27	24	16	18	19	25
Somewhat likely	50	53	60	61	63	12
Not at all likely	20	19	23	18	18	60

Source: Zogby International, *Six-Nation Arab Opinion Poll*, November 1–18, 2009. Sample size: 3,989 adults.

Given the centrality of the Arab–Israeli conflict in a region in which the United States is heavily invested, we must figure out how to reconcile these two divergent narratives and begin the process of healing the wounds. In the earliest days of his administration, President Obama inspired great hope among Arabs that he intended to do this. On his second full day in office in January 2009, while announcing George Mitchell as his special envoy in the Middle East, Obama stunned Arab audiences by showing respect for both sides of this conflict. The president spoke with compassion about Palestinian needs and acknowledged both Israeli and Palestinian suffering:

> Now, just as the terror of rocket fire aimed at innocent Israelis is intolerable, so, too, is a future without hope for Palestinians. Our hearts go out to Palestinian civilians who are in need of immediate food, clean water, and basic medical care, and who've faced suffocating poverty for too long. . . . As part of a lasting cease-fire, Gaza's border crossings should be open to allow the flow of aid and commerce. . . . The United States will fully support an international donor's conference to seek short-term humanitarian assistance and long-term reconstruction for the Palestinian economy.[10]

President Obama also showed other signs that he might give credence to the Palestinian narrative of dispossession, urging Israel to stop what he called "illegitimate" settlement construction. In turn, he called on the Palestinians to control violence and anti-Israeli incitement. Obama also urged other Arab states to make gestures of normalization toward Israel. That is the right way to insert America into both narratives, but doing so requires consistency, and on that front the Obama team has stumbled more than once.

The first indication Arabs received that the Obama administration might let them down came in September 2009 during the meeting of the United Nations General Assembly in New York. It was here that the U.S. president appeared to back away from pressing the Israelis to halt settlement construction as a way of building trust with Palestinians before the start of negotiations. Perhaps because Obama realized that the Israelis would not accept a total freeze on settlements, the president publicly called on Israelis and Palestinians to begin talks "without preconditions."[11] What the United States failed to consider was how important this issue was to the Palestinian side. Israeli settlements have more than tripled in size since the signing of the Oslo Accords in 1993. Without a complete and verifiable freeze, Palestinians lack confidence in Israeli intentions to withdraw from the occupied territories.

Then, one month later, in October 2009, the U.S. administration again disappointmented the Arab World when it summarily rejected the findings of a U.N. Human Rights Commission report on war crimes committed by both sides during the Gaza War. The United States pressured the Palestinian leadership to withdraw its backing for the report, causing the Palestinians to lose support with their own public that wanted both Israel and Hamas to be held accountable for their actions.

This let down was compounded when in November 2009, Secretary of State Hillary Clinton enthusiastically accepted an Israeli offer of a ten-month, limited "restraint" in West Bank settlement construction. The loopholes implied by the term "restraint" made it clear that the United States was backing down from its earlier demands and that this would be a blow to the Palestinians.

Not surprisingly, then, hope in Obama, which had been so high early in his term, declined somewhat by the time of our 2009 year-end survey of Arab opinion. Most Arabs, with the exception of Saudis, were no longer confident that this administration could make a critical difference in finding a solution (see Table 13.5).

Even more telling, two separate Palestinian polls conducted during the same period found even less confidence in the Obama administration's efforts. Of those surveyed, 87% believed that the United States was not committed to the peace process, and only 21% thought that the Obama administration was dedicated to helping Palestinians end the occupation. Just 36% of Palestinians saw the Obama administration as representing positive change when compared with the Bush administration (60% saw no change at all).[12]

The Obama administration's early miscues in the Middle East resulted from the same problems we have seen before. Despite an early promise of being different, the Obama administration sometimes failed to listen equally to Israeli and Palestinian narratives and give equal weight to the sensibilities of both, a situation they attempted to remedy in March of 2010 when the administration confronted and condemned Israel's settlement program in occupied East Jerusalem while making clear the United States' continued commitment to Israel's security. But as our April 2010 poll demonstrated, this effort had only marginal success with a wary Arab public. In that survey we found a significant decline in confidence, with only one-quarter of Saudis, one in ten Egyptians, Lebanese, and Jor-

TABLE 13.5   EVALUATION OF OBAMA ADMINISTRATION'S HANDLING OF THE
ISRAELI–PALESTINIAN ISSUE (in %)

*The Obama administration will be evenhanded when dealing with the
Israeli–Palestinian issue.*

	Morocco	Egypt	Lebanon	Jordan	Saudi Arabia	UAE
Agree	35	42	24	29	62	13
Disagree	41	43	52	38	26	68
No U.S. president will be evenhanded	20	11	20	18	9	19

Source: Zogby International, *Arab Opinions on President Obama's First 100 Days: A Six-Nation
Survey,* April 21–May 11, 2009. Sample size: 4,087 adults.

Note: "Agree" is the aggregation of "strongly agree" and "somewhat agree." "Disagree" is the
aggregation of "strongly disagree" and "somewhat disagree." Percentages do not add to 100%
because numbers were rounded, and the percentage responding "not familiar" or "not sure" has
not been included.

danians, and less than one per cent of Palestinians indicating that they
now had "more confidence in the ability of the Obama Administration to
be evenhanded in dealing with the Israeli–Palestinian conflict."[13]

In the end, what is required is not choosing one side over another or favoring one people's heartbreaking story of victimhood. Instead, Americans
must loudly demand what polls suggest they already favor: a U.S. policy that
demonstrates a balanced approach to peacemaking. When asked whether
U.S. policy should "lean toward Israel," "lean toward Palestine," or "steer a
middle course," a strong majority of Americans favors striking a balance. And
when asked which is most important—"relations with Israel," "relations with
Arab nations," or "both are equally important"—an even greater majority
says that both are equally important (see Tables 13.6 and 13.7).

In the early years of the Oslo peace process, I was not alone in believing
that the time was right to end the Israeli–Palestinian conflict. Following
the signing of the accords in September 1993 on the White House lawn,
Arab Americans, American Jews, and leaders across the world shared the
belief that the conflict was ripe for a solution. But to have achieved that

TABLE 13.6   U.S. POLICY FOR PURSUING ISRAELI–PALESTINIAN PEACE

Which describes how the United States should pursue peace?

U.S. policy	Percentage approving
Lean toward Israel	22
Lean toward Palestine	3
Steer a middle course	70

Source: Zogby International, *Poll of American Voters,* November 30–December 8, 2009. Sample size: 1,006 adults.

TABLE 13.7   IMPORTANCE OF U.S. RELATIONS WITH ISRAEL AND ARAB NATIONS

In your view, which is a more important objective for the United States to pursue?

Objective	Percentage approving
U.S. relations with Israel	11
U.S. relations with Arab nations	6
Both are equally important to the United States	80

Source: Zogby International, *Poll of American Voters,* November 30–December 8, 2009. Sample size: 1,006 adults.

goal would have required stronger leadership than was forthcoming at the time. Instead, the cycles of violence, fear, and anger have escalated to the point where it is unlikely that Israeli or Palestinian leaders can, on their own, resolve this problem. That puts an even greater burden on the United States and the West to listen to the voices on both sides and frame policy that respects the narratives and needs of both peoples. No doubt, some will balk, but if U.S.-led peacemaking efforts are to move beyond merely "taking sides," it is important that we change the way we understand this conflict. Until then, there will be no winners, only victims.

In addition, it is critical to consider the observation made by General David Petraeus, commander of the United States Central Command, who noted that failure to resolve this conflict will continue to jeopardize Western interests in the Middle East. Testifying in March of 2010 before the Senate Armed Services Committee, Petraeus said, "The enduring hostilities between Israel and some of its neighbors present distinct challenges to our ability to advance our interests. . . . The conflict foments anti-American sentiment, due to a perception of U.S. favoritism for Israel. Arab anger over the Palestinian question limits the strength and depth of U.S. partnerships with governments and peoples . . . and weakens the legitimacy of moderate regimes in the Arab world. Meanwhile, al-Qaeda and other militant groups exploit that anger to mobilize support. The conflict also gives Iran influence in the Arab world."[14]

14
ARAB AMERICANS
BRIDGING THE DIVIDE

IN 2005 AND 2006, I was invited to Prague, Warsaw, Berlin, and London to speak on the situation of Arab and Muslim immigrants in the United States. Concern was growing in Europe that the deepening alienation of its diverse Muslim communities was leading some young people into extremism. Because I had spent a professional lifetime bringing Arab Americans into the U.S. political mainstream and also frequently interacting with Arabs and Muslims in Europe, I knew both the problems my own community faced in the United States and the profound differences between the American and European experiences.

I've met third-generation Kurds in Germany, Algerians in France, and Pakistanis in the United Kingdom who have all complained that they remain on the margins of their societies. They may become citizens and, in some cases, highly successful ones. In too many instances, however, they are still considered "Turks," "Arabs," or "Pakis," in large measure owing to the conjoining of ethnicity and nationality across Europe.

America, by contrast, is a never-ending experiment in *inclusion,* unique as a nation of immigrants. Men and women who have come from the ends of the Earth have, within a generation, become Americans. Waves of new arrivals have brought varying cultures, experiences, and religions to U.S. shores. The absorption of immigrants into the mainstream does not erase or dilute those differences but enriches the texture and the very meaning of America. It is this openness to diversity that is one of the enduring and positive qualities of the evolving American character.

To be sure, nativist movements are no stranger to America. Since the country's founding, there have always been those who argued in favor of the dominance of one race, ethnicity, or religion. These groups sought to close the doors, shut down the experiment, and limit the ongoing expansion of freedom. During the past century, there were pressures either to keep out immigrants or to demean the newest Americans. But in the end, the "open America" has always won out, with diverse communities of immigrants becoming citizens, transforming the nation, and making America unimaginable without them. However, this has not happened without some hardship and struggle.

At the turn of the last century, for example, many people viewed Irish immigrants as practically subhuman. In the 1920s, Italians were scorned, and some were even lynched in the South. Jews were victims of discrimination, as were Poles and Eastern Europeans, who were looked upon with suspicion and subjected to violence by nativist movements of "real Americans." By 1960, when John F. Kennedy overcame voters' doubts about his Catholic faith to emerge as the elected icon of a young, sophisticated, and idealistic nation, the country was already changing. Recall, though, that even in that watershed election, many African Americans couldn't cast a vote for (or against) Kennedy. All this is true, but America's story is inconceivable without the contributions of African Americans, American Jews, Irish, Italians, and so many others who have irrevocably written themselves into the nation's history.

Arab Americans, too, have faced discrimination. The post–World War I era brought efforts in Congress to limit immigration from southern European and Asian countries. Because most Arab Americans traced their ancestry to Lebanon or Syria (Mediterranean countries on the Asian continent), quotas for both were severely limited. In defending his position on quotas, Senator David Reed (D-PA, 1922–1935), the author of the immigration bill that bore his name, decried the presence of what he called "Syrian trash" coming into the United States. In 1929, my mom's best friend, my Aunt Lila Mandour, wrote an angry letter to Reed, taking him to task. Reed responded:

> I did not say that all Syrians are "trash." I said that in former years we had received "the trash of the Mediterranean," and that much of it had come from Syrian and Turkish provinces. I do think that in our immigration of recent years we have admitted a great many undesirables from the Mediterranean region, among them some Syrians who, unlike yourself and some other members of your race, could not be classified as good immigrant stock.[1]

Like Aunt Lila, my mother believed in standing up to this kind of bigotry and wanted her generation to be proud of its heritage. When she was just twenty-one, my mother wrote an article in an Arab American magazine about the need for the Syrian Americans—as Arab Americans were largely called then—to be proud of their heritage. She also criticized the behavior of some of her generation, writing:

> [M]any of the young generation, and even some of the old, who are in this country only a few years, are ashamed to acknowledge that they are Syrians. They refuse to learn the Arabic language, and if they know it they are reluctant, through shame, to be heard speaking it. They shun Syrian companionship and become inadvertent to Syrian ideals and customs, thinking that by doing so they are becoming Americanized. How, then, can we ever aspire to win the admiration and esteem of our American friends if we do not respect ourselves?[2]

Mom was absolutely right, and her message still inspires me. Indeed, there have been more than a few times in my life when her words have helped me.

In the late 1960s when I was a graduate student at Temple University in Philadelphia, I took the stage at an anti–Vietnam War rally. In the middle of my speech, another student started screaming: "Why are they letting the Arab talk?" At first, I didn't even know he was yelling at me; I was stunned when I figured it out.

A few years later, my heckler had formed a Jewish Defense League (JDL) chapter on campus, and I was a teaching assistant in the religion department. One day, I received a letter that threatened, "Arab dog you will die," warning me not to set foot on campus again. When I went to teach my class the next day, several JDL members showed up hell-bent on violence; they were eventually removed by campus security. Though still puzzled by all this, I was starting to get the point.

Let me be clear: I did not consider myself an Arab. There were Arab students on campus—people from Lebanon, Syria, and Egypt. They were among my friends, but I was born in Utica, New York, and though proud of my Arab heritage, I've always considered myself an Arab American. However, for some of my fellow citizens, the "Arab" seems to cancel out the "American."

Over the years, my ethnic background came up in other situations as well. In 1972, I went for a job interview in the history and philosophy department at Shippensburg State College, now Shippensburg University, in south-central Pennsylvania. I was also qualified to teach about the Middle East and Islam, but the interviewers made it clear I wouldn't be teaching either of those subjects. They told me that it would be too controversial to have me in that role. A few years later, while teaching a special course on the Middle East at nearby Dickinson College, an administrator asked me if I was interested in teaching more courses and—hint, hint—if I would be able to help them get "Arab" funding to cover it.

These two anecdotes highlight what was curious about being Arab American. Being of Arab descent set off political warning lights in some situations and made me a potential money magnet in others. Whether born of bigotry, ignorance, or insensitivity, this legacy was unfortunately not something I was able to leave behind in the 1970s. Sometimes it is expressed in the hate mail I receive at my office. On other occasions, it comes from those who ought to know better, as in this on-air exchange with John McLaughlin, the host of the NBC political program *One on One*, in 1999:

> McLaughlin: Don't you want presence and authority in Jerusalem as the capital of your forthcoming Palestinian state?
> Zogby: Well, it's not my forthcoming Palestinian state . . .
> McLaughlin: Well you're an Arab . . .
> Zogby: I'm an American citizen. My capital is here in Washington.[3]

Let me hasten to add that the unique process of becoming American is often not understood in the Arab World either. In early September 2002, I was invited to address the foreign ministers' meeting of the Arab League at their headquarters in Cairo, Egypt. They wanted to hear firsthand about the post-9/11 experiences of Arab Americans. I used the opportunity to challenge them to engage the American public more directly to help combat the anti-Arab and anti-Muslim stereotypes that had been fueled by the terrorist attacks. I then warned that there was the growing danger of a war with Iraq. I chastised the Iraqis, noting that their bluster and stubborn insistence on noncompliance with weapons inspectors were not helping to defuse the situation. "Complain," I said, "if you feel you must, but comply." When one minister argued that this was not fair, I replied that "unfortunately politics is not about fair. If it were, the Indians would be running America." At that, the Libyan foreign minister said, "You sound like an American." To which my friend Prince Saud al-Faisal, the Saudi foreign minister, said, "Exactly, that's what he is."[4]

Saud's gentle rebuke apparently did not register with everyone, because in February 2009, I received an invitation from the Arab League to speak at a conference of "Arab expatriates." I politely declined the offer, saying that I could not accept because I am not an expatriate. I am an American.

This annoying need to remind others that I am American, born and bred, describes an uncomfortable reality I share with many other Arab Americans born and raised in the West, especially those of my generation. Growing up inspired by the American values we all cherish, I was shaped by my involvement with the peace and civil rights movements. But applying what I learned from these experiences to my empathy for the people of the Arab World has made me politically threatening to some. Of course, I realize and accept that my participation in teaching, activism, and political causes has made me a lightning rod for criticism and hatred in a way that an Arab American businessmen or doctor might not encounter. But as frustrating and painful as the journey has sometimes been, it is a challenge I accept because ultimately I believe that hearing Arab American voices will make America stronger and smarter. As Mom put it all those years ago, "How can we ever aspire to win the admiration and esteem of our American friends if we do not respect ourselves?"

Today, on most levels, Arab Americans are fully integrated into American life. Data show Arab Americans among the nation's leaders in income and education; and in recent decades, we've produced three four-star generals, four governors, five senators, and more than a dozen members of Congress. The last three U.S. presidents have each had an Arab American in his cabinet.

Beneath the surface, though, the picture is less rosy. In the post-9/11 period, many recent immigrant Arab Americans have faced hatred and discrimination. Many were profiled by law enforcement, resulting in widespread fear among the broader Arab American community. And many, including Darrell Issa—a Lebanese American who serves as a Republican congressman from California—and myself, have had their lives threatened by hate crimes. In three separate instances, individuals who threatened my life in the years since 9/11 have been arrested by the FBI and convicted for their threats.[5]

Thankfully, the story doesn't end there. Soon after the September 11 attacks, President Bush spoke out in defense of Arab Americans, as did members of both houses of Congress. I will personally never forget how humbled I was walking into a Democratic Party executive committee meeting in New York City after 9/11 to find my party voting in support of a resolution denouncing hate and discrimination against Arab Americans. And in communities across the country, churches, civic groups, and ordinary citizens stood up and defended their Arab American and American Muslim neighbors.[6]

Despite this progress, Arab American voices are still largely excluded in one area where they can make a unique and significant contribution: bridging the gap between our country and the nations of the Middle East. When I first came to Washington in the mid-1970s, I began the Palestinian Human Rights Campaign (PHRC) to advocate for victims of torture and political prisoners. I would have considered working through or with an established human rights group, but because of the domestic politics involved, the American chapter of Amnesty International would not adopt these cases. They were afraid it would cost them support. Although Amnesty is the world's premier human rights group, only its London chapter will deal with Palestinian victims.

So I started the PHRC, relying mainly on church-based support with strong endorsements from the United Church of Christ and the Methodists. I was fortunate enough to tap into a lot of the civil rights and peace movement leadership that had surrounded Reverend Martin Luther King, including influential people like Reverends Walter Fauntroy and Joseph Lowery, as well as legendary folk singer Pete Seeger.

Having gotten our organization up and running, I applied for membership in the Coalition for a New Foreign Military Policy, an umbrella organization for other advocacy groups. The vote was overwhelmingly in favor of our application. However, the three groups that voted against our entry threatened to leave the coalition if we were admitted. These were groups that had been very active in the civil rights movement and remain committed to other kinds of liberal advocacy, but they absolutely refused to let in a Palestinian human rights group.

I returned three years later, even pledging not to raise the issue of the Middle East during coalition meetings. However, I said I would debate freely if the topic were raised by others. Again, our membership was denied because of fears that "letting the Arabs in" would undercut the group's congressional lobbying on, say, Guatemala or El Salvador.

Dealing with these organizations wasn't the only situation in which simply being an Arab American advocating for more understanding of Arab concerns created deep problems. Two and a half decades ago, I opened up the *Washington Post* and saw in the television listings that one of Sunday's interview programs would feature a discussion of the Israeli–Palestinian conflict with "terrorism experts." These were individuals who were part of what was the emerging cottage industry of pro-Israel advocates promoting themselves as "experts" on all things Arab and Palestinian. By then I was the founder and director of the American Arab Anti-Discrimination Committee, whose mission was to fight defamation and promote greater balance in our nation's discussion of Middle East issues. So I called the show's producer to propose that additional voices be included in the conversation. I was told they knew my perspective but were looking for "experts."

The point I gathered was that if you were somebody else, you could be an expert—a dispassionate observer. But if you were an Arab American, you had a "point of view."

This reaction crystallized for me what it meant to run an Arab advocacy group. It wasn't just that annoying sense of someone not *really* listening; it was, at times, being shamelessly and thoroughly excluded from the discussion. I was not begrudging or even questioning the invited guests' right to speak, but they were no better equipped than an informed Arab American to explain and analyze Arab or Palestinian motives, opinions, and desires. And no one else was being asked to provide that side of the story to Americans, to our country's detriment.

This problem of political exclusion takes other forms as well. For decades, individuals of Arab descent had been active in American politics—running for elective office and serving in all branches of government. When they organized as Lebanese or Syrian-Lebanese, they were accepted. But beginning in the 1970s, as an all-inclusive and politically aware Arab American community brought together its diverse parts, difficulties resulted. Although the first formal acceptance of Arab Americans did not happen until 1984 when Jesse Jackson and Ronald Reagan formed Arab American committees to support their candidacies, the problems of exclusion did not end there. In 1987, I documented dozens of instances in which politicians from both parties returned contributions from respected Arab American business leaders and rejected the endorsements or inclusion of Arab Americans in their campaigns.[7]

When we organized the Arab American Institute (AAI) in 1985, it was precisely to deal with this problem of exclusion. Like so many other ethnic communities before us, we sought through voter registration and political engagement to break down barriers. We wanted to ensure that Arab Americans were empowered and that our voices would be heard in critical policy debates.

In 1988, again under the umbrella provided by Jesse Jackson's presidential campaign, we elected more than 400 Arab Americans as delegates to state party conventions and more than 50 to the national conventions. Working together with allies in the progressive Jewish community, we went to the Democratic National Convention in Atlanta with a platform plank that called for "mutual recognition, territorial compromise, and self-determination for both Israelis and Palestinians."[8] The language in our proposal actually came from an ad that had been signed by numerous Jewish intellectuals and run in the New York Times. But the resistance to even opening a debate on the issue was enormous.[9] At the convention, when I made my case to a Jewish leader who had signed the New York Times ad, he said, "When I signed the ad, I knew what I meant. I'm not sure you mean the same thing."[10]

He never clarified exactly what he thought I *did* mean. But again, there was that strange sense of being considered an alien by my own countrymen. If I were to list the positions held by the majority of Arab Americans on most Middle East issues, they would not be that different from those of most American Jews or members of the Israeli left. As Table 14.1 shows, both groups support a two-state solution and want security for both Israel and Palestine. Arab Americans and American Jews also oppose settlements and want deeper American engagement in pressing for a negotiated solution to

TABLE 14.1   ARAB AND JEWISH AMERICAN SUPPORT FOR MIDDLE EAST ISSUES (in %)

Do you support . . .	Jewish Americans	Arab Americans
Israelis' right to a secure, independent state?	98	88
Palestinians' right to a secure, independent state?	90	96
A negotiated peace that establishes two independent states and resolves Jerusalem and refugees?	87	94
Freezing settlements?	63	77
The Arab League peace initiative?	70	82

Source: Zogby International, *Seeing Eye to Eye: A Survey of Jewish American and Arab American Public Opinion,* survey commissioned by Americans For Peace Now and The Arab American Institute, May 22–23, 2007. Sample size: 501 adults.

the conflict. Nonetheless, being of Arab descent somehow casts a suspicious light on our opinions and scrambles our words into some bizarre code.

Throughout my adult life, this silencing of alternative voices on Middle East issues has been a deeply troubling constant. It has affected so many of my colleagues, and not only Arab Americans. American Jews who have a balanced understanding of these issues and dedicated foreign-service officers who have been accused of becoming "Arabists" have also been sidelined. All this has been hurtful, of course, but in a larger sense, it has also been damaging to the American policy debate, denying the entry of new voices and perspectives into the discussion of critical problems facing America in the Arab World.

There would, of course, still be an America if the country had refused to fully embrace Irish, Japanese, Jewish, German, Mexican, Hawaiian, or African Americans as fully American. But were the United States populated solely by descendants of the English settlers who first arrived here in the early 1600s, it would be a smaller, considerably poorer, and markedly less vibrant place.

Likewise, full integration of Arab Americans into all aspects of political life should be a priority of U.S. policy. Many of the same prejudices that prevent complete acceptance of Arab Americans into U.S. society also create and foster costly blind spots in U.S. foreign policy in the Middle East. These prejudices can be addressed by increasing education about and awareness of Arab language, culture, and history. Such efforts would go a long way toward defeating both the resistance Arab Americans run up against in their day-to-day lives *and* the larger strategic blunders the United States makes abroad.

Arab Americans also can play a crucial role in America's quest to improve and promote U.S. policy overseas. They can help explain the realities of American life and the possibilities that the United States offers to the Arab World. Likewise, cultural insights and linguistic abilities are desperately needed for everything from economic development initiatives to business negotiations to fighting terrorism. Incorporating Arab American input into U.S. policy will make us markedly smarter actors in the region. Among the many critical areas where increased Arab American assistance can immediately be employed is in refocusing our efforts for a lasting peace between Israelis and Palestinians.

The Irish Troubles of the past century had more than a few things in common with the Israeli–Palestinian conflict: both featured age-old battles over land between two seemingly irreconcilable groups; both were driven by religious differences and completely different narratives. Like Israel today, the United Kingdom held an overwhelming military advantage. As with some Palestinians, some Irish groups utilized bombings to terrorize British civilians. The difference in American reaction is this: Americans were much more aware of the stories told by both the British and the Irish.

It's true that U.S. history already held close parallels to the Irish quest for freedom—America's foundational moment was throwing off the British yoke. But our awareness of and sympathy for the Irish story was facilitated by the large number of proud Irish Americans who financed and publicly advocated for Ireland's cause. Because of this vocal presence of Irish Americans, the United Kingdom could not dominate the narrative struggle, as Israel now does. Although the U.S. government correctly criticized the Irish Republican Army and similar groups for terrorist attacks, the Irish people could never be pigeonholed as "just a bunch of terrorists." And when President Bill Clinton enlisted the support of Irish Americans in the peacemaking effort, they proved to be an invaluable moderating force in advancing the peace process and finally, in 1998, achieving what has thus far proved to be a lasting accord.

On the opening page of the U.S. passport, that prized possession of many American travelers, it states quite clearly: "The Secretary of State of the United States of America hereby requests all whom it may concern to permit the citizen/national of the United States named herein to pass without delay or hindrance and in case of need to give all lawful aid and protection."

This is a simple statement but one that the United States has failed to uphold and defend when Arab Americans travel to Israel and the Palestinian lands. Although the United States and Israel are among the closest of allies, Arab *Americans*—and particularly those of Palestinian descent—are routinely treated as second class by the Jewish state. Over the past several decades, these U.S. citizens have been detained at entry and exit, humiliated, interrogated, and in some instances forced to surrender their U.S. passports. This treatment has even been directed at some Arab Americans with U.S. diplomatic passports.

This is behavior that one might expect from some past Cold War adversary, not one of America's closest allies. Although the U.S. government intervened in some cases, for years it refused to unequivocally rebuke Israeli behavior. Worse, in tacit acknowledgment of this shameful attitude, the State Department issued a travel advisory warning Americans who wanted to visit their Palestinian relatives that they could not expect Israel to treat them as U.S. citizens.

Finally, in 2008, in response to my repeated complaints to then Secretary of State Condoleezza Rice, I received the forceful reply one might expect from the world's sole superpower: "Our view," said a State Department spokesperson, "is that an American citizen is an American citizen is an American citizen. There are no second classes. . . . You have a blue American passport, you should be treated like an American citizen. . . . We expect all American citizens to be accorded the rights that any other American citizen would be accorded."[11] It had taken thirty years, but I could add only, "Amen."

My advocacy of Arab American issues and my role in founding and directing AAI have brought me many rewards, tangible and intangible. One of the nicest has been the chance to know and work with people at the highest levels of American government. When I met then Vice President Al Gore in 1993—he had tapped me to head up, with former Congressman Mel Levine, a project to promote businesses in the West Bank and Gaza— he asked me to tell him a little about myself. I related the trajectory of my family's story and how remarkable it was that the son of an immigrant, who had been born in a one-room stone house in the hills of Lebanon, was now sitting in the West Wing office of the vice president of the United States.

I've never lost that feeling of wonder. Nor have I ever forgotten the debt my family and I owe America, the country that provided us—and many other Arab Americans—the opportunity to excel. I grew up proudly reading letters that my godfather, Faris, and my Uncle Albert sent back from the European theater where they served during World War II. Reading them, I was able to literally trace their path across Europe—even walking into the camps they had helped liberate.

The day after my mother died in 1998, I got a call from President Clinton. Like me, Clinton had been largely raised by his mom, and both our mothers had left big impressions on us. I also received calls from Vice President Gore and Reverend Jesse Jackson, who reached me at a low point and offered a pastor's wisdom in consolation. "Don't give in," he said. "The measure of her success as a mother will be your ability to rise above the pain to continue to do the great things she inspired you to do."[12]

That is exactly what my mother, a proud Arab American, would have said. Likewise, the measure of America's success as a multiethnic democracy lies in its continued ability to fully integrate the talents and skills of various people and accept the dignity of their heritage. Doing that will point us toward a more unified, smarter, and stronger America—a country true to its promise of inclusion. The United States can still be a model from which Europe and the Arab World can learn how to broaden their national self-definitions and incorporate all their citizens. In the end inclusion is the antidote to alienation and the lure of extremism.

PART 4
GETTING IT RIGHT

15
WHAT GOVERNMENT CAN DO

IN JUNE 2009, WHEN President Obama traveled to the heart of the Arab World and delivered his historic address to Muslims from a podium at Cairo University, he was taking an important first step in getting it right. His appeal for understanding, partnership, and honest dialogue was a nuanced but resolute call to move beyond the stereotypes and distortions that have often complicated and derailed American involvement in the Middle East. In so doing, President Obama appeared to be setting a course away from past failures. This represented a change of direction celebrated not only in the Arab World but also in European capitals, where leaders and the public alike were eager to see an end to American unilateralism and a new approach to the Middle East.

As he had in his critically acclaimed 2008 Philadelphia speech on the tensions and misunderstandings that have long characterized America's history of race relations, in his Cairo address Obama took on the wide gulf separating the West and Islam. Just as the Philadelphia speech had been directed at both white and African American audiences, his remarks in Cairo posed challenges to both Western and Muslim listeners worldwide.

In Cairo, and in his earlier interview with Al Arabiya, the president spoke of the need to listen in the Middle East rather than dictate: "We meet at a time of tension between the United States and Muslims around the world—tension rooted in historical forces that go beyond any current policy debate. . . . [T]ension has been fed by colonialism that denied rights and opportunities to many Muslims, and a Cold War in which Muslim-majority countries were too often treated as proxies without regard to their own aspirations."[1]

The president then recounted how the terror of 9/11 was not merely a cause of these strains but also, to a degree, a symptom of the climate of misunderstanding and fear that has long characterized Arab–American relations. "Violent extremists," he pointed out, "have exploited these tensions in a small but potent minority of Muslims. The attacks of September 11th, 2001 and the continued efforts of these extremists to engage in violence against civilians has led some in my country to view Islam as inevitably hostile not only to America and Western countries, but also to human rights. This has bred more fear and mistrust."[2]

Obama then called for an end to diplomacy built on misunderstanding and thus controlled by the forces of violence. "So long as our relationship is defined by our differences, we will empower those who sow hatred rather than peace, and who promote conflict rather than the cooperation that can help all of our people achieve justice and prosperity. This cycle of suspicion and discord must end."[3]

Once he had established the problems that have historically clouded the West's relations with Muslims and, by extension, much of the Arab World, the president spoke of his commitment to remaking this partnership: it would be "one based on mutual interest and mutual respect; and one based upon the truth that America and Islam are not exclusive, and need not be in competition."[4]

For his part, the president pledged to "fight against negative stereotypes of Islam wherever they appear."[5] At the same time, he challenged Muslims to reject anti-Americanism. "Just as Muslims do not fit a crude stereotype, America is not the crude stereotype of a self-interested empire. The United States has been one of the greatest sources of progress that the world has ever known."[6]

Central to Obama's argument for a new partnership was the simple acceptance that in today's globalized world, all of our fates are entangled. "For we have learned from recent experience," he said, "that when a financial system weakens in one country, prosperity is hurt everywhere."[7]

Obama called for both sides to move beyond the pitfalls of past actions: "whatever we think of the past, we must not be prisoners of it. Our problems must be dealt with through partnership; progress must be shared."[8] And finally, he noted the limitations of even his impressive rhetorical abilities: "No single speech can eradicate years of mistrust. . . .

Words alone cannot meet the needs of our people. These needs will be met only if we act boldly in the years ahead."⁹ How right he was.

As a public address, the Cairo speech was very effective. Across the Arab World our polling showed expectations toward the United States were raised dramatically, maybe too high. In Europe, the speech was cited by the Nobel Committee as one of the reasons Obama was deemed worthy of receiving its prestigious Peace Prize. But as the president's stated goals ran into the profound challenges presented by the spread of extremism, the instability of Afghanistan and Pakistan, and the hardening of positions on both sides of the Israeli–Arab divide, reality set in, and Arab hopes were deflated by the lack of change. Meanwhile, at home, the president's outreach was confronted almost immediately by a deep partisan divide and accusations that he had gone "soft" on confronting terror and extremism.

All that, in a way, was to be expected—the soaring hopes, the deflated expectations, and highly partisan reactions. But just because change won't be easy doesn't make getting it right impossible or any less of an imperative. In the next chapter, I'll cite examples of private entities—nongovernmental organizations, businesses, media figures, and individuals—that are helping improve and refine our understanding of Arabs and their world. The following are public-sector initiatives that are doing the same thing.

THE IRAQ STUDY GROUP

No clearer example exists of how the United States has gotten it wrong with Arabs than in the way it led coalition partners into the war in Iraq. Even as the world's attention now shifts to Afghanistan, Iran, and other hotspots, Iraq remains a challenge that cannot be ignored. Getting into Iraq was relatively easy: the U.S.-led effort was able to invade and occupy Iraq on its own terms, without the involvement of Iraq's neighbors. Getting out has proven to be another matter entirely, one that will require the active engagement and cooperation of countries in the region.

During the 2008 presidential campaign, then candidate Obama repeatedly rejected calls to abandon Iraq, insisting instead that we be "as careful getting out as we were careless getting in."¹⁰ Now, as the clock counts down on the U.S. military departure date, there is a limited window in which to craft a responsible exit. The key concern to keep in mind is not the date the troops will leave, but what will be done between now and then. The best guidelines for withdrawal from Iraq remain those spelled out in the recommendations of the Iraq Study Group, a thoughtful, bipartisan panel created by Congress in March 2006 and led by veteran hands James Baker, a former secretary of state, and former Congressman Lee Hamilton.

Despite the best efforts of many Iraqi leaders, the country is fractured, with 20% of its population either refugees or internally displaced. Strong sectarian and ethnic divisions have left Iraq prone to renewed civil conflict and vulnerable to the machinations of other countries seeking to exploit these differences as they work to advance their own interests. The Iraq Study Group calls for establishing a regional security framework in the form of a contact group anchored by Turkey and Saudi Arabia, with Syria, Jordan, and Kuwait also involved. Most controversially, Iran must also by necessity be included in this group.[11] Although the West is right to confront Iran over its nuclear program and challenge its regional meddling, Iran cannot be excluded from efforts to stabilize the future of Iraq. Iran is, in fact, already quite involved with its neighbor. Therefore, it is far better for Iran to be sitting around a table working with the rest of Iraq's neighbors than manipulating events through the back door. Because Iraq's internal political situation remains fragile, with the potential for domestic tensions to spill over beyond its borders, the creation of a regional security framework could be a significant force for maintaining the peace.

And finally, even with U.S. combat forces out of Iraq, it will be important to understand that Iraq cannot be abandoned. The United States has become a part of Iraq's history and will need to craft a responsible long-term relationship with that country, supporting its reconstruction, development, and national reconciliation.

THE POWELL DOCTRINE AND INCREASED TRANSPARENCY

In 1992, then U.S. Chairman of the Joint Chiefs of Staff Colin Powell enumerated what came to be known as the "Powell Doctrine," a model to be followed in any future military operation.[12] Powell laid out essential preconditions that should be met before sending U.S. troops into combat: military and political objectives should be clearly delineated; there must be a reasonable expectation that Congress and the American people understand the costs of the commitment and will support it for a sustained period; the question of whether military action would be effective and at what cost should be answered first; and all possible peaceful means of resolving the conflict should be exhausted.

The Powell Doctrine was conceived as a universal checklist to be completed before any military engagements begin. However, as a safeguard against military adventurism, it is extremely relevant to the Arab World. For one, the United States' most significant recent armed conflict has been fought in the region. Second, because the Arab World remains misunderstood territory, it is difficult for Congress, much less the American people, to fully comprehend the costs and responsibilities of a military commitment in a place many Americans can't even locate on a map. Without a doubt, the preconditions of the Powell Doctrine were not met in Iraq, and I fear they have not been fully considered as the United States ramps up its mission in Afghanistan.

For this reason, I suggest that the Powell Doctrine be extended. With Americans and Europeans so fatigued by wars in Iraq and Afghanistan and wary of future entanglements in other areas, governments more than ever need to ensure that their citizens are involved in the public discussion. Governments also must earn their people's support and do so without resorting to lies and distortions. The best way to guarantee such earnest, long-term support of U.S. troops enmeshed in any future conflict is for Congress to hold open hearings on the goals, costs, and expected commitment of the military campaign. These hearings should include not only government testimony, but also that of nongovernmental organizations and regional experts in order to guarantee a full and open debate.

What's more, these hearings should not only occur prior to military action but continue at regular intervals along the way to review progress. Such public evaluation should not be limited to areas where the country is involved in combat—any engagement in a Middle East hotspot should be thoroughly assessed.

Because of unrest in the United Kingdom over its involvement in the Iraq War, Prime Minister Gordon Brown launched the Iraq Inquiry in July 2009. The Inquiry held a number of public sessions featuring a range of official and nonofficial witnesses in an examination of how and why their country entered the Iraq War and what lessons can be learned from it. Such transparency would have been even more useful and proper *before* committing troops, but Britain's Iraq Inquiry is still an important development that can provide instruction from which other governments can learn.

A perfect model for this type of process in the United States can be found in the series of ten hearings convened in 2008 by Congressman William Delahunt (D-MA), then chairman of the House Foreign Affairs

Subcommittee on International Organizations, Human Rights, and Oversight. These proceedings examined America's image overseas and featured expert witnesses on each of the several regions where U.S. interests are at stake. Following the hearings, Congressman Delahunt issued a comprehensive and insightful report on his subcommittee's findings.[13]

Continued hearings of this sort would create valuable channels for debate and the presentation of contrary views that have too often been swept under the rug when discussing critical Arab World policy issues. In 2005, Senator Richard Durbin (D-IL) took the Senate floor to read aloud a statement by an FBI agent describing the torture of prisoners at Guantanamo Bay. Durbin noted that the techniques described by the agent called to mind those used by repressive regimes, including the Nazis and Soviets.[14] Immediately subjected to attacks by Republicans and largely abandoned by his own Democratic Party, Durbin's courage to call out these abuses has outlasted the torrent of criticism that initially sought to bury him. Indeed, President Obama was elected on a policy of ending torture and closing Guantanamo Bay, and he has taken steps to do both.

In another effort to increase governmental transparency, the U.S. Department of Justice has released the internal memoranda used by the Bush administration to justify the use of "enhanced interrogation techniques" (i.e., torture). These documents describe in disturbing detail the techniques that were to be allowed. But there has been no action taken to hold accountable the officials who wrote these legal opinions. At the same time, the push to close Guantanamo has been slowed by both legal and political complications. Dozens of Guantanamo detainees either hail from countries that do not want to repatriate them or are individuals who cannot easily be tried in court because the evidence against them resulted from coerced confessions. The most likely outcome, at this point, appears to be that the remaining Guantanamo prisoners will be moved to another location and kept in legal limbo—a partial solution that will continue to weaken America in Arab eyes.

PALESTINIAN PROGRESS

Even with the frustrations and policy miscues of the Obama administration, the president was right to recognize early on the centrality of the Arab–Israeli conflict. Obama spoke with compassion about the suffering of Palestinians. Even more impressive, he put his finger on the fear and sense of vulnerability that defines the narratives of both sides and helps sustain the conflict: "The only resolution is for the aspirations of both sides to be met through two states, where Israelis and Palestinians each live in peace and security."[15]

Once again, the key is translating this well-honed rhetorical sketch of the problem into action. It will, of course, not be easy to undo the damage done by years of neglect. Positions have hardened among Israelis and Palestinians. Jaded Arab and Israeli populations both want peace but don't believe the other side is willing to take the steps necessary. But as Zogby International's polling repeatedly shows, if the United States and the West are to build bridges of understanding with the Arab World, resolving the Israeli–Palestinian issue is the critical place to begin.

Solving the conflict is important not just in its own right; it will also give the United States and other concerned governments the opportunity to build the alliances necessary for us to confront extremism and promote needed reform. With most Americans supporting a more balanced policy—and with strong majorities of Arab Americans and American Jews endorsing a two-state solution—the Obama administration has the backing it needs to face down opponents from all quarters.

Arabs have long felt that an asymmetry characterizes the current Palestinian–Israeli policy of the United States. Israelis receive compassion, and Palestinians get little; Palestinians feel U.S. pressure, and Israelis do not. To his credit, President Obama has attempted to correct this imbalance.

Our polling shows that Arabs want the West to apply a consistent approach in dealing with bad behavior by Israelis and Palestinians. This does not mean abandoning Israel, but it does mean insisting on serious negotiations, applying balanced pressure to both sides, and coupling our firm stance against Palestinian violence with concrete assurances to defend Palestinians against any further loss of land and rights.

A useful guide as we move forward can be found in *Negotiating Arab-Israeli Peace: American Leadership in the Middle East*. This work is a well-documented look at past negotiating efforts issued by the U.S. Institute for Peace (USIP), a congressionally funded entity dedicated to the study and promotion of peacemaking.[16] It was based on the work of a study group headed by Daniel Kurtzer (former U.S. ambassador to both Israel and Egypt). The group interviewed more than a hundred officials and experts from seven countries, including those involved in the peacemaking efforts of the last five U.S. administrations. Too often, the reports of study groups are of little consequence, but this one is different: its assessment of past successes and failures and its recommendations for moving forward are important and should be taken to heart.

DEMAND-DRIVEN ASSISTANCE AND REFORM

In 1994, a year after the signing of the Oslo Accords, an international conference in Casablanca was organized to support the ongoing Israeli–Palestinian peace process. As cochair of Vice President Al Gore's Builders for Peace, I moderated a session on building the Palestinian economy that featured a number of Palestinian ministers and business leaders including Minister of Economic Planning Nabil Sha'ath. During the discussion, the Palestinians described both their needs and the problems they might encounter as they sought to grow their economy.

Following the panel, a young and excited American approached me. He told me that he had just been awarded a $12 million contract from the U.S. Agency for International Development (USAID) to promote entrepreneurial skills among Palestinians in the occupied territories. He didn't know many of the Palestinian businesspeople and ministers in the region, but he was eager to meet them.

When I mentioned this to Sha'ath, he was both surprised and furious. The $12 million USAID grant was a large chunk of the $75 million the Clinton administration had promised for all of Palestine that year. Yet as Sha'ath told me, the Palestinians had never been consulted as to how the USAID money should be spent, or whether areas other than entrepreneurialism represented more pressing needs. Later, one Palestinian businessman laughed at this story, telling me: "We don't need some American to teach us how to be entrepreneurs; we are a society of entrepreneurs. We need loans and we need to be freed from the occupation, so we can have access to markets."[17]

I wish that this were just an old story about an isolated instance of failed policy, but it's not. To date, the West has spent billions of dollars on reform throughout the Arab World, but the programs created and offered have not always been the ones asked for or needed by Arabs. (Another infamous USAID clunker was the multimillion-dollar Gaza apartment complex built with U.S. tax dollars. Each apartment cost around $100,000 even though annual per capita income in Gaza was less than $800.)

Finally, however, there does seem to be hope on the horizon. Although some problem areas remain, a new government culture is seeking to get it right by partnering with groups in other countries to promote reform and development. In late 2009, Secretary of State Hillary Clinton announced a series of promising partnerships with grassroots, community-based organizations and entrepreneurs to promote civil society and job creation. These arrangements include projects designed to develop joint ventures in science and technology, support educational development and job creation to meet the needs of the region's burgeoning youth sector, and improve the delivery of social services and the effectiveness of local governance. Then, while announcing the confirmation of the new USAID director in January 2010, Clinton noted:

> In the past, we have sometimes dictated solutions from afar, often missing our mark on the ground. Our new approach is to work in partnership with developing countries that take the lead in designing and implementing evidence-based strategies with clear goals. Development built on consultation rather than decree is more likely to engender the local leadership and ownership necessary to turn good ideas into lasting results.[18]

This large-scale reorientation toward demand-driven programs is extraordinarily positive. We already know that foreign aid can work wonders when it meets local wants and needs. In fact, one of the shining lights of U.S. capacity-building efforts is the Center for International Private Enterprise (CIPE), one of four programs working with the National Endowment for Democracy.[19]

CIPE is a nonprofit affiliate of the U.S. Chamber of Commerce that has for twenty-five years worked with partners worldwide "to build the civic institutions vital to a democratic society."[20] CIPE has a long record of working across the Middle East. It is a small operation, spending only about $6 million in this region, but it makes a difference because it empowers local organizations, building their capacity to make change from the bottom up. Working with business groups, chambers of commerce, and other area NGOs, CIPE has funded projects across the Arab World: promoting anticorruption initiatives, empowering the business community to advocate for governmental transparency, and promoting corporate citizenship and ethics.

A CHANGE IN PROGRAMMING

For a powerful example of the difference between partnering with Arabs on demand-driven projects versus cramming expensive, unilateral efforts down their throats, look no further than the way Western television- and radio-based public-relations initiatives are used. Since 2004, U.S. taxpayers have been funding al Hurra, a government-run television station, to the tune of $650 million. Unfortunately, al Hurra (along with SAWA, its sister radio station) is based on the outdated, twentieth-century Radio Free Europe model. Today's Arab World is not behind an iron curtain where people are denied access to information from the outside world. As we've seen, many Arabs have access to the Internet and a variety of satellite TV networks, and that access is mushrooming year by year.

Because the U.S. government did not have a preexisting respected international news brand with a seasoned staff of professionals—like, for example, the British Broadcasting Corporation (BBC)—al Hurra had to be created out of whole cloth. So, instead of a BBC-like initiative, the United States has been left with a low-quality propaganda network—one in which a former right-wing partisan from Lebanon runs the news operations and a leading official in a pro-Israel think tank hosts a weekly show.

When al Hurra launched, our polling showed that Arabs were already watching many American television programs via Arab satellite networks. Likewise, "American television" and "American people" were viewed very favorably across the Arab World—as much as five times higher than "the U.S. government."[21] Why, I wondered, would we spend $100 million annually to create a government-sponsored television station to compete with some of our own best products?

Polling also showed that exposure to U.S. television and films resulted in more favorable opinions toward Americans. Clearly, expanding Arab access to quality American television was a worthwhile objective, but it was also one that could be better achieved by partnering with Arabs. After more than a decade of working with and advising three different Arab satellite networks, I have found that these outlets are open to cooperation, coproduction agreements, purchasing rights to air American shows, and training programs with U.S. networks. This has been the case with all three of the Arab networks (MBC, ART, and now Abu Dhabi TV) with which I have worked.

Given this diversity and openness, it would be better to create a government fund to encourage public–private coproduction arrangements between Arab and U.S. networks and other opportunities for Arab network journalists to work with their American counterparts. Instead of the United States wasting hundreds of millions of dollars on a poorly conceived competitor, the Middle East region would be better served by receiving U.S. technical support and partnerships with existing Arab networks, enhancing their capacity and programming.

KNOWING US IS LIKING US: INCREASE U.S.–ARAB EXCHANGE PROGRAMS

Although I love hosting policy makers and prominent analysts on my weekly TV show, there is one program I especially look forward to. Each year, I invite a group of college-age students from across the Arab World for a discussion.[22] The group of twenty or so young people appears right after they have completed a U.S. government–sponsored visitor program. During their time in the United States, they attend classes, meet American counterparts, visit the U.S. students' homes, and spend some time on a guided tour of the United States. Each group I've met is energized and excited by their experiences. The Arab students' attitudes toward Americans are often changed, and they are pleased by their opportunity to change the perceptions of the Americans they've met.

Programs like this are part of a range of efforts sponsored by the United States that annually bring more than 2,000 international visitors to this country through Fulbright scholarships, professional or cultural exchanges, and high school and college study programs. Budgets for initiatives like these have increased since 9/11, and they should be expanded further because they are worth every dollar spent. Not only have these young people had life-changing experiences that have empowered them, but our polling shows that Arabs who have been to the United States or who know Americans give the country significantly higher favorable ratings than those who have not been here.[23] But these government-sponsored efforts represent only a fraction of the Arabs who come or want to come to the United States, and there are problems here we must address.

Although most Americans maintain that we are an open and welcoming country, scores of Arabs who have been denied visas feel otherwise. This is a list that includes visiting scholars, doctors, patients seeking medical care, and respected businesspeople. Since 9/11, America has confused immigration policy with counterterrorism policy. As a result, we have inadvertently shut out tens of thousands of deserving Arabs from visiting and working in this country. A Fulbright recipient, a doctor seeking a J-1 visa, and a businessman with partners in the United States are not terrorist threats. Common sense should prevail, and America's visa policy and procedures for entry into the United States should be changed. To stand in line for long hours at an embassy abroad and then to be treated harshly or dismissively by a visa officer does little to repair America's image overseas. The arbitrary and oftentimes insulting behavior meted out by border officials at points of entry into our country also is counterproductive.

Though this hostile treatment occurs one person at a time, the overall impact of these policies has been dramatic. Before 9/11, more than 150,000 Arabs from Egypt, Saudi Arabia, Lebanon, Jordan, and Morocco came to the United States every year as students, tourists, and businesspeople. By 2003, that number had dropped precipitously to around 50,000, only climbing back to 85,000 in 2008. Misguided profiling of entire groups of people is wasteful and pointless. It ties up needed law enforcement resources and work hours, making these jobs more difficult. It also widens the divide between Arabs and the United States, creating resentment that plays into the hands of extremists.

Without a doubt, we have to provide security protection at U.S. points of entry. Of course, visas shouldn't be handed out indiscriminately. But our public officials have to realize that who we let into America is often as important as who we keep out. If America wants its democracy to be the envy of the world, we have to allow people—Arabs included—to experience it firsthand.

A NEW IDEA

In 1957, the United States was shocked when the Soviet Union made it into space first, successfully launching Sputnik, the first satellite. Resolved to defeat the West's Cold War rival, the U.S. Congress passed the National Defense Education Act (NDEA) in 1958. Although the focus of the Act was to provide resources to universities to increase programs in math and science, Title VI of the NDEA provided funding for "Critical Area Studies"—including Arabic language and Middle East studies. Over the years, these programs have been augmented by the Fulbright Scholar program and by funds to open additional centers at universities in other area studies. After 9/11, monies devoted to Arabic language study have increased but not enough—as we have seen—to meet the need.

Zogby International's polling shows that Americans know too little about the Arab World and that too few colleges and universities offer advanced Arabic language study and programs in Middle East studies. Therefore, the government should facilitate a rapid expansion of educational opportunities in both areas. Using the Cold War–era NDEA as a model, Congress should appropriate funds needed to provide critical language and area studies for U.S. students interested in the Arab World. Congress should also dramatically expand the Fulbright program, which provides exchange opportunities for U.S. and Arab students pursuing advanced degrees.

ARAB AMERICANS AS ASSETS TO POLICY
AND PUBLIC DIPLOMACY

As I argued at the end of Part III of this book, the Arab American and American Muslim communities also can play a critical role in bridge-building efforts and should be more fully engaged. Truly, Arab Americans' unique cultural skills and backgrounds are an underused asset, one we can't afford to waste. More Arab Americans should be appointed to government posts dealing with policy and public diplomacy and assistance programs. Similarly, an Arab American advisory commission should be established at the State Department to allow these communities direct input into the public diplomacy effort.

The issue here isn't quotas or fairness. The issue is common sense. Government needs to do everything it can to ensure that Arabs are being heard—whether they are Arabs in the Middle East or Arab Americans at home. It should use all the resources at its disposal. And then, most importantly, government in all its many forms and manifestations must learn to listen to what is being said. Happily, the private sector, from corporations to columnists, offers some excellent examples of how to do just that.

16
WHAT WE CAN DO

GOVERNMENTS, OF COURSE, have a big responsibility to get it right in shaping and promoting policies in the Arab World. But in a democracy, other sectors of the society also have important contributions to make. Businesses heavily invested in the Middle East, educational institutions charged with preparing the next generation of global citizens, and news media that inform the public and define the West's history of engagement in the Arab World—they all need to get it right, too. But the challenge doesn't stop there. The rest of us, citizens throughout the Western democracies, also have a duty to become informed and participate in the public debate about the many ways our governments are involved on our behalf in pursuing policies across the Arab World.

CORPORATE CITIZENS

One day when I was thirteen, I cringed as the woman who lived next door to my father's grocery store picked over the peaches I had just put on display. She was pinching each one, bruising them in the process. I was about ready to confront her when my father stopped me. He had a different approach. He walked up to her and said, "Mrs. Metzger, your hair is beautiful—did you change it?"

"Oh, you think so?" she asked. "Thank you."

"I notice you were looking at the peaches," noted my father.

"Yes, but they're bruised," countered Mrs. Metzger.

Now, that almost pushed me over the edge, but my father responded calmly, "Yes, but smell them. Don't just feel them, smell them. And because they're bruised, I'll give them to you at a discount."

By the time he was done, Mrs. Metzger was buying peaches and more. The way my father—or any savvy businessperson—can resolve a situation so that everyone is happy is really the essence of mutually beneficial partnerships. Because closing a deal is so central to commercial success, I've often marveled at the way this kind of partnering seems second nature to many businessmen and businesswomen—yet it completely escapes others.

I was reminded of the lessons I'd learned in my father's grocery store when, in 2002, I was asked by former Ambassador Ed Djerijian from the Baker Institute for Public Policy to join in a U.S.–Syria dialogue in Houston. A second session followed a few years later in Damascus, Syria. Djerijian invited me to be part of the American team that would meet with our Syrian counterparts for three discussions on business, politics, and cultural exchange.

The business roundtable was first. Like my father, the businesspeople on both sides knew how to talk to each other in ways that helped move issues forward. After that meeting, I went to the political discussion. This talk did not move so smoothly. Before long, comity broke down, people started pointing accusatory fingers across the table, and the conversation went nowhere at all. As I headed over to the cultural exchange meeting, which I was chairing, all I could think about was how fascinatingly divergent the first two sessions had been. My father could have taught those political negotiators on both sides a lot about getting to know the other side before making demands.

Over the years, I've come to believe that if our politicians conducted diplomacy the way our businesspeople handle commerce, the world would be doing a lot better right now. (Likewise, if we applied our political model to our business ventures, we'd all be broke.) No one satisfies customers by insisting that purchasers buy a product because it's the only one available— or by pointing fingers and hurling epithets. That sounds pretty basic, I know. But joint sessions like the one I just described drive home an important point: when it comes to diplomacy and much else, the public sector has a great deal to learn from the private one.

In 2005, I was the guest speaker before the international board of an American corporation that was opening franchises across the Arab World. I commended them, noting that in many ways—and without even knowing it—they and other similar companies (especially those with brand names) were serving on the front lines of public diplomacy efforts in the Middle East.

Just as my one-time travel companion—Mahmood, the Boston-bred Palestinian businessman—had pointed out, Western businesses market more than their products abroad; they market a way of life. And no one does that more effectively than American name brands. When a Jordanian goes to a Starbucks in Amman, or a Saudi visits a Pizza Hut in Riyadh, it's not necessarily just because the coffee or pizza are better than the local fare—often they are not. Arabs frequent these franchises because they are buying a piece of America and are part of the worldwide fascination with the way of life conveyed through these products.

For decades, major Western corporations have benefited handsomely both from this lifestyle image they create and from their business partnerships in the Middle East. But this is a two-way street: Western companies doing business across the Arab World not only have a responsibility to provide quality products and services, they also face the challenge of being accountable, honest corporate citizens. Many already are, but much more can be done.

EXXONMOBIL

While reaping substantial profits from its investment in the Arab World, ExxonMobil has made an effort to get it right by investing in community programs to promote understanding. This was true even before the 1999 merger of the two oil giants. Going back decades, Mobil Oil had a long tradition of supporting efforts to present Arab and Islamic civilization to the West; for example, it compiled marvelous resource material on Arab and Islamic contributions to the Renaissance.[1]

More recently, ExxonMobil has devoted a substantial part of its foundation's budget to sponsoring a range of activities that benefit both Arabs and Americans. This includes the Middle East and North Africa Scholars Program, administered by the Institute of International Education.[2] Open to Arabic-speaking citizens of fourteen Arab nations, this program awards full scholarships to pursue master's degrees in geoscience at U.S. universities.

Much of this may sound like enlightened self-interest, but not all of ExxonMobil's giving has been immediately related to petroleum and geology. The company also sponsored a three-year, $1 million grant to the British organization Save the Children's Ishraq Program in Egypt. This fund helps to provide 1,000 Egyptian girls between the ages of 12 and 17 a second chance at education. And the corporation continues to support a wide array of educational and cultural programs sponsored by a number of U.S. universities and institutes.

STARBUCKS

Through a licensing agreement with Kuwait's M. H. Alshaya, Starbucks Coffee operates 280 stores in the Middle East, including the Gulf Arab states and several countries in the Levant and North Africa. These retail ventures employ more than 2,700 people, with a commitment to hiring local nationals: in Lebanon, Jordan, and Egypt, 100% of the employees are local citizens.[3]

Starbucks has also bolstered its corporate image in the Middle East through a number of ecological activities. For example, a tree-planting project in Lebanon replaced 500 pine trees in an area devastated by a forest fire. Likewise, in the UAE, Kuwait, and Saudi Arabia, Starbucks sponsored and participated in beach cleanups. The company also partnered with Dubai Cares in an effort to provide school supplies and hygiene kits for 50,000 Palestinian children affected by the 2008–2009 Gaza War. Another case of enlightened self-interest? Perhaps, but Starbucks's emphasis on hiring locally and supporting regional charities ends up doing as much for America's overall image as it does for the global coffee chain. Corporations can do good while doing well—and the best often do.

CISCO SYSTEMS

Cisco has twelve offices in eight Middle East countries, employing more than 628 people. The company's corporate social responsibility efforts have largely focused on education and economic development. Cisco has gained recognition for these activities—including the U.S. Secretary of State's Award for Corporate Excellence in 2005 for its participation in the Jordan Education Initiative.[4]

Other significant examples of Cisco's Middle East initiatives include a January 2008 announcement of a three-year, $10 million investment to seed a sustainable model for desperately needed job creation and economic development in the Palestinian territories. In Egypt, Cisco partnered with the World Economic Forum to create the Egypt Education Initiative, a trailblazing project that utilizes computer technology to help reform and improve educational standards in developing countries. Finally, in Lebanon, Cisco created a similar project called Partnership for Lebanon with an investment of $20 million over three years. The initiative is designed to expand the reach of education and workforce training, create jobs, and build technology infrastructure to connect communities.

This corporate giving creates goodwill toward the companies. But because ExxonMobil, Starbucks, and Cisco are recognized as American corporations, this funding also fosters and maintains positive opinions about the West's businesses and citizens in general. Likewise, the millions of dollars invested in job creation, education, and ecological activities are ultimately a recognition that building better, more respectful relations with the Arab World isn't just the right thing to do—it's in the West's own best interest. Understanding fosters understanding—and a better business environment.

UNFINISHED BUSINESS

Although good corporate citizenship is alive and well in the Arab World, much more can be done. For example, it is shocking that despite the growing importance of the Middle East, few U.S. colleges and universities offer students the opportunity to learn Arabic or study Islamic and Arab history. And though the United Nations–sponsored Arab Human Development Report correctly chides the Arab World for the scarcity of English books translated and published in Arabic, it is disturbing how few Arabic classics are available in English. These are areas in which corporations can be helpful. Businesses with a strong presence and investment in the Arab World should be encouraged to run their own exchange programs and fund chairs at Arab universities to promote American studies and chairs in Arab studies at U.S. universities.

SISTER CITIES: CHICAGO STYLE

Sister Cities International is a program that partners U.S. cities with communities across the world, providing opportunities for cultural exchanges and the development of commercial and educational ties. In all, almost 1,000 American cities have established relationships with more than 2,500 cities in 135 countries—but only a handful of these are cities from the Arab World.[5]

Chicago, under the leadership of Mayor Richard Daley, has been a major proponent of the Sister City program and of outreach to Arab cities. Chicago already has ties with Amman, Jordan, and Casablanca, Morocco, and will soon add Abu Dhabi, UAE, as its newest Sister City. In 2008, Chicago hosted the first U.S.–Arab Cities Forum, with fifty municipal leaders from seventeen nations participating. A follow-up summit will take place in Amman.

Building on this commitment to promoting understanding of and engagement in the Arab World, Chicago launched an Arabic language program in its elementary and secondary schools in 2004. Today more than 2,000 students are enrolled.

In describing his goals as mayor, Daley identified the need to "make cultural connections and expand our working relationships . . . to build strong, diverse local economies that . . . are competitive in the new global society . . . [and that] lead to greater understanding among cultures and greater friendship among nations."[6]

MEDIA: BRINGING THE ARAB WORLD TO AMERICA

Reporters covering conflicts take great risks, but they have a critical role to play in informing the public about crises as they unfold. When the only network coverage comes from journalists "embedded" with the U.S. or British military in Iraq or ensconced in the Green Zone (or from outside of Gaza, receiving briefings from Israeli military press officers), then the stories they report will be inherently skewed. The same is true of correspondents in prewar or even peaceful conditions: only by engaging the Arab World fully can reporters help Western readers and viewers better understand this region.

Fortunately, there are some shining examples of television, Web, and print journalists who understand the region, its history, and its people. These individuals don't settle for rewording a military press officer's briefing. As with the businesses engaged in corporate relations initiatives, these journalists make a significant contribution to U.S. efforts in the Arab World simply by doing their jobs well.

Viewers in the United Kingdom and global audiences with access to the BBC benefit tremendously from this world-class news service. The BBC provides extensive coverage not only of crises as they occur but of day-to-day Arab World events ignored by most U.S. networks. France 24, CNN International, and Al Jazeera English are worthy competitors, but unfortunately for U.S. viewers, no comparable news organizations are widely available in the United States.

Major U.S. networks provide just a half hour of nightly news, with much of this domestically focused and too much of it "soft" human-interest stories. The three major cable news networks in the United States (CNN, Fox News, and MSNBC) have become overly self-absorbed and partisan even when they cover global issues.

Much the same holds true with print media. The United Kingdom, for example, features a number of competing national newspapers with outstanding correspondents providing in-depth coverage of Arab World issues. Roula Khalaf of the *Financial Times*, Brian Whitaker of *The Guardian*, and Max Rodenbeck of *The Economist* regularly bring readers not only the region's news but also expert analysis that comes from a lifetime of experience in the Middle East. Of the few U.S. national newspapers, only the *New York Times* brings readers regular coverage of the Arab World.

Still, there are some bright lights in the U.S. media—reporters who get it right time and again. Christiane Amanpour, formerly of CNN, is one such example. Her extraordinary series "Generation Islam," which aired on CNN in August 2009 (and remains available on CNN's Web site), provides an inside look at the lives, attitudes, and aspirations of young Muslims from across the Middle East and Central and South Asia.[7] This is television at its best, taking viewers on a journey to understand the despair of a young person in Gaza, the joy and pride an Egyptian teenager derives from wearing her hijab, and how *Sesame Street* is educating a generation of Iraqis and Palestinians. The voices of the young Arab Muslims need to be heard in the West, and thanks to Amanpour's thoughtful journalism, they are.

Many Western reporters have covered the Iraq War or the wars in Gaza and Lebanon, either embedded with military personnel or from a safe distance. However, the *Washington Post*'s Nora Boustany; the *New York Times*'s Taghreed El Khodary; and Anthony Shadid, formerly of the *Washington Post* and now with the *New York Times*, have taken great personal risks in getting the stories on the ground. Boustany was in Lebanon during Israel's 2006 attacks on the country. Her in-depth coverage, with a human touch, was the best reporting of that war. Shadid won two Pulitzer Prizes for his efforts to bring Americans the images and voices of Iraqis he encountered while walking the streets of Baghdad during the early years of the war. For her part, El Khodary covered the Gaza War from deep within the combat zone. She visited hospitals, interviewed families, and delivered to *Times* readers the human dimension of the conflict.

All three of these reporters courted great danger, and their work provided invaluable information on the human costs of these wars and a more complex picture of what was happening as events unfolded. Ultimately, major media have a responsibility to take these types of risks: to assign journalists who understand the region they are covering so their stories have context and to position them so they can get the full story. This is simply good journalism, but without such basic reporting, all of us operate in an information vacuum.

Amanpour's primary medium—twenty-four-hour cable news—has an additional responsibility. Too often, in the midst of a developing crisis, the networks tend to fall back on their in-house stable of talking heads for commentary and analysis. Although some of these individuals may be prominent ex-politicians or accomplished in other fields, it is unhelpful to cast them as "Afghanistan experts," "Iraq experts," or more recently, "Iran experts." In reality, they know nothing more about these countries than what they read in the newspapers. They serve as mere purveyors of conventional wisdom, rather than as educated analysts. This lazy trend does a disservice to the public's need to know. Cable news network producers need to fatten their Rolodexes and make regular use of regional experts representing a variety of viewpoints on critical issues. Democracy is predicated on an informed population; getting it right in the Arab World requires that major media thoughtfully examine topics and events there that affect the United States.

THE CHALLENGE TO EDUCATION

Better educating students about the Arab World is a joint effort. Government can play a part by distributing resources to expand Middle East studies programs. Though several corporations operating in the Arab World already provide support in this area, too few of their business peers seem to realize how urgently needed—and mutually beneficial—this work is. Getting it right requires that American and European educational systems prepare students to engage with the Arab World and understand its complexities. Remembering the injunction of the UAE's Sheikh Abdullah, with which I began this book, the first step in helping the Arab World understand the West is for policy makers and the Western public to reciprocate and learn about the Arab World. To do this, current curricula need to be expanded to provide more opportunities for learning Arabic and studying Middle Eastern history.

Because funding is so crucial to improving education, it is important to resist efforts to stigmatize donations from Arabs to Western universities—especially when these gifts are offered with no strings attached. Prince Al-waleed bin Talal of Saudi Arabia has endowed two major programs, the Georgetown University Center for Muslim–Christian Understanding and Harvard University's Islamic Studies Program.[8] (Being a committed bridge-builder, Alwaleed has also funded the American Studies programs at the American Universities of Beirut and Cairo.[9]) As a result of his efforts, hundreds of students have been afforded an opportunity that would have otherwise been denied to them. But in too many other cases, institutions of higher learning have been forced by rabid anti-Arab campaigns to return contributions to Arab donors—even when the donations were completely legitimate.[10]

Universities with large Arab and Muslim student populations should take advantage of their presence to create dialogues and exchange opportunities. Programs like the National Council on U.S.–Arab Relations' Model Arab League (MAL) should be supported and expanded.[11] The National Council has been in existence since 1983 and has over the years brought hundreds of U.S. teachers and students on educational tours to countries in the Middle East. Since its inception, the council has also sponsored MALs in eleven cities across the United States, involving more than 30,000 students. Based on the Model United Nations programs, MALs assign college and university participants an Arab country whose history and culture they are to study and whose positions they are to defend at a Model Arab League meeting. Students not only develop leadership and negotiating skills, but they also receive an immersion in understanding the Arab country they are given and the others with which they interact.

CITIZENS: ENGAGED AND INFORMED

In 2005, shortly after Israel unilaterally withdrew from Gaza, I was a guest on C-SPAN's *Washington Journal,* taking calls from viewers about the situation.[12] One man asked a question that suggested a quick history lesson might be helpful. But instead of lecturing on air, I recommended a short but authoritative history written by the United Nations on the origins of the Israeli–Palestinian conflict. I told the caller that he could e-mail me or go to my organization's Web site to download the document, and then I moved on to the next call.[13]

When I got back to my office an hour later, I had already received 400 e-mails requesting the document. By day's end, another 2,000 had downloaded the document from our Web site. (This link, along with others, is available in this book's Appendix.) So I am not surprised when our polling consistently shows that about two in three Americans say they want to learn more about the Arab World. If you've gotten this far, then you are probably one of this group.

Getting it right in a democracy ultimately requires enlightened individuals who support government policies when they are productive and challenge them when they are misdirected. Citizens can become public diplomats by listening and engaging more effectively on key issues affecting America's position in the Arab World. Government, corporations, the media, and educators need to do more. But in the Information Age, an informed populace can be remarkably effective in forcing additional change.

INCREASING EXCHANGE

I'm always challenging Arab governments to promote greater understanding and pointing out that they should send citizen delegations to visit and engage in conversations with communities around the world. Our polling shows that 60% of Americans would welcome such an opportunity to meet Arab visitors, seeing it as a chance to learn more.[14] Arabs should also sponsor more programs, like the Kennedy Center's "Arabesque," to bring their culture to Western audiences. Arabs also ought to provide more materials to teachers and community groups who seek greater understanding. Some efforts have been made, but not enough to respond to the urgent need before us.

There are also a number of ways for American citizens to become informed and engage in conversations with others about critical policy questions facing the United States in the Middle East. World Affairs Councils of America (WACA) can be found in more than 100 U.S. cities. These councils comprise a national grassroots effort seeking "to involve as many citizens as possible in an exchange of ideas, knowledge and understanding of global issues."[15] The councils host visiting speakers, including many from the Arab World. There are also discussions on crucial foreign-policy topics that provide those interested with the means to become better educated and to air their concerns.

I also recommend the Great Decisions program operated by the Foreign Policy Association.[16] Each year, Great Decisions involves an estimated

350,000 citizens in more than 800 communities in sessions about vital matters. Topics to be debated are announced at the beginning of each year, and materials—in the form of a briefing book—are sent to all participants. During the year, the groups meet and discuss the assigned subjects. At the year's end, the Foreign Policy Association conducts a national ballot on the issues that have been deliberated.

The bottom line is this: Listen to Arab voices, and hear what they are saying, not just what the pundits are thinking. Engage in whatever ways you can with this often troubled region of the world. An enlightened and aware public that better understands the Arab World can not only help change the ways that Arabs see us, but can also help to transform the way Western governments relate to the Arab World. Therein lies the formula for a brighter future for the Arabs and for the West. As the news shows us every day, our fates are too closely linked to do otherwise.

AFTERWORD

IN MID-JANUARY 2011, after thirty-five events in twenty U.S. cities, my book tour finally brought me to the Middle East. The string of up-risings that would become known as the "Arab Spring" was just beginning. Demonstrators had already brought an end to the twenty-three-year rule of Tunisia's Zine el Abidine Ben Ali, and protesters in that country, embold-ened by their success in forcing the dictator and his family into exile, were still in the streets, demanding more far-reaching changes from the military, which remained in control. Although scattered protests had begun in other Arab countries, we had only a hint as to what would soon unfold.

Meanwhile, in Lebanon, the fragile coalition government of Prime Minister Saad al Hariri was unraveling, with a Hizbullah-led coalition waiting in the wings. At issue was the much-anticipated report of the International Tribunal that had been charged with investigating the assassi-nations of Saad's father, Rafiq, the former prime minister, and many of his aides and supporters. Early leaks suggested that the Tribunal would find that elements affiliated with Hizbullah had been responsible for the killings. There were fears that if members of Hizbullah were actually in-dicted, the group's heavily armed militia might once again (as they had in 2008) use their weapons to force the government to disassociate itself from the Tribunal, blocking it from carrying out its mandate.

One night, in the midst of all this, I found myself at the home of a friend in Riyadh, Saudi Arabia. There were ten of us sitting in the family's living room, watching the news coverage of these dramatic events. The re-mote control was getting a workout as they flipped back and forth between two channels—Al Arabiya (a Saudi-owned pro-Western channel) and Al Jazeera (a Qatari-owned channel, known to advocate a more radical point of view). It was akin to switching between MSNBC or CNN and Fox News during a critical moment in American politics. Arabs generally know their news sources and understand their biases, so they like to see what everyone is saying about important events. The reports sparked a heated debate among those assembled, with some declaring the developments in Tunisia to be positive or taking a position on Lebanon's domestic crisis, and others worried that both situations might be spiraling out of control.

At one point in the evening, the twenty-eight-year-old son of my host entered the room, seized the remote, announced "It's on," and promptly changed the channel to a favorite regional show, *Arabs Got Talent*—a knockoff of *America's Got Talent*. For the next hour, we watched this lighthearted, gimmicky contest show. The debate over who should win was as heated as the Tunisia/Lebanon debate that it had temporarily, and without protest, displaced. In the midst of such radical change, my friends, though deeply concerned with the political developments unfolding around them, could still take a break to be entertained and have fun— just like people everywhere.

The uprising in Tunisia was both dramatic and inspiring. Beginning in December 2010 with the shocking self-immolation of a young, distraught, and humiliated Tunisian street vendor, it quickly grew into a peaceful mass revolt. It persisted in the face of repression and violence, ultimately bringing down a dictator and a government in a marvelous display of "people power."

We have rarely seen such mass mobilization in the Arab World. Generations ago, there were the uprisings against colonial domination across North Africa. More recently, the region witnessed the first Palestinian Intifada and the massive street demonstrations in Lebanon that followed the assassination of Prime Minister Rafiq Hariri. But acts like these have been few and far between, and—more to the point—the hopes that have accompanied them have gone largely unfulfilled.

The impact of colonial domination and imperial manipulation (the Sykes-Picot Agreement, the Balfour Declaration, etc.) has taken a toll. The region has been occupied, deeply wounded, dismembered, and transformed against the will of its inhabitants. Scars remain. Among the most pervasive is a gnawing sense that history was made by others—that their destinies are out of their control. In the face of this malaise, the uprisings in Tunisia, and later in Egypt, serve as strong medicine.

A few weeks later, on February 10, I sat in London with a friend, the author Patrick Seale, watching an amazing scene unfold on the BBC. On one half of a split screen, Egyptian president Hosni Mubarak was making a last-ditch effort to save his rule. On the other half, throngs filled Tahrir Square. The disconnect went deeper than a screen split. Addressing an imagined audience of supporters, Mubarak played every card at his disposal: the caring father, patriot, xenophobe, reformer, and more—every card except the one that responded to the concerns of the Tahrir Square crowd. His performance served only to inflame them and deepen their resolve. This was the immovable object squaring off against the irresistible force. In the end, the force won. The protesters rejected Mubarak's appeal as "too little, too late" and began to pour out beyond the square to further demonstrate their discontent.

The next day, Mubarak was gone and the people in the streets were empowered to seek more change. It was not the end—just the beginning of a process whose outcome is still uncertain.

By the time I returned to the United States to resume my book tour, Libya, Yemen, and Bahrain were also boiling; Lebanon's divide was being rubbed raw; Syria was breaking into the headlines; and Palestine remained an open wound. There was much to discuss, and people were eager to have the discussion. Over the next two months, I appeared at forty more book events in seventeen cities, and at virtually every one of them, I was asked the same two questions: Had I anticipated this Arab Spring? And, in light of the changes that were occurring, did I feel the need to rewrite any section of my book? The answer to the first question was, I had not—and to the second, I did not.

The uprisings, in fact, caught just about everyone off guard. Not only was the region unprepared, U.S. policy makers were mostly confounded as well. As F. Gregory Gause III, a leading scholar on the Arab Gulf states, wrote in *Foreign Affairs*, so, too, were "the vast majority of academic specialists on the Arab world."[1] Not only that, but from my conversations with some of the young leaders who launched the protests in Egypt, I learned that even they had been surprised by the success of their efforts. Said one, "It just kept growing. We soon realized that this was going to be bigger than we had dreamed."[2]

If I was surprised by the events, though, I wasn't at all surprised by the reaction to them in much of the West. *Arab Voices* wasn't intended as a history of the Arab World or a political report on developments in the region; my purpose in writing it was to establish that we in the West don't know enough about the Arab World, especially given the challenges we face with our military, political, and economic entanglements in this critical region. We don't know because we don't listen to what Arabs themselves are saying about their lives, their aspirations, and how they feel about the way the West has treated them. And because we don't listen, all too often our involvements have gone awry.

Even with the new urgency of the moment, we in the West *still* do not understand this region, its history, culture, or people. Analysts discussing these events on the fly are like blind men in a dark room. They frequently view Arabs or evaluate developments in the Arab World through the lens of long-held biases and cultural stereotypes or by attempting to force fit parallels. What they come up with might appear on the surface to make sense, but it's largely born of mistaken assumptions, leading to erroneous conclusions and further misunderstanding.

For too many commentators, for example, the analogy of the fall of the Iron Curtain became a comfortable way of understanding the Arab Spring. Tunisia became Gdańsk, and Tahrir Square the dismantling of the Berlin Wall. With the dictators in Tunisia and Egypt gone, these talking heads and op-ed columnists assumed that—*à la* Eastern Europe—the rest of the Arab World would soon follow suit. And from there, they imposed their ideological convictions on motives, events, and outcomes.

In this instance, though, evidence barely matters. Among neoconservatives, it is an article of faith that Arabs are drawn to extremism either because they labor under repressive regimes or because autocratic leaders have used anti-Americanism to deflect from their own failed rule. Hence, the neoconservatives—and many liberals—posited that with the dictators overthrown, the Arab masses would now embrace America and forget their "imagined" grievance over Palestine. As evidence, some proudly noted that no demonstrators were burning American or Israeli flags.

But these assumptions were dead wrong in at least two regards. First, although American flags were not being burned on the streets of Cairo, they weren't being cheerfully waved either. Second, the Arab World was not Eastern Europe behind the Iron Curtain. During the Soviet occupation, the peoples of Poland, Lithuania, and elsewhere looked ardently to the West, and to the United States in particular. Arabs, as we have already seen, admire many aspects of American values and culture but feel betrayed by American behavior toward their region. Hosni Mubarak, for one, had become deeply unpopular, in large part, because he supported the United States and our policies that are so wildly out of touch with the needs, feelings, and aspirations of his people.

The Iron Curtain analogy also betrayed a dangerous tendency to look at the Arab World as a monolithic whole, ignoring the distinct political dynamics at work in each country. Yes, the contagion that began in Tunisia and then spread to Egypt and other Arab countries did provide evidence of the "Arab" connectedness that binds together the region's peoples. For example, although the mass mobilizations that roiled Pakistan in 2009 and the inspiring pro-democracy demonstrations by Iranian youth later the same year had both provoked interest and sympathy in the Arab World, they produced little reaction. But it was a very different story when Arabs saw those with whom they share a cultural and political identity rise up and demand change.

Although this connectedness is important to recognize, so, too, are the differences that exist across the region.

The underlying causes behind the frustration and unrest in Tunisia and Egypt, for example, are quite distinct from the factors that triggered the revolts in Yemen, Bahrain, Syria, and Libya. In Egypt and Tunisia, the presidents in power had emerged from a military establishment. The patronage-based political systems they had created had ossified, becoming corrupt, overly bureaucratized, and remote. The economies of these two countries had continued to grow at impressive rates, but the benefits of this new wealth had gone to a small circle of family members and cronies of the regimes, creating social unrest. As polling data demonstrate, the principal drivers behind the unrest in Egypt and Tunisia were jobs and economic opportunity, followed by corruption and the regime's loss of legitimacy. In both instances, the presidents had been deposed, but the armies, seen by many as neutral institutions, retained control.

Some of these elements were also at work in Libya, Yemen, Syria, and Bahrain, but other factors mattered, too. In Libya, there were tribal rivalries, leading the country into a NATO-backed civil war; in Yemen, tribal and long-standing regional disputes were also key; in Syria, the country and the economy had stagnated under the repressive rule of an army and a party dominated by a minority sect; while in Bahrain, the trigger was the history of discrimination experienced by that country's majority, members of the Shi'a sect of Islam.

And then there were those Arab states in which little or no unrest occurred and in which there was no great push for change. In some of these countries, the governments had sufficient legitimacy to generate a strong support base; in others, the public's satisfaction levels were high enough to offset any demand for change. In Saudi Arabia and the United Arab Emirates, for example, it was not just the governments' ability to spend on social programs that won public support. The ruling families in these tribal-based societies retained significant legitimacy, as they were descendants of the countries' revered founders and were both accessible to their compatriots and responsive to their needs. Their rule, therefore, was largely unchallenged.

As I hope I have clearly shown in these pages, the problem of not listening to Arab voices goes well beyond those Arab leaders who have fallen or those who are still in power; it is a problem for the West as well. For too long, the United States, Great Britain, and others have ignored the concerns and sensibilities of Arab people. Arabs have been treated as if they were pawns to be moved about on a board. While we paid attention to our own needs and politics, Arabs were left to make do or accommodate themselves to realities we created for them, as we sought to protect our interests and were not responsive to theirs.

Now, with the Arab Spring, all of this must change. When Tunisians and Egyptians organized themselves demanding to be heard, they introduced a new and potentially transformative factor into the political equation of the region. It will no longer be possible to operate as if Arab public opinion doesn't matter. It will no longer be possible to act as if imposed policies will be blindly accepted.

Arabs have been inspired by Tunisia and Egypt and empowered to believe that their voices must be heard and respected. Inevitably, that will make life more complicated for Western and some Arab policy makers. President Obama recognized as much on February 11, 2011, when he said that this is just the beginning and, after today, nothing will be same.[3] Even those words, though, don't express the full effect of the transformation now underway in the Arab World. In truth, the change that is coming will be bigger than any of us can imagine.

Here's the key thing to recognize: the developments that have unfolded since Tunisia have all been generated *internally*. For years, U.S. policy toward the Arab World has been founded on the patronizing mythology of the neoconservatives and their ilk, which stated that change could only happen if induced by external—that is, Western—pressure. Now, that mythology has been exposed for the nonsense it always was.

The movements that have been rocking the Arab nations were inspirational, creating a new pride among publics who have long felt deflated and powerless to make change. These movements were contagious, with tactics and slogans copied or adapted to local settings. And they were purely Arab and, it bears repeating, self-generated. No would-be "Lawrences of Arabia" or "Cheney/Rumsfelds" were leading or pulling the puppet strings in any of these uprisings, fashioning themselves as the shapers of an Arab destiny.

The path forward will have its obstacles and there will be setbacks, but the journey will continue. And when the history of this seminal period is written, what will be most noted is that the movements that launched it all and carried it through were started by Arabs and sustained by Arabs ready to create and claim their own futures, not cede them to the whims of outside powers.

One immediate indicator of this new sense of Arab self-empowerment can be seen in the results of the first post-Arab Spring poll conducted by Zogby Research Services.[4] When we asked respondents in six countries whether they felt they would be better off or worse off in the next five years, the optimism levels were quite high, especially in Morocco, Egypt, and Saudi Arabia (see Table 17.1).

The poll also demonstrates that there is uncertainty and some insecurity, but none of this dampens their sense of optimism about the future.

It is also instructive to look at Arab attitudes toward America in the post-Arab Spring. What we find is that, even with the changes taking place in many countries across the region, U.S. ratings were at a very low level, in large measure because the hoped-for changes in American policy have not materialized. As Table 17.2 demonstrates, the postelection euphoria in 2009 that caused America's favorable ratings to surge upward in most Arab countries has now evaporated.

TABLE 17.1: ARAB OPTIMISM/PESSIMISM, 2011

Do you think you will be better or worse off in the next five years?

	Better/Worse/Same (%)
Morocco	76/14/10
Egypt	85/7/2
Lebanon	23/32/18
Jordan	34/34/31
Saudi Arabia	67/23/9
UAE	38/9/37

Source: Zogby Research Services, *Arab Attitudes, 2011*

TABLE 17.2: U.S. FAVORABLE RATING IN ARAB COUNTRIES (IN %)

	Morocco	Egypt	Lebanon	Jordan	Saudi Arabia	UAE
2011	12	5	23	10	30	12
2009	55	30	23	25	41	21
2008	26	9	21	16	13	22

Source: Zogby International, *Six-Nation Arab Opinion Poll,* November 1–18, 2009. Sample size: 3,989 adults; Zogby International, *Six-Nation Arab Opinion Poll,* March 13–23, 2008. Sample size: 4,090 adults, Zogby Research Services, *Arab Attitudes, 2011.*

When we then asked respondents in the six countries in which we have regularly polled over the past decade to evaluate how effectively Iran, Turkey, Saudi Arabia, and the United States "contribute to peace and stability in the Arab World,"[5] the United States received the lowest rating in every country except Saudi Arabia. Interestingly, Saudi Arabia, a country virtually untouched by the Arab Spring, gave the United States the highest positive score—though still a low 24% (see Table 17.3).

When asked what they believed were the major obstacles to "peace and stability in the Middle East," the top two responses were the "continuing occupation of Palestinian lands" and "U.S. interference in the Arab World" (see Table 17.4).[6]

TABLE 17.3: CONTRIBUTORS TO PEACE AND STABILITY IN THE ARAB WORLD (IN %)

Do you agree or disagree that each of the following countries contribute to peace and stability in the Arab world?

	Morocco	Egypt	Lebanon	Jordan	Saudi Arabia	UAE
Iran	16/83	32/68	57/42	22/72	4/95	12/80
Turkey	82/14	65/35	85/15	58/35	76/21	61/28
United States	11/87	10/89	16/84	5/95	24/71	8/87
Saudi Arabia	69/27	82/17	61/39	57/42	99/1	66/25

Source: Zogby Research Services, *Arab Attitudes, 2011.*

TABLE 17.4: RANK OF MAJOR OBSTACLES TO PEACE AND STABILITY IN THE MIDDLE EAST*

	Morocco	Egypt	Lebanon	Jordan	Saudi Arabia	UAE
Continuing occupation of Palestinian lands	1	1	4	1	1	5
U.S. interference in the Arab World	2	2	1	2	1	1
Lack of democracy in Arab countries	3	3	2	5	4	2
Economic inequality	4	4	3	4	5	3
Iran's interference in Arab affairs	5	4	5	3	1	4

Source: Zogby Research Services, *Arab Attitudes, 2011.*
Note: Respondents were asked to select "the greatest obstacle to peace and stability." Ratings are based on the percentages of those who chose each.

If anything, the Arab Spring uprisings served to reveal how out of touch the United States is with developments in the Arab World and what little leverage we have to influence the course of events there. With conservative critics accusing the White House of not doing enough to support the pro-democracy movements, President Obama responded in a State Department address on May 19, 2011, reaffirming American interests in the Arab World but also acknowledging the limits of American influence. "We must proceed with a sense of humility," Obama said. "It's not America that put people into the streets of Tunis or Cairo—it was the people themselves who launched these movements and it's the people themselves that must ultimately determine their outcome."[7] The contribution America could make, the president noted, was to be supportive of transformation by assisting emerging democracies with job-creation investments and capacity building.

The president concluded his May 19 remarks on just the right note: by making it clear that one other area where the United States could make a real contribution to regional stability in the Middle East would be the promotion of a resolution of the Arab–Israeli conflict on the basis of the internationally recognized 1967 borders. Palestinian rights not only loom large for peace and stability in the Middle East, but also remain the main issue that contributes to negative perceptions of the United States.

While the Arab World was undergoing profound changes, the quality of the discussion in the United States about the Middle East and the Arab and Muslim peoples was moving in a decidedly negative direction. At the end of 2010, the Texas Board of Education—acting on a wildly biased anti-Arab review—passed a resolution decrying the "pro-Islamic/anti-Christian bias [that] has tainted . . . Texas Social Studies textbooks."[8] Given the state's enormous influence with textbook publishers, the resolution threatened to widen the knowledge gap that has put the United States at risk in the Arab and Muslim Worlds.

The last half of 2010 also witnessed a national uproar in the United States against plans to build an Islamic community center in southern Manhattan. Although the site of the center was a considerable distance from Ground Zero—the former location of the World Trade Center destroyed by terrorist attacks on September 11, 2001—the same group of anti-Arab, anti-Muslim activists who had successfully blocked the Khalil Gibran International Academy in Brooklyn began a campaign to stop the project, arguing that it would desecrate "sacred ground." Soon, a number of national Republican leaders and the National Republican Congressional Committee joined in the campaign, blurred the issues (the proposed center became a "mosque"), and broadened the movement from opposition to a particular building in a particular location to a broad-based attack on Islam itself.

In dozens of congressional campaigns, Republican candidates sought to make the "mosque" an issue. In North Carolina's Second Congressional District, for example, Republican Renee Ellmers defeated incumbent Bob Etheridge with ads like this one: "After the Muslims conquered Jerusalem and Cordoba and Constantinople, they built victory mosques. And now, they want to build a mosque by Ground Zero. Where does Bob Etheridge stand? He won't say; won't speak out; won't take a stand. The terrorists haven't won and we should tell them in plain English: No! There will never be a mosque at Ground Zero."[9]

In Missouri, Republican Ed Martin, running against Congressman Russ Carnahan, made the following statement echoing some of the same themes: "I absolutely oppose the so-called mosque at Ground Zero and believe those who are patting themselves on the back as paragons of religious liberty are either deeply naïve or incredibly cynical."[10]

National Republican figures like 2008 vice presidential candidate Sarah Palin and former House Speaker Newt Gingrich also chimed in, with Palin referring to the center as a "stab in the heart"[11] and Gingrich equating it to "putting a Nazi sign next to the Holocaust Museum."[12] Soon,

Islam, Muslims, and Arabs generally were fair game for Republican presidential aspirants all across the increasingly narrow ideological spectrum of the party. Speaking before thousands of followers of John Hagee—founder of Christians United for Israel—Gingrich expressed the bizarre conviction that "if we do not decisively win the struggle over the nature of America, by the time [my grandchildren are] my age they will be in a secular atheist country, potentially one dominated by radical Islamists and with no understanding of what it once meant to be an American."[13]

Pizza king–turned–presidential aspirant Herman Cain joined the fray. When asked if he would consider appointing a Muslim American to his cabinet or to a federal judgeship should he be elected president, Cain responded, "No, I will not. And here's why. There is this creeping attempt, there is this attempt, to gradually ease Sharia law and the Muslim faith into our government. It does not belong in our government."[14]

Staying on message, Tim Pawlenty, the former governor of Minnesota, boasted that he disbanded a program in his state that had provided home buyers the opportunity to secure Islam-compliant mortgages. Through a spokesman, Pawlenty asserted that he did so because "the United States should be governed by the U.S. Constitution, not religious laws."[15]

Not surprisingly, such political exploitation has exacerbated a disturbing partisan divide on matters related to Arabs and now, especially, Muslims. In our most recent poll of U.S. voters, attitudes toward Arabs and Muslims were roughly evenly divided between "favorable" and "unfavorable," but the split masked a vast underlying partisan divide that Palin, Gingrich, Pawlenty, and others have worked so hard to feed in recent months (see Table 17.5).[16]

TABLE 17.5: ATTITUDES TOWARD ARABS AND MUSLIMS

	All (Fav/Unfav %)	Democrats (Fav/Unfav %)	Republicans (Fav/Unfav %)
Attitudes toward Arabs	45/40	59/28	30/56
Attitudes toward Muslims	41/49	57/29	22/71

Source: Zogby Interactive, *National Poll of Likely Voters,* June 28–30, 2011. Sample size: 1,804 adults.

When we began polling on American views toward Arabs and Muslims over a decade ago, more than three-quarters of Americans would tell us that they "didn't know enough" or that they "needed to know more" about Arabs and Muslims. In our more recent efforts, the number dropped to just over one half. And once again, it is the partisan divide on this question that is most disturbing, with 68% of Democrats saying that they "don't know enough" or "need to know more" and 66% of Republicans saying that they "know enough" and "don't need to know more."

All this political posturing has an inevitable reverse effect. America's favorable ratings across the Arab World are back to Bush-era lows, and the post-Cairo optimism that America would change its approach to the region has all but evaporated. America, it bears repeating, is not unpopular among many Arabs because we have supported their leaders; rather, some Arab leaders have become unpopular because of their own deeds and because they have supported our policies. America has dealt itself out of the game by refusing to hear what is actually happening in the region. In seeking change in their own countries, Tunisians, Egyptians, and other Arabs no longer look to us. This is their movement, not ours.

What is required now is to recognize the degree to which our failed policies of the past have alienated Arab public opinion, undercut our stated values, and put at risk those who sought to be our friends. Unless our political leaders can put aside "politics as usual" and end their callous disregard for the suffering of Palestinians; unless leaders are willing to challenge their political fears and do what is right, instead of what is convenient; unless we can stand up against the Islamophobes who threaten to tear apart the fabric of our nation; unless we can restore our commitment to fundamental freedoms and constitutional protections; and unless we stop ignoring Arab concerns and truly listen to what Arab voices are telling us about their needs and aspirations, we will continue to operate clumsily and, at times, brutally on the wrong side of history.

As Arabs seek change at home, the challenge we face is to question how we can bring real change to America and to the way America deals with the Arab World and its people. This is what Barack Obama promised when he said that he would lead the effort to change Washington and, in the process, change America and change the world. This is still the transformation we need. Unfortunately, it hasn't happened yet.

Amid the gloom, though, there are hopeful signs. In the course of promoting *Arab Voices*, I have been especially pleased to discover how many students and community groups have been closely following events in the Middle East and how many had, on their own, taken steps to "get it right." A group of students at Rice University, for example, had formed their own Arab World outreach effort. To enrich their learning experience, they traveled to Egypt in the summer of 2010. While there, they lived with Arab students from the American University in Cairo. They followed up in 2011 by hosting their new Egyptian friends in Texas.

I found much the same at Davidson College, except its study program had taken students to Damascus. Listening to these students describe what they saw, the lessons they learned, and their feelings about the Syrian families they had come to know, I could feel their excitement and knew their lives had been transformed by the experience. Students at Millersville University in Pennsylvania have formed a Middle Eastern Studies Organization to support their study of Arabic and their participation in the Model Arab League. And back in Washington, I met an inspiring group of young Egyptians and Americans, brought together by LearnServe Egypt. This project not only builds bridges by introducing students to each other's worlds, but also empowers young people by assisting them in designing start-up business ventures. I found their projects fascinating but was even more impressed by the bonds that had been forged by their partnerships.

In the end, this is how true and lasting change will come: one changed mind at a time.

APPENDIX:
RESOURCES

NOT EVERYONE LIVES in a city where there's a chapter of World Affairs Councils of America or a Great Decisions group. The good news is that in our Information Age, opportunities are available on the Internet providing immediate access to Arab views.

Most Arab countries have English-language newspapers that are available online. Many of these news outlets are quite good at providing not only the stories from their countries and the wider region but also Arab commentary on Western policies and international affairs. Most also host comment sections encouraging discussion and debate.

Here are some of the best papers available to an English-speaking audience:

The Daily Star (Lebanon) http://www.dailystar.com.lb

An excellent source of news about Lebanon.

The Jordan Times (Jordan) http://www.jordantimes.com

Valuable for following developments in Jordan and Palestinian affairs.

Al-Ahram Weekly (Egypt) http://weekly.ahram.org.eg

The Arabic parent of this weekly is the largest circulated daily in the Arab World and an authoritative source of news about Egypt. This weekly digest features thoughtful commentary about developments in the country and the Arab World, as well as in African and international affairs.

The National (UAE) http://www.thenational.ae

One of the newest papers in the region. It is strong on Gulf affairs and domestic UAE issues.

Gulf News (UAE) http://gulfnews.com/

The largest circulation English language daily in the UAE.

Gulf Daily News (Bahrain) http://www.gulf-daily-news.com/

Bahrain's daily English language newspaper.

Arab News (Saudi Arabia) http://www.arabnews.com

Carrying stories and commentaries about issues in the kingdom with sections carrying news relevant to the country's South Asian expatriate communities.

Al Hayat (London) http://www.daralhayat.com/morenews/english

The English Web site carries articles and commentaries from its Arabic-language parent paper. *Al Hayat* is one of the Arab World's major pan-Arab dailies.

Asharq al Awsat (London) http://www.aawsat.com/english

Another English-language Web site featuring stories and commentaries from a major pan-Arab, Arabic-language daily.

Al Jazeera (Qatar) http://english.aljazeera.net

The English-language news site of the Arab satellite television network. A useful source for updates on Arab and international news.

Haaretz (Israel) http://www.haaretz.com

A liberal Israeli daily. This English-language site includes news and opinion translated from Hebrew. It is an excellent source for news on Israeli affairs.

In addition to these newspaper Web sites from the Middle East, American television viewers with Dish Network or DirecTV can also see translations of select Arab television news programs on Link TV's *Mosaic* program. Link also carries my weekly Abu Dhabi TV call-in program *Viewpoint* live on Thursday afternoons. For information visit: http://www.linktv.org/mosaic.

There are also a number of Web sites hosted by U.S.-based Arab, Muslim, Jewish, and Christian organizations that are worth consulting because they provide useful information.

The Arab American Institute (http://www.aaiusa.org)

The organization I founded in 1985. It is the "political and policy arm of the Arab American community." A useful source of Arab

American policy concerns and initiatives and Arab American demographic data. (On this Web site you can also see my TV show dialogue with Iraqi students.)

The American-Arab Anti-Discrimination Committee (http://www.adc.org)

> A group I cofounded in 1980. It is the nation's premier Arab American civil rights organization. This site also features up-to-date details on policies that affect Arab Americans and contact information for ADC's chapters across the United States.

J Street (http://www.jstreet.org)

> The newest of the pro-peace, pro-Israel lobbies. This organization has, in a short time, been able to project an alternative voice representing a pro-peace perspective in Washington.

The Muslim Public Affairs Council (http://www.mpac.org)

> A smart and forward-looking advocacy organization bringing Muslim American voices into the U.S. policy debate.

Americans for Peace Now (http://peacenow.org)

> An American Jewish organization supporting the efforts of Peace Now in Israel. The best source of information on Israeli settlement policies and on U.S. congressional efforts on Middle East issues affecting Israel and peace in the region.

Churches for Middle East Peace (http://www.cmep.org)

> A coalition of U.S. mainstream Christian churches supporting peace in the Middle East and Christians in the Holy Land.

Holy Land Christian Ecumenical Foundation (http://www.hcef.org)

> An organization committed to the well-being of the Christians of the Holy Land, with programs to build solidarity between them and Christians elsewhere.

A number of organizations specializing in foreign affairs are invaluable sources of information and analysis about the Arab World.

Council on Foreign Relations (http://www.cfr.org)

Foreign Policy magazine (http://www.foreignpolicy.com)

> In particular, the Mideast Channel.

International Crisis Group (http://www.crisisgroup.org)

> Produces the most definitive background resource material on critical issues worldwide.

I have mentioned in this book a number of groups that sponsor programs engaging citizens in education and discussion on a range of issues including those in the Arab World. The Web sites for these organizations are included below for readers interested in the location of their local chapters, how to join, and dates of upcoming events.

World Affairs Council (http://www.worldaffairscouncils.org)
Great Decisions (Foreign Policy Association: http://www.fpa.org)
National Council on U.S.–Arab Relations (http://www.ncusar.org)

One group that deserves special recognition is Business for Diplomatic Action (BDA). Formed by leading executives from major U.S. corporations, BDA supports programs that promote global citizenship and cross-cultural understanding. Their annual Arab and American Business Fellowship program provides opportunities for dozens of young professionals to benefit from "the only private-sector exchange program that focuses on cultivating today's global leaders." For more information: http://www.businessfordiplomaticaction.org/

Finally, although I am loath to provide a long list of books, there are a few I want to suggest, which interested readers can consult. Some are classics from which I have personally benefited; others are gems written by authors I have hosted on my weekly program.

Albert Hourani, *A History of the Arab Peoples* (Cambridge: Belknap Press, 1991).

> The classic and comprehensive history of the region and its people from the time of Muhammad to the present day.

Edward Said, *The Question of Palestine* (New York: Times Books, 1979).

> Said was the preeminent Arab American scholar. This book remains the most authoritative treatment of the Palestinian issue and its importance to the Arab people.

Edward Said, *Covering Islam: How the Media and the Experts Determine How We See the Rest of the World* (New York: Pantheon Books, 1981).

> A treatise on how Western media and popular culture have perpetuated stereotypes of Islam.

Karen Armstrong, *Islam: A Short History* (New York: Modern Library, 2000).

The best treatment of Islam in one book.

Juan Cole, *Engaging the Muslim World* (New York: Palgrave Macmillan, 2009).

A useful survey of U.S. policies across the Muslim World.

Jimmy Carter, *Palestine: Peace Not Apartheid* (New York: Simon and Schuster, 2006).

It shouldn't have been as controversial as it was, but the overreaction is indicative of the difficulty of having reasoned discourse about this issue.

John Mearsheimer and Stephen Walt, *The Israel Lobby and U.S. Foreign Policy*, (New York: Farrar, Strauss and Giroux, 2007).

Jehan Sadat, *My Hope for Peace* (New York: Free Press, 2009).

A short but insightful insider's look at the life of her husband (Anwar Sadat), Egypt, and Islam today.

Queen Noor, *Leap of Faith: Memoirs of an Unexpected Life* (New York: Miramax, 2003).

And here are three invaluable and comprehensive works I have cited in this book:

James Baker and Lee Hamilton (cochairs), *The Iraq Study Group Report: The Way Forward, A New Approach* (New York: Vintage Books, 2006).

Daniel C. Kurtzer and Scott B. Lasensky, *Negotiating Arab-Israeli Peace* (Washington: United States Institute of Peace, 2008).

And that excellent short history on the origins of the Israeli–Palestinian conflict I recommended to the C-SPAN audience in 2005 can be found online: United Nations, *Question of Palestine*, http://www.un.org/Depts/dpa/qpal.

ACKNOWLEDGMENTS

IT ALL BEGINS WITH my family. My father, Joseph; my mother, Celia; my sister, Selwa; my brother, John; and a wonderful extended family of uncles, aunts, and cousins provided me with my initial and continuing immersion into my heritage and taught me the need to listen and learn.

Forty years ago, my wife Eileen and I traveled together to the Arab World with our firstborn. We stayed in several different places: my father's mountain village, West Beirut, a Bedouin campsite, and a Palestinian refugee camp. These experiences transformed us. Since then, Eileen and I and our five now-grown children—Joseph, Elizabeth, Sarah Hope, Matthew, and Mary Margaret—have traveled at different times to eleven Arab countries. I have benefited from seeing the region through their eyes and listening to their keen observations.

Over the years, I have been blessed with the opportunity to meet and learn from a number of remarkable people across the Arab World—some of whom have made a lasting impression. Rafiq Hariri and Doctor Amal Shamma (Lebanon); Tawfiq Zayyad and Father Elias Chacour (Israel); Zahi Khouri, Hanna Nasir, Abdul Jawad Saleh, Hanan Ashrawi, Hatem Husseini, and Faisal Husseini (Palestine); Prince Turki al-Faisal, Prince Alwaleed bin Talal, Abdulrahman al-Zamil, Sheikh Sulayman Olayan, and Abdul Aziz al-Tuwaiji (Saudi Arabia); Sheikh Abdullah bin Zayed and Anwar Gargash (UAE); Mohamed al-Sager (Kuwait); and here in the United States, Edward Said, Ibrahim Abu Lughod, Kamal Boullata, and Ismail al-Faruqi.

This book would not have been possible without the support of a number of individuals: my agents, Rafe Sagalyn and Bridget Wagner, who believed in it; as did Reem al Hashemi, from the beginning; Palgrave's Alessandra Bastagli, whose guidance helped shape it; Howard and Nathan Means, whose insightful suggestions helped bring it to life; my daughter Liz Zogby, whose watchful eye and attention to detail were invaluable; and Kyle Haley, my assistant, who aided the project from beginning to end. Additional support came from Ashraf Fouad Makkar, Amal Mudalali, and my son Joseph Zogby, who read portions and offered important ideas.

And finally, of course, to my brother, John Zogby, whose insights and backing are always so crucial, and my colleagues at Zogby International, especially Joe Mazloom and Sam Rogers. Thanks to my dedicated staff at the Arab American Institute, who put up with my absence, and the folks at Shelly's, who tolerated my presence and cigar smoke.

NOTES

INTRODUCTION

1. Edmond Moutran, Memac Ogilvy's Web site "splash page," http://www.memacogilvy.com/main.html.
2. Jarrett Murphy, "U.S. Propaganda Pitch Halted," *CBS News,* January 16, 2003, http://www.cbsnews.com/stories/2003/01/16/world/main536756.shtml.
3. James Zogby, personal notes from meeting with Arab Gulf ministers, November 13, 2001.

CHAPTER 1. THE DAY THAT DIDN'T CHANGE EVERYTHING

1. *NBC News Special Report: America Remembers,* NBC, September 11, 2002.
2. *Viewpoint Special: The Roots of 9/11,* Abu Dhabi TV, September 11, 2002.
3. Steven Emerson, interview by Anthony Mason, *CBS Evening News,* CBS, April 19, 1995.
4. David McCurdy, interview by Natalie Allen, CNN, April 19, 1995.
5. Anonymous caller, interview by James Zogby, *A Capital View,* Arab Network of America, April 19, 1995.
6. Thanassis Cambanis, "Threat to Arab-American Admitted," *Boston Globe,* June 7, 2002, B1; United States Department of Justice, "Zachary J. Rolnik Pleads Guilty to Federal Hate Crime Violations Against Dr. James J. Zogby," news release, June 6, 2002.
7. U.S. Commission on Civil Rights, *Briefing on Boundaries of Justice: Immigration Policies Post-September 11,* Washington, DC, October 12, 2001.

CHAPTER 2. LISTENING IN THE LEVANT

1. *Times (London),* "Palestine for the Jews," November 2, 1917.
2. Woodrow Wilson, "Address to the Diplomatic Corps" (speech, Mt. Vernon, Washington, DC, July 4, 1918).

3. *The King-Crane Commission Report—Report of the American Section of Inter-allied Commission of Mandates in Turkey,* August 28, 1919, http://www.ipcri.org/files/kingcrane.html. First printed as "King-Crane Report on the Near East," *Editor & Publisher* 55, no. 27 (1922), 2d.

4. "Memorandum by Mr. Balfour Respecting Syria, Palestine and Mesopotamia, 1919," in E. L. Woodward and Rohan Butler, eds., *Documents on British Foreign Policy, 1919–1939,* Third Series, vol. VII, 1939 (London: Her Majesty's Stationery Office, 1954), 340–347.

5. William T. Ellis, "Crane and King's Long-Hid Report on the Near East," *New York Times,* December 3, 1922, 33.

6. John Kampfner, "NS Interview—Jack Straw," *New Statesman,* November 18, 2002, http://www.newstatesman.com/200211180010/.

7. Personal notes from a meeting with Arab Gulf Ministers, November 11, 2001.

8. James J. Zogby, *What Arabs Think: Values, Beliefs and Concerns* (Utica, NY: Zogby International/The Arab Thought Foundation, 2002).

CHAPTER 3. KNOWLEDGE WARS

1. Zogby International, *Poll of American Opinion,* November 30–December 8, 2009. Sample size: 1,006 adults.

2. Among these materials were: *Arab Americans: Making a Difference* by Casey Kasem—a listing of famous Arab Americans who had made a contribution to American life; *Who Are Arab Americans?* from Grolier's Multimedia Encyclopedia; *Who Are Arabs?* from the Center for Contemporary Arab Studies; and *Arab Contributions to Civilization.* These were distributed to thousands of school districts and individual educators seeking information in the immediate aftermath of 9/11.

3. William J. Griswold, *The Image of the Middle East in Secondary School Textbooks* (New York: Middle East Studies Association of North America, 1975), 1.

4. Ibid., 3.

5. Ibid., 11.

6. Ibid., 5, 12.

7. Elizabeth Barlow, ed., *Evaluation of Secondary-Level Textbooks for Coverage of the Middle East and North Africa: A Project of the Middle East Studies Association and the Middle East Outreach Council* (Tucson, AZ: Middle East Studies Association, 1994).

8. The Chicago Council on Foreign Relations, *A Post-September 11th Curriculum for the Chicago Public Schools,* April, 2002.

9. Ibid.

10. Toni Locy, "For Linguists, Job Is Patriotic Duty," *USA Today,* November 11, 2003, http://www.usatoday.com/news/washington/2003-11-11-linguists_x.htm.

11. Jerry L. Martin and Anne D. Neal, "Defending Civilization: How Our Universities Are Failing America and What Can Be Done About It," rev. ed., (Washington, DC: American Council of Trustees and Alumni, 2002), https://portfolio.du.edu/portfolio/getportfoliofile?uid=85865.

12. Ibid., 7.

13. Stanley Kurtz, "Studying Title VI: Criticisms of Middle East Studies Get a Congressional Hearing," *National Review Online*, June 16, 2003, http://article.nationalreview.com/269123/studying-title-vi/stanley-kurtz.

14. Kristine McNeil, "The War on Academic Freedom," *The Nation*, November 11, 2002; Campus Watch, http://www.campus-watch.org/.

15. *International Studies in Higher Education Act of 2003*, HR 3077, 108th Cong., 1st sess.

16. Michelle Goldberg, "Osama University," *Salon*, November 6, 2003, http://dir.salon.com/story/news/feature/2003/11/06/middle_east/.

17. *Higher Education Opportunity Act of 2008*, Public Law 110–315, 100th Cong.

18. Martin Kramer, "Qui custodiet ipsos custodes? Campus Watch," *Sandbox*, September 18, 2002, http://sandbox.blog-city.com/sandstorm_qui_custodiet_ipsos_custodes_campus_watch.htm.

19. Daniel Pipes, "A Madrassa Grows in Brooklyn," *New York Sun*, April 24, 2007, http://www.nysun.com/foreign/madrassa-grows-in-brooklyn/530 60/.

20. Seth Wessler, "Silenced in the Classroom," *ColorLines*, http://www.color lines.com/article.php?ID=456.

21. For example, Stop the Madrassa, http://stopthemadrassa.wordpress.com and Militant Islam Monitor, http://militantislammonitor.org.

22. Pipes, "Madrassa Grows in Brooklyn."

23. Daniel Pipes, "New Approach Needed for Arab School," *New York Sun*, August 15, 2007, http://www.nysun.com/new-york/new-approach-needed-for-arab-school/60542/.

24. Wessler, "Silenced in the Classroom."

25. JTA Staff, "What Your Kids Are Learning about Israel, America and Islam," *Jewish Journal*, October 27, 2005, http://www.jewishjournal.com/world/article/what_your_kids_are_learning_about_israel_america_and_islam_20051028/.

26. Nelly Furman, David Goldberg, and Natalia Lusin, *Enrollments in Languages Other Than English in United States Institutions of Higher Education, Fall 2006* (New York: The Modern Language Association of America, 2007), http://www.mla.org/2006_flenrollmentsurvey.

27. Nancy C. Rhodes and Ingrid Pufahl, *Foreign Language Teaching in U.S. Schools: Results of a National Survey* (Washington, DC: Center for Applied Linguistics, 2009).

28. United States Government Accountability Office, *U.S. Public Diplomacy: Key Issues for Congressional Oversight*, GAO–09–679SP (Washington, DC: May 2009).

29. Dan Eggen, "FBI Agents Still Lacking Arabic Skills: 33 of 12,000 Have Some Proficiency," *Washington Post,* October 11, 2006, http://www.washingtonpost.com/wp-dyn/content/article/2006/10/10/AR2006101001388.html.

30. Richard Willing, "Arabic Speakers Answer FBI Call for Translators," *USA Today,* April 24, 2002, http://www.usatoday.com/news/nation/2002/04/25/us-arabs-fbi.htm.

31. Zogby International, *Poll of American Opinion,* 2009. Sample size: 1,006 adults.

32. Jack Shaheen, *Guilty: Hollywood's Verdict on Arabs After 9/11* (New York: Olive Branch Press, 2008).

CHAPTER 4. LORD BALFOUR, THEN AND NOW

1. United Nations General Assembly, *Resolution 181, Part III, The City of Jerusalem,* November 29, 1947.

2. Israeli Knesset, *Basic Law: Jerusalem, Capital of Israel,* July 30, 1980.

3. United Nations Security Council, *Resolution 478,* August 20, 1980.

4. Council of Foreign Ministers, Organization of the Islamic Conference, *Resolutions on the Cause of Palestine, The City of Al-Quds Al-Sharif, and the Arab-Israeli Conflict,* Kampala, Uganda, June 18–20, 2008.

5. Executive Committee, Organization of the Islamic Conference, *Final Communiqué on the Israeli Aggressions Against the Blessed Al Aqsa Mosque,* Jeddah, Kingdom of Saudi Arabia, November 1, 2009.

6. Shibley Telhami, "If at First You Don't Succeed, Postpone," *Los Angeles Times,* July 14, 2000, http://articles.latimes.com/2000/jul/14/local/me–52987.

7. Foundation for Middle East Peace, "Europe Affirms Support for a Corpus Separatum for Greater Jerusalem," *Settlement Report* 9 (May 1999), http://www.fmep.org/reports/special-reports/israels-uncertain-victory-in-jerusalem/europe-affirms-support-for-a-corpus-separatum-for-greater-jerusalem.

8. See a survey of Democratic and Republican Party platforms going back to 1972 in: James Zogby, "Washington Watch: The 1996 Democratic and Republican Platforms" (Arab American Institute, August 26, 1996), http://www.aaiusa.org/washington-watch/1297/w082696.

9. Republican National Convention Committee, *2008 Republican Platform,* 12.

10. Democratic National Convention Committee, *The 2008 Democratic National Platform: Renewing America's Promise,* 39.

11. Douglas Bloomfield, "Jerusalem Football Is in the Air Again," *The Jewish State,* November 13, 2009, http://thejewishstate.net/nov13090pedbloomfield.html.

12. *Jerusalem Embassy Act of 1995,* Public Law 104–45, 104th Cong., 1st sess. (November 8, 1995).

13. *Jerusalem Embassy Relocation Act of 2009,* S 2737, 111th Cong., 1st sess. (November 5, 2009).

14. Letter from 71 senators to President Barack Obama, sponsored by Senator Evan Bayh (D-IN) and Senator James Risch (R-ID), August 7, 2009.

15. Ibid.

16. U.N. Human Rights Council, Twelfth Session, Official Records, Agenda Item 7, *Human Rights in Palestine and Other Occupied Arab Territories: Report of the United Nations Fact Finding Mission on the Gaza Conflict*, A/HRC/12/48, September 15, 2009.

17. Laura Friedman, "Americans for Peace Now Legislative Round-Up for the Week Ending September 18, 2009," *Americans for Peace Now*, September 18, 2009, http://peacenow.org/entries/apn_legislative_round-up_for_the_week_ending_september_18_2009.

18. Office of U.S. Representative Gary Ackerman, "Ackerman Blasts Goldstone as 'Pompous, Tendentious, One-sided Political Diatribe,'" news release, September 16, 2009.

19. Office of U.S. Representative Eliot L. Engel, "Reps. Engel, Berkley Slam U.N. 'Goldstone' Report on Gaza Conflict," news release, September 17, 2009.

20. Representative Burton of Indiana, speaking on the Goldstone Report, on September 16, 2009, in the House of Representatives, 111th Cong., 1st sess., *Congressional Record* 155, Extensions: E2295–96.

21. Representative Tiahrt of Kansas, speaking on the Goldstone Report, on September 23, 2009, in the House of Representatives, 111th Cong., 1st sess., *Congressional Record* 155, Extensions: E2350.

22. Representative Ros-Lehtinen of Florida, speaking on the United Nations, on September 22, 2009, in the House of Representatives, 111th Cong., 1st sess., *Congressional Record* 155: 9741–42.

23. Laura Friedman, "Americans for Peace Now Legislative Round-Up for the Week Ending November 6, 2009," *Americans for Peace Now*, November 6, 2009, http://peacenow.org/entries/legislative_round-up_november_6_2009.

24. Daniel C. Kurtzer and Scott B. Lasensky, *Negotiating Arab-Israeli Peace: American Leadership in the Middle East* (Washington, DC: United States Institutes of Peace, 2008), 53.

25. David Aaron Miller, *The Much Too Promised Land* (New York: Bantam Dell, 2008), 75.

26. Boutros Boutros-Ghali, interview by James Zogby, *A Capital View*, Arab Network of America, November 20, 1996.

27. James Zogby, "Washington Watch: Boutros Boutros-Ghali, the U.S. and the U.N.," *Arab American Institute*, November 25, 1996.

28. A. M. Rosenthal, "The No-Win Gamble," *New York Times*, November 12, 1996.

29. Barbara Crossette, "White House Steps Up Effort To Deny U.N. Chief a 2d Term," *New York Times*, November 7, 1996, http://www.nytimes.com/1996/11/07/world/white-house-steps-up-effort-to-deny-un-chief-a-2d-term.html.

30. UNICEF, "Iraq Surveys Show Humanitarian Emergency," news release, August 12, 1999, http://www.unicef.org/newsline/99pr29.htm.

31. Madeleine Albright, interview by Lesley Stahl, *60 Minutes*, CBS, May 12, 1996.

32. Madeleine Albright, *Madam Secretary: A Memoir* (New York: Hyperion, 2003), 274.

33. Miller, *Much Too Promised Land.*

34. Zogby International, *Impressions of America Poll*, March 4–April 3, 2002. Survey included ten nations, including five Arab countries: Saudi Arabia (700 respondents), Lebanon (500), UAE (500), Egypt (700), and Kuwait (500).

35. James Zogby, personal notes, November 19, 2002.

36. Democratic Policy Committee, "In Their Own Words: Bush Administration Officials Predict Iraqis Will Greet U.S. Soldiers as Liberators," July 22, 2004, http://democrats.senate.gov/dpc/dpc-new.cfm?doc_name=fs-108-2-211.

37. Karl Zinsmeister, "What Iraqis Really Think," *AEI Online*, September 1, 2003, http://www.aei.org/issue/19192. Report on the poll commissioned by the American Enterprise Institute for Public Policy and conducted by Zogby International. Zogby International, *Iraq Opinion Poll*, August 3–19, 2003. Sample size: 600 adults.

38. Dick Cheney, interviewed by Tim Russert, *Meet the Press*, NBC, September 14, 2003, http://www.msnbc.msn.com/id/3080244.

39. Ibid.

40. Ibid.

41. Ibid.

42. James Zogby, "Bend It Like Cheney," *Guardian*, October 29, 2003, http://www.guardian.co.uk/world/2003/oct/29/usa.iraq.

43. Zinsmeister, "What Iraqis Really Think."

44. Zogby International, *Five-Nation Survey of the Middle East*, November 11–21, 2006. Sample size: 3,500 adults.

45. Dick Cheney, Washington, DC speech to the American Enterprise Institute, May 21, 2009; Elizabeth Cheney, interview by Norah O'Donnell, MSNBC, April 24, 2009.

46. Zogby International, *Arab Opinions on President Obama's First 100 Days: A Six-Nation Survey*, April 21–May 11, 2009. Survey included respondents in Morocco, Egypt, Saudi Arabia, UAE, Lebanon, and Jordan, with a total sample size of 4,087 adults.

47. *Situation Room with Wolf Blitzer*, CNN, June 4, 2009, http://transcripts.cnn.com/TRANSCRIPTS/0906/04/sitroom.02.html.

48. Ibid.

49. President Barack Obama, interview by Hisham Melhem, *Al Arabiya*, January 27, 2009.

50. E. B. Solomont, "US 'Concerned' With Goldstone Report," *The Jerusalem Post*, September 18, 2009; M. J. Rosenberg, "It's Time to Pressure Ne-

tanyahu," *Media Matters Action Network,* January 22, 2010, http://media
mattersaction.org/blog/201001220002.

51. M. J. Rosenberg, "Why Did We Pressure Palestinians To Deep Six
Goldstone Report?" *Talking Points Memo,* October 6, 2009; Rami G.
Khouri, "Enough of Blaming the Goldstone Report!" *The Daily Star,* De-
cember 16, 2009.

52. Barak Ravid, "In Jerusalem, Clinton Hails 'Unprecedented' Israeli Settlement Concessions," *Haaretz,* November 1, 2009; "Obama's Abandoned Principles," *Middle East Mirror,* November 2, 2009 (a collection of
editorials from seven major Arab newspapers expressing condemnation
or concern over U.S. backtracking on a settlement freeze).

53. Zogby International, *Six-Nation Arab Opinion Poll,* November 1–18, 2009.
Sample size: 3,989 adults.

54. Abdul Rahman Al-Rashed, "The Harassment of Passengers from 10
Muslim Nations," *Asharq Alawsat,* January 7, 2010, http://www.asharq-e.
com/news.asp?section=2&id=19430.

55. Elias Harfoush, "What Obama After Detroit?" *Al-Hayat (UK),* January
10, 2010, http://www.daralhayat.com/portalarticlendah/95886.

CHAPTER 5. SUPER MYTH ONE: THEY'RE ALL THE SAME

1. James Zogby, personal notes from trip to Cairo, July 6, 1989.

2. Thomas L. Friedman, "Fire, Ready, Aim," *New York Times,* March 9, 2003,
http://www.nytimes.com/2003/03/09/opinion/09FRIE.html.

3. Thomas L. Friedman, "Mideast Rules to Live By," *New York Times,* December 20, 2006, http://select.nytimes.com/2006/12/20/opinion/20
friedman.html.

4. Ibid.

5. Ibid.

6. Ibid.

7. Ibid.

8. Ibid.

9. Glenn Kessler, "Rice Stresses the Positive Amid Mideast Setbacks,"
Washington Post, December 20, 2006.

10. Raphael Patai, *The Arab Mind,* rev. ed. (New York: Hatherleigh Press,
2007).

11. Ibid.

12. Ibid.

13. Norvell De Atkine, "Foreword," in *The Arab Mind,* rev. ed., by Raphael
Patai, (New York: Hatherleigh Press, 2002).

14. James Pinkerton, "A Culture Gap Complicates U.S. Task in Iraq," *Newsday,* July 9, 2003, http://www.newamerica.net/publications/articles/
2003/a_culture_gap_complicates_u_s_task_in_iraq.

15. Ibid.

16. Seymour M. Hersh, "The Gray Zone: How a Secret Pentagon Program Came to Abu Ghraib," *The New Yorker*, May 24, 2004, http://www.new yorker.com/archive/2004/05/24/040524fa_fact.

17. Ibid.

18. Smith, Lee, *The Strong Horse: Power, Politics, and the Clash of Arab Civilizations* (New York: Doubleday, 2010), 6.

19. Zogby International, *Six-Nation Arab Opinion Poll*, November 1–18, 2009. Sample size: 3,989 adults.

20. Zogby International, *Morocco Opinion Poll*, November 1–18, 2009. Sample size: 820 adults.

21. Zogby International, *Egypt Opinion Poll*, November 1–9, 2009. Sample size: 810 adults.

22. Zogby International, *Lebanon Opinion Poll*, November 1–14, 2009. Sample size: 508 adults.

23. Zogby International, *Jordan Opinion Poll*, November 2–17, 2009. Sample size: 515 adults.

24. Zogby International, *Saudi Arabia Opinion Poll*, November 3–18, 2009. Sample size: 815 adults.

25. Zogby International, *United Arab Emirates Opinion Poll*, November 2–17, 2009. Sample size: 521 adults.

CHAPTER 6. SUPER MYTH TWO: THERE IS NO ARAB WORLD

1. "The World of the Arabs," in "Waking From Its Sleep: A Special Report on the Arab World," *The Economist*, July 25, 2009: 2.

2. "Waking From Its Sleep" in "Waking From Its Sleep: A Special Report on the Arab World," *The Economist*, July 25, 2009: 4.

3. "World of the Arabs," 2.

4. Samuel P. Huntington, *Who Are We? The Challenges to America's National Identity* (New York: Simon & Shuster, 2004); Stanley Allen Renshon, *The 50% American: Immigration and National Security in an Age of Terror* (Washington, DC: Georgetown University Press, 2005).

5. Zogby International, *Six-Nation Arab Opinion Poll*, November 1–18, 2009. Sample size: 3,989 adults.

6. Zogby International, *Arab Update Poll*, April 3–30, 2010. Sample size: 4,658 adults.

7. Zogby International, *Poll of American Opinion*, November 30-December 8, 2009. Sample size: 1,006 adults.

8. Zogby International, *Arab Views of Leadership, Identity, Institutions and Issues of Concern*, January 1–December 25, 2007. Sample size: 6,506 adults.

CHAPTER 7. SUPER MYTH THREE: THE ANGRY ARAB

1. President George W. Bush, "Address to a Joint Session of Congress" (U.S. Capitol, Washington, DC, September 20, 2001).

2. Michael Ledeen, interview by Newt Gingrich, *Fox News Special, Not If, But When: America and the Axis of Evil,* Fox News, July 13, 2002.

3. Bernard Lewis, "The Roots of Muslim Rage," *The Atlantic,* September 1990.

4. Lee Smith, *The Strong Horse: Power, Politics, and the Clash of Arab Civilizations* (New York: Doubleday, 2010),6.

5. *Meet the Press,* NBC, March 3, 2002.

6. *The 2002 Gallup Poll of the Muslim World,* December 2001–January 2002, conducted in Saudi Arabia, Iran, Pakistan, Indonesia, Turkey, Lebanon, Kuwait, Jordan, and Morocco. Sample size: 10,000 adults.

7. *Meet the Press,* NBC, March 3, 2002.

8. Zogby International, *The Ten-Nation Impressions of America Poll,* March 4–April 3, 2002. Conducted face-to-face interviews in five Arab nations (Saudi Arabia, Lebanon, UAE, Egypt, and Kuwait), three Muslim non-Arab nations (Pakistan, Iran, and Indonesia), France, and Venezuela. Sample sizes: Saudi Arabia (700), Lebanon (500), UAE (500), Egypt (700), Kuwait (500), Pakistan (1,045), Iran (700), Indonesia (700), France (700), Venezuela (700).

9. James Zogby, "It's the Policy, Stupid!" *Washington Watch,* April 15, 2002, http://www.aaiusa.org/washington-watch/1614/w041502.

10. Jonathan Turley, "Camps for Citizens: Ashcroft's Hellish Vision," *Los Angeles Times,* August 14, 2002.

11. Zogby International, *Impressions of America,* June 2004. Sample size: 3,286 adults.

12. Ibid.

13. Zogby International, *Five-Nation Survey of the Middle East,* November 11–21, 2006. Sample size: 3,500 adults.

14. James Zogby, personal notes, June 12, 2003.

15. James Zogby, personal notes, 2003.

16. Rick Salutin, interview by Bill O'Reilly, "Canada Gets Al-Jazeera But No FNC!" *The O'Reilly Factor,* Fox News, July 20, 2004, http://www.foxnews.com/story/0,2933,126500,00.html.

17. David Tusing, "Toon In as Emirati Grannies Look to World Domination," *Emirates Business,* January 11, 2010.

18. Zogby International, *Poll for Arab Broadcast Forum, Abu Dhabi, UAE,* March 11–26, 2008. Sample size: 4,046 adults. In our six-nation survey for the ABF, for example, when we asked which kind of television news Arabs watched to learn about the U.S. elections, local news channels outpolled the larger satellite networks in Lebanon, Saudi Arabia, and UAE. And in our November 2009 *Six-Nation Poll,* when asked which TV network Arabs watched for international news, viewership was evenly divided between local channels and the larger satellite networks.

19. Zogby International, *Impressions of America,* 2004.

20. Zogby International, *Arab Opinions on President Obama's First 100 Days: A Six-Nation Survey,* April 21–May 11, 2009. Sample size: 4,087 adults.

CHAPTER 8. SUPER MYTH FOUR: THE LENS OF ISLAM

1. Peter Gottschalk and Gabriel Greenberg, *Islamophobia: Making Muslims the Enemy* (Lanham, MD: Rowman & Littlefield Publishers, 2008); James Zogby, *The Other Anti-Semitism: The Arab As Scapegoat* (Washington, DC: American-Arab Anti Discrimination Committee, 1980).

2. William F. Buckley Jr., "Things We're Not Ready For," *Reading Eagle Company*, July 11, 1993, B10.

3. James R. Woolsey, jacket note for *Stealth Jihad: How Radical Islam Is Subverting America without Guns or Bombs* by Robert Spencer (Washington, DC: Regnery Press, 2008).

4. Paul Johnson, "Relentlessly and Thoroughly: The Only Way to Respond," *National Review*, October 15, 2001.

5. President George W. Bush, "Remarks on the War on Terror" (speech to Military Officers Association of America, Washington, DC, September 5, 2006).

6. Paul Vitello and Kirk Semple, "Muslims Say F.B.I. Tactics Sow Anger and Fear," *New York Times*, December 17, 2009, http://www.nytimes.com/2009/12/18/us/18muslims.html.

7. Bernard Lewis, "Second Acts," *Atlantic*, November 2007, http://www.theatlantic.com/doc/200711/lewis-islam.

8. President George W. Bush, "President Bush and Secretary of State Rice Discuss the Middle East Crisis" (press conference, Crawford, TX, August 7, 2006).

9. Pat Robertson, *The 700 Club*, CBN, November 9, 2009.

10. The Virginia Public Access Project, http://www.vpap.org; James Zogby, "Another Robertson Outrage: Time for Accountability," *Huffington Post*, January 19, 2010, http://www.huffingtonpost.com/james-zogby/another-robertson-outrage_b_427994.html.

11. Virgil Goode, in a letter to constituents, December 7, 2006.

12. Erik Ose, "Pro-McCain Group Dumping 28 Million Terror Scare DVDs in Swing States," *Huffington Post*, September 12, 2008, http://www.huffingtonpost.com/erik-ose/pro-mccain-group-dumping_b_125969.html.

13. "Approbations," *Obsession: Radical Islam's War Against the West*, http://www.obsessionthemovie.com/about_approbations.html.

14. John Robinson, "Why We Didn't Distribute 'Obsession,'" *News & Record*, September 21, 2008, http://blog.news-record.com/staff/jrblog/2008/09/why_we_didnt_di.shtml.

15. President Barack Obama, interview by Hisham Melhem, *Al Arabiya*, January 27, 2009.

16. U.S. Senate Committee on Foreign Relations, *Engaging with Muslim Communities Around the World*, hearing, 111th Cong., 1st sess., February 26, 2009.

17. Ian Traynor, "Profile: Geert Wilders," *The Guardian*, October 16, 2009, http://www.guardian.co.uk/world/2009/feb/12/profile-geert-wilders.

18. Nicolien Den Boer, "'Qur'an should be banned'—Wilders strikes again," *Radio Netherlands*, August 8, 2007, http://static.rnw.nl/migratie/www.radio netherlands.nl/currentaffairs/ned070808mc-redirected.

19. *Situation Room with Wolf Blitzer*, CNN, June 4, 2009, http://transcripts. cnn.com/TRANSCRIPTS/0906/04/sitroom.02.html.

20. James Zogby, interview by Erica Hill, *The Early Show*, CBS, June 6, 2009.

21. President Barack Obama, "A New Beginning" (speech at Cairo University, Egypt, June 4, 2009), http://www.whitehouse.gov/the_press_office/ Remarks-by-the-President-at-Cairo-University-6-04-09.

CHAPTER 9. SUPER MYTH FIVE: IMMUTABILITY, OR THE FROZEN CAMEL

1. Bernard Lewis, "The Middle East, Westernized Despite Itself," *Middle East Quarterly*, March 1996, http://www.meforum.org/290/the-middle-east-westernized-despite-itself.

2. Danielle Pletka and Mustafa Hamarneh, "Arab Reform and the West," *Dialogue* 3, June 2005, http://www.bitterlemons-dialogue.org/dialogue3.html.

3. Thomas L. Friedman, "Winds of Change?" *New York Times*, June 13, 2009, http://www.nytimes.com/2009/06/14/opinion/14friedman.html.

4. Zogby International, *Six-Nation Arab Opinion Poll*, November 1–18, 2009. Sample size: 3,989 adults.

5. United Nations Development Programme, Regional Bureau for Arab States, *The Arab Human Development Report 2002: Creating Opportunities for Future Generations* (New York: United Nations Publications, 2002), http:// www.arab-hdr.org/publications/other/ahdr/ahdr2002e.pdf.

6. Ibid.

7. Michael Slackman, "In a New Age, Bahrain Struggles to Honor the Dead While Serving the Living," *New York Times*, September 17, 2009, http://www.nytimes.com/2009/09/18/world/middleeast/18bahrain. html.

8. Zogby International, *Six-Nation Arab Opinion Poll*.

9. Ronald Reagan and Jimmy Carter, presidential debate, October 28, 1980.

10. Zogby International, *Poll of American Voters*, November 30–December 8, 2009. Sample size: 1,006 adults. (Note: The Arab World "better off/ worse off" ratios in Table 9.1 compare quite favorably with recent U.S. numbers. When asked if they were better off or worse off than they were ten years ago, 41% of Americans say "better off," while 46% say "worse off." And "how will you be ten years from now?" 48% expect to be "better off," while 22% say they will be "worse off.")

CHAPTER 10. IRAQ: HISTORY CUTS LIKE A KNIFE

1. James Zogby, personal notes from trip to Riyadh, Saudi Arabia, June 10, 2003.

2. Steven R. Weisman, "Saudi Women Have Message for U.S. Envoy," *New York Times*, September 28, 2005, http://www.nytimes.com/2005/09/28/international/middleeast/28hughes.html.

3. Ibid.

4. Karen P. Hughes, "Sinking in the Polls," *Washington Post*, September 17, 2007.

5. Zogby International, *Five-Nation Survey of the Middle East*, November 11–21, 2006. Sample size: 3,500 adults.

6. James A. Baker III, Lee H. Hamilton, Lawrence S. Eagleburger, Vernon E. Jordan Jr., Edwin Meese III, Sandra Day O'Connor, Leon E. Panetta, William J. Perry, Charles S. Robb, and Alan K. Simpson, *The Iraq Study Group Report*, Washington, DC, December 2006.

7. For example: "I believe demolishing Hussein's military power and liberating Iraq would be a cakewalk," in Ken Adelman, "Cakewalk in Iraq," *Washington Post*, February 13, 2002, A27; "My own judgment based on my time as secretary of Defense, and having operated in this area in the past, I'm confident that our troops will be successful, and I think it'll go relatively quickly. . . . Weeks rather than months," from Dick Cheney, interview by Bob Schieffer, *Face the Nation*, CBS, March 16, 2003; "We are talking about a country that can really finance its own reconstruction and relatively soon," from Paul Wolfowitz, testifying before the defense subcommittee of the House Appropriations Committee, March 27, 2003.

8. Bill O'Reilly, *The O'Reilly Factor*, Fox News Channel, January 29, 2003.

9. Bill Kristol, interview by Terry Gross, *Fresh Air*, NPR, April 1, 2003.

10. Fred Barnes, Fox News Channel, April 10, 2003.

11. National Geographic-Roper, *2002 Global Geographic Literacy Survey*, prepared by RoperASW for National Geographic Education Foundation, November 2002, http://www.nationalgeographic.com/geosurvey2002/download/RoperSurvey.pdf. Sample size: 800 young adults ages 18–34 in the United States.

12. Rep. Jesse Jackson Jr. and James Zogby, "A resolution of the Democratic National Committee supporting and honoring the men and women who serve in our Armed Forces, opposing a pre-emptive U.S.-led military action against Iraq, and urging President Bush to sustain diplomatic efforts to resolve the United States' issues with Iraq," introduced February 21, 2003, http://archive.democrats.com/view.cfm?id=12226.

13. James J. Zogby, "Unanswered Questions," *Baltimore Sun*, February 20, 2003.

14. Zogby International, *America Poll*, March 14–15, 2003. Sample size: 1,129 U.S. voters.

15. James Zogby, personal notes from a conversation with Davidson student, March 12, 2003.

16. *Viewpoint with James Zogby*, Abu Dhabi TV, March 12, 2003.

17. Ibid.

18. *Viewpoint with James Zogby*, Abu Dhabi TV, May 8, 2003.

19. Ibid.

20. James Zogby, personal notes of postshow conversation, May 8, 2003.

21. Lou Dobbs, *Moneyline,* CNN, May 1, 2003.

22. Gwen Ifill, *Washington Week,* PBS, May 2, 2003.

23. Baker et al., *Iraq Study Group.*

24. Ibid., 61.

25. Anwar Sadat Chair for Peace and Development, *2009 Annual Arab Public Opinion Survey,* April–May 2009. Survey conducted in Egypt, Jordan, Lebanon, Morocco, Saudi Arabia, and UAE. Sample size: 4,087 adults. Report includes numbers for 2008 and 2009 annual surveys.

26. Ibid.

27. Ibid.

28. *Viewpoint with James Zogby,* "Four Years Later," Abu Dhabi TV, May 10, 2007.

29. James Zogby, personal notes, May 10, 2007.

30. Zogby International, *Arab Update Poll,* April 3–30, 2010. Sample size: 816 Iraqi adults.

31. Ted Barrett, "Lott: Bush Barely Mentioned Iraq in Meeting with Senate Republicans," *CNN,* September 28, 2006.

CHAPTER 11. LEBANON: HEARING HALF THE STORY

1. *Hardball with Chris Matthews,* MSNBC, March 8, 2005.

2. Ibid.

3. President George W. Bush, "President Discusses the War on Terror" (speech to National Defense University, Washington, DC, March 8, 2005), http://georgewbush-whitehouse.archives.gov/news/releases/2005/03/20050308-3.html.

4. Zogby International/Information International (ZI/II), *Hariri Poll,* February 19–24, 2005. Sample size: 1,250 adults.

5. Jefferson Morley, "The Branding of Lebanon's 'Revolution,'" *Washington Post,* March 3, 2005.

6. James Zogby, personal notes from a conversation with Dr. Amal Shamma, September 29, 1985.

7. James Zogby, personal notes from a meeting with my cousin Jack Zogby and Rafiq Hariri, July 6, 2001.

8. James Zogby, personal notes from a conversation with Rafiq Hariri, October 23, 2000.

9. James Zogby, personal notes from a conversation with Rafiq Hariri, July 6, 2001.

10. Zogby International/Information International, *Hariri Poll.*

11. Zogby International/Information International, *Lebanon Poll,* April 7–14, 2005. Sample size: 1,250.

12. Ibid.

13. Zogby International, *Arab Update Poll,* April 3–30, 2010. Sample size: 817 Lebanese adults.

CHAPTER 12. SAUDI ARABIA: THEIR REFORM, NOT OURS

1. James Zogby, personal notes from meeting, March 20, 2004.
2. Shibley Telhami, "Arab Public Opinion: A Survey in Six Countries," *San Jose Mercury News,* March 16, 2003.
3. World Economic Forum, "What is the Origin of Arab People Power?— The World Economic Forum in Jordan Debate," news release, May 21, 2005.
4. Zogby International, *Five-Nation Survey of the Middle East,* November 11–21, 2006. Sample size: 3,500 adults.
5. James Zogby, personal notes, November 4, 2004.
6. For example, "It is the spread of freedom, democracy, and justice that is the antidote to Islamic extremism." Stephen Hadley, "Remarks to the American Israel Public Affairs Committee National Summit" Washington, DC, October 31, 2005, http://georgewbush-whitehouse.archives.gov/news/releases/2005/10/20051031-4.html.
7. Nick Kotz, *Judgment Days: Lyndon Baines Johnson, Martin Luther King Jr., and the Laws That Changed America* (New York: Houghton Mifflin Harcourt, 2005), 418.
8. University of Maryland and Zogby International, *Annual Arab Public Opinion Survey,* April 21–May 11, 2009. Sample size: 4,087 adults.
9. Zogby International, "Arabs Want Reform, U.S. Help in Solving Israeli–Palestinian Crisis," December 6, 2004. Based on poll taken November 6–24, 2004. Sample size: 2,600 adults.

CHAPTER 13. PALESTINE: A WOUND IN THE HEART

1. Phone conversation with Arab journalist in Gaza, January 6, 2009.
2. Phone conversation with Gulf state minister, January 7, 2009.
3. James J. Zogby, "Outside View: History and Peace Making," *United Press International,* May 25, 2005, http://www.upi.com/Business_News/Security-Industry/2005/05/25/Outside-View-History-and-peace-making/UPI-91651117005720/.
4. Leon M. Uris, *Exodus* (New York: Doubleday, 1958); *Exodus,* DVD, directed by Otto Preminger (1960; Los Angeles, CA: MGM, 2002).
5. Jack G. Shaheen, *Reel Bad Arabs: How Hollywood Vilifies a People* (New York: Olive Branch Press, 2001), 189.
6. Colonial Office, Great Britain, 733/297/75156/II/Appendix A, extract from Weizmann's speech, April 23, 1936; *Peel Commission Report,* 96–97, cited in Philip Mattar, *The Mufti of Jerusalem: Al-Hajj Amin-al-Husayni and the Palestinian National Movement* (New York: Columbia University Press, 1988), 73.
7. Philip Paull, "'International Terrorism': The Propaganda War" (master's thesis, San Francisco State University, 1982).
8. James Zogby, personal notes from a conversation with Tawfiq Zayyad, October 2, 1980.

9.   Daniel J. Wakin, "Minuets, Sonatas and Politics in the West Bank," *New York Times,* May 31, 2009, http://www.nytimes.com/2009/06/01/arts/music/01dali.html.

10. President Barack Obama, speech announcing the appointment of George Mitchell as special Middle East peace envoy, U.S. Department of State, Washington, DC January 22, 2009.

11. President Barack Obama, speech to the United Nations General Assembly, September 23, 2009.

12. Palestine Center for Public Opinion, *Poll #168,* November 2009. Sample size: 1,050 adults. Arab World for Research and Development (AWRAD), *Role of the U.S. Government Evaluation of Living Conditions and Institutions, Elections and Reconciliation,* December 8–10, 2009. Sample size: 1,200 Palestinians in the West Bank and Gaza.

13. Zogby International, *Arab Update Poll,* April 3–30, 2010. Sample size: 4,658 adults.

14. General David Petraeus, testifying before the Senate Armed Services Committee, March 16, 2010.

CHAPTER 14. ARAB AMERICANS: BRIDGING THE DIVIDE

1.   David Reed, United States Senator from Pennsylvania, in a letter to Lila Mandour, May 21, 1929, personal files of James Zogby, Washington, DC.

2.   Saleemie A. Zogby, "Syrians Are Respected," *The Syrian World, Volume I* (April 1927): 51.

3.   James Zogby, interview by John McLaughlin, *One on One,* WRC-TV, July 18, 1999.

4.   Personal notes from the League of Arab States Meeting of Arab Foreign Ministers in Cairo, Egypt, September 4, 2002.

5.   United States Department of Justice, "Zachary J. Rolnik Pleads Guilty to Federal Hate Crime Violations Against Dr. James J. Zogby," news release, June 6, 2002, http://www.justice.gov/opa/pr/2002/June/02_crt_342.htm; Federal Bureau of Investigation, Washington Field Office, "Former Foreign Service Officer Sentenced on Federal Civil Rights Charges," July 11, 2008, http://washingtondc.fbi.gov/dojpressrel/pressrel08/wf071108a.htm; United States Department of Justice, "Federal Authorities Arrest Iowa Man for Sending E-mail Threat," October 13, 2004, http://www.justice.gov/opa/pr/2004/October/04_crt_695.htm.

6.   Arab American Institute, *Healing the Nation: The Arab American Experience After September 11* (Washington, DC: Arab American Institute Foundation, September 2002), http://aai.3cdn.net/64de7330dc475fe470_h1m6boyk4.pdf.

7.   James Zogby and Helen Hatab Samhan, *The Politics of Exclusion* (Washington, DC: Arab American Institute, 1987); Samhan expounds on this subject in Helen Samhan, "Politics and Exclusion: The Arab American Experience," *Journal of Palestine Studies* XVI, no. 2 (Winter 1987): 11–28.

8. *Official Proceedings of the 1988 Democratic National Convention* (Washington, DC: DNC Services Corporation, 1988), 259–265.

9. "Let 1987 Be the Year of Peace in the Middle East" (advertisement), *New York Times,* June 7, 1987, E7.

10. James Zogby, personal notes from a conversation at the Democratic National Convention in Atlanta, GA, July 21, 1988.

11. United States Department of State, Bureau of Consular Affairs, "Travel Warning: Israel, the West Bank and Gaza." August 14, 2009, http://travel.state.gov/travel/cis_pa_tw/tw/tw_922.html; Arab American Institute, "AAI Calls on Secretary of State to Protect American Citizen Travelers," news release, September 3, 2009, http://www.aaiusa.org/press-room/4240/aai-calls-on-secretary-of-state-to-protect-american-citizen-travelers; James J. Zogby, "Enough Is Enough," *Washington Watch,* August 31, 2009, http://www.aaiusa.org/washington-watch/4235/enough-is-enough.

12. James Zogby, personal notes, December 1998.

CHAPTER 15. WHAT GOVERNMENT CAN DO

1. President Barack Obama, "A New Beginning" (speech, Cairo University, Egypt, June 4, 2009).

2. Ibid.

3. Ibid.

4. Ibid.

5. Ibid.

6. Ibid.

7. Ibid.

8. Ibid.

9. Ibid.

10. President Barack Obama, interview by Gwen Ifill, *NewsHour,* PBS, March 17, 2008, http://www.pbs.org/newshour/bb/white_house/jan-june08/obama_03-17.html.

11. James A. Baker III, Lee H. Hamilton, and others, *The Iraq Study Group Report* (New York: Vintage Books, 2006), 46ff.

12. Colin L. Powell, "U.S. Forces: Challenges Ahead," *Foreign Affairs* 72, no. 5 (Winter 1992/1993): 32.

13. U.S. House Committee on Foreign Affairs, Subcommittee on International Organizations, Human Rights, and Oversight, *The Decline in America's Reputation: Why?* 110th Cong., 2nd sess., 2008, H. Rep. 42–566.

14. Senator Richard Durbin, speaking on Guantanamo detainees, 109th Cong., 1st sess., *Congressional Record* 151 (June 14, 2005): S 6591–5.

15. Obama, "A New Beginning."

16. Daniel C. Kurtzer and Scott B. Lasensky. *Negotiating Arab-Israeli Peace: American Leadership in the Middle East* (Washington, DC: U.S. Institute of Peace Press, 2008).

17. James Zogby, personal notes, November 2, 1994.

18. Hillary R. Clinton, "On Development in the 21st Century" (speech, The Peterson Institute for International Economics, Washington, DC, January 6, 2010), http://www.state.gov/secretary/rm/2010/01/134838.htm.

19. Center for International Private Enterprise, http://www.cipe.org.

20. Ibid.

21. Zogby International, *Impressions of America*, June 2004. Sample size: 3,300 adults.

22. For example, *Viewpoint with James Zogby*, Abu Dhabi TV, August 13, 2009.

23. Zogby International, *Impressions of America*.

CHAPTER 16. WHAT WE CAN DO

1. John R. Hayes, ed., *The Genius of Arab Civilization: Sources of Renaissance* (Cambridge, MA: MIT Press, 1983).

2. ExxonMobil, *2008 Worldwide Giving Report*, http://www.exxonmobil.com/Corporate/community_contributions_report.aspx.

3. Starbucks, *Facts About Starbucks Coffee Company*, http://me.starbucks.com/NR/rdonlyres/19A33462-4647-4AAB-B000-998F8113C8B9/9182/FactsaboutStarbucksMiddleEastENGLISH.pdf.

4. Cisco, *CSR Report 2009, Middle East*, http://www.cisco.com/web/about/ac227/csr2009/map/middleeast.html.

5. Sister Cities International, http://www.sister-cities.org/.

6. Mayor Richard M. Daley, remarks at Arab American Foundation Dinner, April 21, 2010.

7. "Generation Islam," *Christiane Amanpour Reports*, CNN, August 13, 2009, http://www.cnn.com/SPECIALS/2009/generation.islam/.

8. Prince Alwaleed Bin Talal Center for Muslim–Christian Understanding, Georgetown University, http://cmcu.georgetown.edu/; Prince Alwaleed Bin Talal Islamic Studies Program, Harvard University, http://www.islamicstudies.harvard.edu/.

9. American University of Beirut's Prince Alwaleed Bin Talal Bin Abdulaziz Alsaud Center for American Studies and Research, http://www.aub.edu.lb/fas/casar; Prince Alwaleed Bin Talal Abdulaziz Alsaud Center for American Studies and Research at the American University in Cairo, http://www.aucegypt.edu/ResearchatAUC/rc/casar/.

10. Himdi Heba, "Harvard to Return Zayed's Cash Gift," *Arab News*, July 30, 2004, http://www.arabnews.com/?page=4&section=0&article=49084&d=30&m=7&y=2004.

11. National Council on U.S.–Arab Relations' Model Arab League, http://www.ncusar.org/modelarableague/index.html.

12. *Washington Journal*, C-SPAN, July 28, 2005.

13. United Nations, Division for Palestinian Rights, *Question of Palestine*, http://www.un.org/Depts/dpa/qpal/.

14. Zogby International, *Poll of American Voters,* November 30–December 8, 2009. Sample size: 1,006 adults.

15. World Affairs Councils of America (WACA), http://www.worldaffairs councils.org/.

16. Foreign Policy Association, Great Decisions Program, http://www.great decisions.org/.

AFTERWORD

1. F. Gregory Gause III, "Why Middle East Studies Missed the Arab Spring: The Myth of Authoritarian Stability," *Foreign Affairs,* July/August 2001, http://www.foreignaffairs.com/articles/67932/f-gregory-gause-iii /why-middle-east-studies-missed-the-arab-spring.

2. James Zogby, personal notes, May 5, 2011.

3. President Barack Obama, remarks on Egypt (White House, Washington DC, February 11, 2011), http://www.whitehouse.gov/the-press-office /2011/02/11/remarks-president-egypt.

4. Zogby Research Services, *Arab Attitudes, 2011* (Washington DC: Arab American Institute Foundation, 2011), http://www.aaiusa.org/reports /arab-attitudes-2011.

5. Ibid.

6. Ibid.

7. President Barack Obama, remarks on the Middle East and North Africa (State Department, Washington DC, May 19, 2011), http://www .whitehouse.gov/the-press-office/2011/05/19/remarks-president -middle-east-and-north-africa.

8. Texas State Board of Education, *Resolution Regarding Bias in Texas Social Studies Textbooks* (Austin, TX, passed September 24, 2010), http:// www.tea.state.tx.us/WorkArea/linkit.aspx?LinkIdentifier=id&ItemID =2147487008&libID=2147487006.

9. Renee Ellmers, *No Mosque at Ground Zero,* advertisement produced by Renee Ellmers for U.S. Congress, uploaded September 21, 2010, http:// www.youtube.com/watch?v=0QvKOdiyFaw.

10. Ed Martin, *The "Ground Zero Mosque,"* advertisement produced by Ed Martin for U.S. Congress, posted August 15, 2010, http://edmartinfor congress.com/2782/the-ground-zero-mosque/.

11. Sarah Palin, interview by Greta Van Susteren, *On the Record,* Fox News, August 16, 2010, http://www.foxnews.com/on-air/on-the-record/tran script/palin-obama-039doesn039t-get-it039-ground-zero-mosque -location-039stab-heart039?page=2.

12. Edward Wyatt, "3 Republicans Criticize Obama's Endorsement of Mosque," *New York Times,* August 14, 2010, http://www.nytimes.com /2010/08/15/us/politics/15reaction.html.

13.   Kendra Marr, "Newt Gingrich Talks Faith—Not Affairs—at Corner-
      stone Church in Texas," *Politico,* March 27, 2011, http://www.politico
      .com/news/stories/0311/52023.html#ixzz1I1Exj70T.

14.   Scott Keyes, "Exclusive: Herman Cain Tells ThinkProgress 'I Will Not'
      Appoint a Muslim in my Administration," *ThinkProgress,* March 26, 2011,
      http://thinkprogress.org/politics/2011/03/26/153625/herman-cain
      -muslims/.

15.   Ben Smith, "Pawlenty Shut Down Islam-Friendly Mortgage Program,"
      Politico, March 25, 2011, http://www.politico.com/blogs/bensmith/0311
      /Pawlenty_shut_down_Islamfriendly_mortgage_program.html.

16.   Zogby Interactive, *National Poll of Likely Voters,* June 28–30, 2011. Sample
      size: 1,804 adults.

INDEX

9 780230 120686